Douglas Dunn's eight collections of poetry have won several major literary prizes, including the Somerset Maugham Award, the Hawthornden Prize and a Cholmondely Award. *Elegies* won the Whitbread Prize for 1985, and was followed by *Selected Poems* and *Northlight*. His short stories appear from time to time in *The New Yorker* and he has also published a collection of stories, *Secret Villages*. Most recently, he has edited the *Faber Book of Twentieth Century Scottish Poetry*.

Douglas Dunn was born in 1942 and brought up in Inchinnan in Renfrewshire. He is a Professor of English at St Andrew's University and lives in Tayport in north Fife with his wife and two children.

SCOTLAND

An Anthology

EDITED BY
DOUGLAS DUNN

Fontana
An Imprint of HarperCollins*Publishers*

Fontana
An Imprint of HarperCollins*Publishers*,
77–85 Fulham Palace Road,
Hammersmith, London W6 8JB

Published by Fontana 1992
9 8 7 6 5 4 3 2 1

First published in Great Britain by
HarperCollins*Publishers* 1991

ISBN 0 00 637821 8

Set in Itek Meridien by
Ace Filmsetting Ltd, Frome, Somerset

Printed in Great Britain by
T.J. Press (Padstow) Ltd, Padstow, Cornwall

For Lesley, Robbie and Lillias

CONTENTS

'Oh, look!' she cried. 'What's that? What is it called?'
'The Isle of May,' she was told.
'The Isle of May? I never heard of it! Has it always
been there?'
'Always.'

ERIC LINKLATER, *The Merry Muse* (1959)

Largo, Blebo, Dunino
Into Europe seem to go,
But plainly Scottish we may deem
Auchtermuchty, Pittenweem.

ANON

INTRODUCTION

Anthologizing Scotland was not always a comfortable task, even in the silence of university libraries depopulated by vacations, or in the hermitage of one's own. In recent years Scotland has been experiencing a climate of thought and feeling at the centre of which is the redefinition of Scotland itself. It is a mood that has created an unsettled and exciting cultural and political scene.

What I wanted was a book with deep roots and a topical peak. However, the past is a subject about which to be wary. Robertson Nicoll once said, 'The Scotsman takes long views, and does not find them inspiriting.' One part of me feels tempted to see the truth in it. Another, in a less atavistic or ancestral corner of the brain, suspects it to be a throw-away sooth that disguises the reasons why long views are said to be depressing. It represents the disfiguring zest with which Scotland and Scottishness have often been described, and it is a habit of mind with which many contemporary Scots are impatient.

Instead, I hope to have been guided by Croce's maxim that 'All history is contemporary history'. It is not far from Santayana's warning that a people that chooses to forget its past condemns itself to relive it.

Tom Nairn has evoked Scottish history as one of 'aberrant, self-destructive grandeur'. Over the centuries a feckless habit of snatching defeat from the jaws of victory, usually on a point of principle, has made the Scots seem to be what Mr Nairn calls 'a people of gallant losers and political imbeciles'. Another contemporary writer, Neal Ascherson, points to 'the old contradiction between self-assertion and self-distrust' as a fundamental flaw in Scottish society. These recognitions are essential to Scotland past and present; and the purpose of much recent Scottish thought, literature and art is to turn them around. It

1

has taken a long time to arrange the funeral of the belittling notion that Scottish history is inferior. Worthy of having been buried under the same cairn is the idea of Scottishness as a birthright to be overcome by an English public school, or, if that cannot be arranged, by extraordinary determination and sheer genius.

> Pride in history is pride
> In living what your fathers died,

wrote the Irish poet, Louis MacNeice, and the warning is salutary. Only a morbid braggart would *defend* a national history, let alone Scottish history, which, tradition asks us to believe, is a long view, inducing gloom, and leaving the present raddled and unreliable. It lacks cheer, as much as Mr Nairn says (and he was writing about a recent development in Scottish politics); but a wider perspective ought to suggest that many of the nations of Europe have been equally prone to self-defeating or suicidal strategies, some of them momentous in their awful consequences. Others have found themselves faced with the problem of how to survive beside bigger, grimmer neighbours. A big brutal neighbour alongside a small brutal neighbour is a recipe for trouble. It is not for nothing that Scotland is sometimes said to resemble Czechoslovakia, Poland, or Lithuania.

> Behind every new child . . . stretched a past of bloody battles, desperate uprisings, gallows, deportations . . . and, whether the child willed it or not, all this shaped his subsequent life.

These words are Czesław Miłosz's about Lithuania, but he could just as well have been summarizing the junior beguilements of Scotland's battle-scarred past. Of course, much of Scotland's history *is* vile, valorous, and violent; but to see it as unique in these respects is to indulge in the deficiencies of romanticism.

Early in his career Sir Walter Scott wrote in his commonplace book:

> I was born a Scotsman and a bare one. Therefore I was born to fight my way in the world, with my left hand, if my right hand failed me, and with my teeth if both were cut off.

Scott was born into a relatively favoured level of Scottish soci-

2

ety. Why, then, did he feel compelled to state his resolve in terms of imaginary carnage? His bitterness is as apparent as his pride. Sheer ferocity of expression suggests the power of the prejudices and obstacles against which he believed he would have to struggle. So, did he overstate? I doubt it. For example, Robert Burns's career looks painfully ill-omened by and from birth. 'It is foolish to talk about anyone being a victim who has become the Poet of Man,' it has been said, and it was sensibly put. But without falling for the myth of Burns as Scotland's hero-victim, we might be left wondering why it was that all Burns got in a material way from Scotland in his lifetime amounted to a routine post in the Excise and a strenuous, unprofitable sideline in farming. Robert Louis Stevenson, like Scott, was born to comfortable circumstances; but he, too, related the matter of Scotland in the terrible, triple terms to which Burns's career was subjected as if by nature: 'Poverty, enterprise, and constant ill-luck.' For John Buchan, 'Poverty is the first and biggest fact of our history.'

Should you repeat to yourself often enough that Scotland is defined by its poverty and misfortune, you could end up believing them to be God-endowed, fore-ordained, and probably eternal; you could even grow to like them. Add 'enterprise', however, along with ingenuity, inventiveness and industry, and the outcome must be to question the prestige in which poverty and ill-luck are held in Scotland. A country as productive in men and women of talent and in manufactures is not unlucky; it is more likely to have been cheated, by itself, by the nation to which it is united, and by both working together.

Alastair Reid has pointed out that more whigmaleerie has been committed to print about the peculiarities of Scottish character than about anything else relating to Scotland. 'The odd thing is that almost everything said of the Scots is true,' he continues, 'but never the whole truth – their character has so many sides to it.' Mr Reid's remark banishes simplification; but it could encourage overstatement of a different kind in that it invites an even longer list of 'characteristics' than usual. In truth, the Scots are like any other nationality. What concern them, what, for better or worse, form and deform their temperaments, are located in a particular place, with a climate and a history. If nothing else, that approach leaves room for the exceptional as

well as the commonplace. It might also help to avoid stereo-
types with which Scotland and Scottishness have been beset
for centuries.

For centuries, though, certain aspects of Scottish personality
have been seen as different, or, at least, as identifiably Scottish.
In medieval times, they used to say: *Scotus est, piper in naso* (He is
a Scot, he has pepper in his nose). Proud, touchy, and with a
dignity, real or imagined, to stand on, then; but I can think of
Scots who are not described by such a formula, just as I can
think of others who are neither thrifty, industrious, mean,
shrewd, pragmatic, drunken, maudlin, dour, nor soldierly.

Perhaps it should be left at that, with the suspicion that no
matter how you characterize a country's inhabitants what you
achieve is a description of the features of a few. Aggressive
nationalists might claim that this proves a point, and that Scottish character has dwindled under English and other influences until it is indistinguishable from them. The true surprise
of Scottishness is its continuing existence, and (or so I would
submit) its strength, not the extent to which identity and
nationality have been diminished by the pressures to which
they have been exposed, inevitable, unavoidable pressures,
given the communicativeness of modern life. It is its survival
which indicates that the phenomenon of Scottishness is resis-
tant, as well as resilient, and of value to those who share it.

At the same time it is a subject which refuses to let go. One
aspect of Scotland and its temperaments stands out from
others. It is a country of contrasts, differences, and antitheses,
which lead you to think of them as clues to behaviour, or as tentative explanations of what its people have done in departments of life considered useful and creative, and in other lines
of business usually considered to be anything but. Scotland is
Lowlands and Highlands; it is towns, cities, industry, country-
side, agriculture, mountains, moorland, rivers, lochs and
wilderness. In its cities and suburbs you can see domestic,
municipal and commercial opulence as well as whole districts
where the quality of housing matches in disgrace the notorious
slums of the past. It asserts the New, while, and not always
helpfully, the Old asserts itself. It is Patrick Geddes, the
understander of cities, and it is architects such as the Adams,
'Greek' Thomson, Robert Lorimer and Charles Rennie Mackintosh; and it is those makers of ruins responsible for the High-

4

land Clearances. It is John Logie Baird; it is the multitude addicted to his goggle-box. It is generals and admirals by the score; it is tens of thousands of other ranks. It is Mary Queen of Scots and it is generations of women who brought up their children and worked in factories or weather-beaten farmtouns and who seldom enter history except as fiction or statistics. It is the nutritionist Lord Boyd Orr and it is queues of late-night revellers waiting for fish and chips, fried pizza or carry-out post-Imperial fare. It is Scottish innovations in medicine; it is J. M. Barrie's Peter Pan and the children of Barrie's day with rickets or worse. It is heavy industry and the scientific and technical acumen that made it possible; it is the magnates it enriched and it is the men and women it did not. It is Picts, Scots, Gaels, Norse, Irish, Welsh and English; and it is also Jews, Italians, Poles, Indians, Pakistanis, Bangladeshis, Chinese and Africans. It is men and women who are content with their nationality; and it is others who would sell it for a groat. It possesses terminal squalor, but it is a country of outstanding natural beauty. It relishes its intimate lore, legends, stories, poetry and music; it is celebrated for its science, medicine, mathematics and metaphysics. In 1707 it negotiated a Union with England and parted with an ancient independence which its culture has kept more than notionally alive ever since. Most of the Scots language has been lost to everyday spokenness and is kept in dictionaries and poetry, while Gaelic hangs on in the face of extinction; but Scotland produced the editor of the *Oxford English Dictionary*, and has sustained an aptitude for other languages as part of its Europeanness or universality of outlook. But in spite of the near-evanishment of the Scots vernacular, something close to its spirit persists in accent, in how mind saturates another, available and associated language, English, or in what Stevenson called 'a strong Scotch accent of the mind'.

Instead of contrasts, ironies, contradictions and paradoxes (although they undoubtedly exist) a better image of Scottishness might be the kaleidoscope. It is tempting to think it was no coincidence that that serious, delightful toy should have been invented by Sir David Brewster, a professor at the University of St Andrews, in 1817. It expresses variousness, the illusion of infinity, multiples, and a recurrent but unpredictable symmetry. It seems more positive and at the same time more complicated than the idea of Scottish personality as 'double' or 'divided' which is the conclusion to which hot pursuit of antitheses usually leads.

It is hard to escape from the comprehensiveness, and the unpredictability, of what the Scottish temperament can produce – philosophers, physicians, jurists, soldiers, sailors, saints, theologians, moralists, bigots, libertines, economists, physicists, chemists, geologists, botanists, poets, painters, sculptors, musicians, financiers, industrialists, civil and other engineers, historians, architects, nannies, discoverers, pedants, tyrants, educators, and champions of social justice. All nations can point to their geniuses in many realms of human endeavour; but, for a country of its size, Scotland's contribution is almost disturbing in its scale. It was a restlessness mopped up successfully by the Empire. Of Skye in the nineteenth century A. M. Mackenzie wrote in her *An Historical Survey of Scottish Literature*:

> In the forty years after 1797, *Skye alone* gave the British Army 21 Lieutenant-Generals and Major-Generals, 48 Lieutenant-Colonels, 600 Majors, Captains and Subalterns, and 10,000 private soldiers; and to the Civil Service in the same time, one Governor-General of India, four Governors of Colonies, a Chief Baron of England, and a Lord of Session.

A similar, but perhaps less spectacularly Imperial muster, would be shown by virtually every district of Scotland. It ought to be easy to relate how the past touches on one's own life, and it could be embarrassment that makes the telling harder than it should be. My own native parish of Inchinnan is hardly exceptional. Indeed, it is not well known. Just over three miles long and never more than two miles wide, it is easy to miss on a map of Renfrewshire, never mind Scotland, never mind the globe. However, its first church was founded by an Irish saint in the Dark Ages, a follower of St Kentigern (or Mungo). He is said to have sailed from Ireland on a stone. When it sank by the banks of the River Gryffe, St Conval took this as God's nod as to where he ought to be. I grew up believing this, and don't see any reason to stop now. Sarcophagus covers or sculpted funerary lids (probably tenth-century) survive in a new church, its predecessor All Hallows having been demolished in 1965 to make way for Glasgow airport's flightpath. In the twelfth century David I granted the church to the Knights Templar. In 1164 Somerled the Lord of the Isles was killed and his seaborne army routed at Inchinnan by local levies led by Walter FitzAlan, the royal Steward, whose family founded subsequently the Stewart dynasty. It produced Robert Law, a noted Covenanter, whose *Memorialls* were once widely read. Erskine New Town has been built, much of it over Inchinnan, and Bargarran, where, in the late seventeenth century, Christian Shaw accused local parishioners of witchcraft. Seven of them burned for it, and another hanged himself in his cell rather than face the odium of a public lie. In 1773, 139 enterprising individuals formed the Scots-American Company of Farmers, also known as the Inchinnan Company. Through their countryman Dr John Witherspoon, president of the College of New Jersey (Princeton University), and signatory of the Declaration of American Independence, they were offered land, which they bought, and took up in 1774. William Lockhart (1841–1900) was a local son-of-the-manse; he was knighted and commanded the British Army in India. His elder brother was a soldier and novelist. The industrialist William Beardmore built a factory at Inchinnan for the construction of airships, including the R34, the first to cross the Atlantic. In time it became India Tyres, and, apart from the Egyptianated art deco façade of its office block, that's gone, too.

As with so many other parishes and localities in Scotland, the closeness of antiquity to the here-and-now and the not-long-gone measures a country which is a nation local to itself as well as made up of intimate, particular places. It is a patchwork of times as well as districts.

Dr Johnson's remark that the noblest prospect a Scot ever sees or saw is the high road to England is one that Scots often find offensive. Historically, though, it is closer to reportage than sardonic wit. For example, Thomas Telford, the civil engineer, stated candidly in his autobiography that he had no option but to 'proceed southward, where industry might find more employment and be better rewarded'. While the Treaty of Union might have had its day (a majority of Scottish people believe this), without it Scotland, and the world, would have been the poorer, especially the world, for it is a conspicuous truth that all the ingenuity and inventiveness of Scottish genius did not lay the foundations of a prosperous and contented country. What they would have done *without* the Union might be one of the great unanswerable questions of history.

Most Scottish emigrants left to put intolerable conditions behind them and find a better place of life. Here, too, the subsequent phenomenon is embarrassingly disproportionate to the numbers involved. Whether in Canada, the USA, Australia or New Zealand, men and women of Scottish origin created the conditions that enabled them to establish power and wealth. Some of the stories of their settlements are filled with intrepid endeavour, hardships overcome, daunting challenges met and vanquished, opportunities seized. Some, too, show dispossessed Highlanders engaged in the unsavoury business of dispossessing those native to the lands they came to settle. Like all history it is blemished with worse than man's contest with climate and terrain. Far from all Scottish emigrants founded private empires. Many returned home disillusioned. Other stories are more exotic. My particular favourite is that of James Hastie, a former sergeant in the East India Company's army, who, for reasons best known to Sir James Farquhar, the Governor of Mauritius, was sent in 1817 as a one-man military mission to the court of Radama I in Madagascar at Tananarive. His task was to reorganize and train the Merina armies, which Hastie accomplished with the help of a French soldier and a Jamaican half-caste. He became commander of the army, rose to higher rank and honour under his new name of Rainihasy, and died in Tananarive in 1826, a far cry from whatever parish he was born in, and to whoever his parents were – a Lord Jim indeed.

Individual Scots have had an impact on the histories of countries other than their own. Scotland's substance, though, is Scotland itself, as well as its diaspora and Mac-scatter, its legion of gifted or opportunistic individuals for whom exile was a 'calling' (to use Muriel Spark's phrase).

It would take more than a lifetime to digest the massive library of what has been written about Scotland. Rather than pilfer from books which I have no intention ever of reading to the end, I have tried to stick to what I could get to know. However, I have tried to be fair as well as honest, and, although I have wanted to be positive, I have included material that will fail to flatter those in the habit of ignoring warts. For example, it is taken for granted that Scotland is a country of the Left in culture and politics. While true, it ought not to lead to the neglect of three of its greatest writers, Scott, Stevenson and Buchan, High Tories, but none of them deficient in Scottishness. The warts here are not Scott, Stevenson and Buchan, but stem from the habit of neglecting those who are not actively derided. Scottish culture tends to the rampantly populist on one hand and the abstruse on the other. It can leave the ground in between looking like the home of the timid instead of where tolerant and constructive debate takes place.

What I have tried to do is represent the foundations of Scottish reality, the character of at least some of its people and places, languages, literature, spiritual concerns and industry. Its lore, nature, landscapes and creatures are less controversial, and in finding them permanent and reassuring, I find them a source of life. Obviously, I have had to be selective; and to that extent the point of view is my own. Norman MacCaig once said, 'I hate a man who calls his country his.' I don't call Scotland mine. I call it Scotland.

Having once been a librarian I think I know how to use libraries intensively, and unobtrusively. Help, though, when needed, has always been given by the staffs of the libraries of the universities of St Andrews and Dundee, to whom I give warm and sincere thanks.

Will MacLean and Peter Davidson trusted me with the loan of books, for which I thank them. They trusted me with conversation, which is a better blessing, as did Robert Crawford, Lorn Macintyre and Alex Sinclair. They helped me in ways they might not have known.

DOUGLAS DUNN
Ferry-port-on-craig

A Strong Scotch Accent
of the Mind

To an Englishman something is what it is called: to a Scotsman
something is what it is.

SIR COMPTON MacKENZIE,
'Safety Last' in ed. David Cleghorn Thomson,
Scotland in Quest of her Youth (1932)

'Reality' is a word with which Scots lacerate, or silence, their
deeper selves.

LES A. MURRAY, 'The Bonnie Disproportion'
in *Persistence in Folly: Selected Prose Writings* (1984)

Dundee Cake

For many years, usually when drunkish, I have bored my
friends with the suggestion that the Scots, of all people, are
misunderstood. A glance at their history or literature (and
especially if you count Byron as a Scot, which after dinner, at
least, is permissible) reveals what lies underneath the slow
accent, the respectability and the solid flesh. Under the cake
lies Bonny Dundee.

JAMES KENNAWAY, *Household Ghosts* (1961)

Kaleedoni

Purposing a visit to Kaleedoni, a country integrally united to
Dominora, our course now lay northward along the western
white cliffs of the isle. But finding the wind ahead, and the
current too strong for our paddlers, we were fain to forgo our
destination . . .

And now, some conversation ensued concerning the country we were prevented from visiting. Our chronicler narrated many fine things of its people; extolling their bravery in war, their amiability in peace, their devotion in religion, their penetration in philosophy, their simplicity and sweetness in song, their loving-kindness and frugality in all things domestic:— running over a long catalogue of heroes, metaphysicians, bards, and good men.

But as all virtues are convertible into vices, so in some cases did the best traits of these people degenerate. Their frugality too often became parsimony; their devotion grim bigotry . . .

In Kaleedoni was much to awaken the fervour of its bards. Upland and lowland were full of the picturesque; and many unsung lyrics yet lurked in her glens. Among her blue, heathy hills, lingered many tribes, who in their wild and tattooed attire still preserved the garb of the mightiest nation of old times. They bared the knee, in token that it was honourable as the face, since it had never been bent.

HERMAN MELVILLE, *Mardi* (1849)

Patriotism

I

Breathes there the man, with soul so dead,
Who never to himself hath said,
    This is my own, my native land!
Whose heart hath ne'er within him burn'd,
As home his footsteps he hath turn'd,
    From wandering on a foreign strand!
If such there breathe, go, mark him well;
For him no Minstrel raptures swell;
High though his titles, proud his name,
Boundless his wealth as wish can claim;
Despite those titles, power, and pelf,
The wretch, concentred all in self,
Living, shall forfeit fair renown,
And, doubly dying, shall go down
To the vile dust, from whence he sprung,
Unwept, unhonour'd, and unsung.

12

O Caledonia! stern and wild,
Meet nurse for a poetic child!
Land of brown heath and shaggy wood,
Land of the mountain and the flood,
Land of my sires! what mortal hand
Can e'er untie the filial band,
That knits me to thy rugged strand!
Still as I view each well-known scene,
Think what is now, and what hath been,
Seems as, to me, of all bereft,
Sole friends thy woods and streams were left;
And thus I love them better still,
Even in extremity of ill.
By Yarrow's stream still let me stray,
Though none should guide my feeble way;
Still feel the breeze down Ettrick break,
Although it chill my wither'd cheek;
Still lay my head by Teviot Stone,
Though there, forgotten and alone,
The Bard may draw his parting groan.

SIR WALTER SCOTT, *The Lay of the
Last Minstrel*, Canto 6, I-II (1805)

'Plurals'

Behind all this is the peculiarity of the Scottish character, and
there is probably more whigmaleerie written about that than
about anything else. Scots are supposed to be dour, canny,
pawky, coarse, fly, stingy, pedantic, moralistic, and drunken
all at once, combining the severity of Calvin with the lasci-
viousness of Burns. They are characterized as a mixture of the
legendary Sawney Bean, the grotesque Galloway rogue who
consumed human corpses and lived in a cave, and David
Livingstone (an ancestor of mine), who darned his own frock
coat neatly in the African jungle. They are, as the saying goes,
like dung – no good unless spread – and there is no doubt that
Scots do get spread to a quite amazing degree over the face of
the earth. There has always been a drift away from the stony

barrenness of the home ground out into the expansive world; yet for wandering Scots the homeland never quite disappears. The odd thing is that almost everything said about the Scots is true, but never the whole truth – their character has so many sides to it.

ALASTAIR REID, The New Yorker (1964)

John Buchan at a Lectern

Poverty is the first and biggest fact in our history, and from that poverty the Scottish race learned certain qualities which only come from a hard school. It learned that nothing comes without effort, and that we value most what costs us most. The homes our forefathers made for themselves were hard won, and therefore they were deeply loved, for love of home has always been a notable Scottish quality. The fireside is all the cheerier for the black weather out of doors and the long hard day in the rain. Then again, poverty teaches self-reliance and effort. It hardens the fibre of a man and toughens his character. And most of all, it makes a man take risks in life. The more comfortable we are the more likely we are to be sluggish and unenterprising and timid. The complaint against Moab in the Bible is that she was 'settled upon her lees'. The Bible thought very little of the comfortable man.

The second great fact in Scottish history is its unsettlement. The last wars in Great Britain were fought on her soil. England, you may say, has been at peace ever since the Restoration. But in Scotland we had the long strife of the Covenant, we had Dundee's campaign, which ended at Killiecrankie, we had the Jacobite wars of 1715 and 1745. And for generations before that you had Scotland a kind of cockpit. In most of the English shires there has been no fighting since the Wars of the Roses. Hence a peaceful society grew up and unfortified manor houses were built as early as the sixteenth century. But Scotland had no rest. More than once an English army marched to the walls of Edinburgh. A herd in Teviotdale never went to bed without the possibility of being roused to defend his master's cattle, amid blazing ricks and roof-trees, against a foray from Northumberland. That was for the Southern Lowlands, while in the Northern Lowlands there was the same risk of attack

14

from the Highland glens. Till a late period in her history Scotland was perpetually being emptied from vessel to vessel. I think such a discipline could only have one result. Dwellers on a border are proverbially a bold race, and the whole of Scotland in this sense was a border. If poverty made us hard and careful, the ancient unsettlement of our land made us enterprising and adventurous.

It is to our history that we must look for the source of what seem to me the two master elements in the Scottish character, as we have seen it in history and as we know it today. These elements are hard-headedness on the one hand and romance on the other: common sense and sentiment: practicality and poetry: business and idealism. The two are often thought to be incompatible, but this is wrong. Almost everybody has got a little of both. It is the peculiarity of the Scottish race that it has both in a high degree . . .

We will take the prosaic side first. We Scotsmen are a commonplace folk, fond of sticking close to the ground, and asking a reason for things and a practical justification. We take a pleasure, a malicious pleasure, I am afraid, in pricking bubbles; and, though we are very sentimental ourselves, we like to pour cold water on other people's sentiment. You remember the shepherd to whom a tourist was dilating on the beauties of a certain hill. 'Why, from the top of it,' said the tourist, 'you can see Ireland.' 'Ye can see far further than that,' said the shepherd, 'you can see the mune.'

Now I want you to turn to the other side of the Scottish character, the side which is as far distant as possible from the cautious, prosaic, worldly-wise side I have been talking about. With all our prudence, our history is a record of the pursuit of lost causes, unattainable ideals, and impossible loyalties. Look at the long wars of independence which we fought under Bruce and Wallace. If we had had any common sense we would have made peace at the beginning, accepted the English terms, and grown prosperous at the expense of our rich neighbours. Look at the wars of religion, when for a refinement of dogma and a nice point of Church government the best of the Lowland peasantry took to the hills. Look at the Jacobite risings. What earthly sense was in them? Merely because Prince Charlie was a Stewart, and because he was young and gallant, we find sober, middle-aged men, lairds, lawyers, and merchants, risking their necks and their fortunes to help a cause which was doomed from the start. We have, all of us, we Scots, a queer *daftness* in our blood. We may be trusted to be prudent and sensible beyond the average up to a certain point. But there comes a moment when some half-forgotten loyalty is awakened, and then we fling prudence to the winds.

The truth is that we are at bottom the most sentimental and emotional people on earth. We hide it deep down, and we don a mask of gravity and dour caution, but it is there all the time, and all the stronger because we hide it so deep . . .

JOHN BUCHAN, 'Some Scottish Characteristics'
in W. A. Craigie *et al.*, *The Scottish Tongue* . . . (1924)

The Princess of Scotland

'Who are you that so strangely woke,
    And raised a fine hand?'
Poverty wears a scarlet cloke
        In my land.

'Duchies of dreamland, emerald, rose
    Lie at your command?'
Poverty like a princess goes
        In my land.

'Wherefore the mask of silken lace
    Tied with a golden band?'
Poverty walks with wanton grace
        In my land.

'Why do you softly, richly speak
    Rhythm so sweetly-scanned?'
Poverty hath the Gaelic and Greek
        In my land.

'There's a far-off scent about you seems
    Born in Samarkand.'
Poverty hath luxurious dreams
        In my land.

'You have wounds that like passion-flowers you hide:
        I cannot understand.'
Poverty hath one name with Pride
            In my land.

'Oh! Will you draw your last sad breath
        'Mid bitter bent and sand?'
Poverty begs from none but Death
            In my land.

RACHEL ANNAND TAYLOR, *The End of Fiammetta* (1923)

The Foreigner at Home

The fact remains: in spite of the difference of blood and language, the Lowlander feels himself the sentimental countryman of the Highlander. When they meet abroad, they fall upon
each other's necks in spirit; even at home there is a kind of
clannish intimacy in their talk. But from his compatriot in the
south the Lowlander stands consciously apart. He has had a different training; he obeys different laws; he makes his will in
other terms, is otherwise divorced and married; his eyes are not
at home in an English landscape or with English houses; his
ear continues to remark the English speech; and even though
his tongue acquire the Southern knack, he will still have a
strong Scotch accent of the mind.

ROBERT LOUIS STEVENSON,
'The Foreigner at Home' (1882)

Genius and Universality

The last half of the eighteenth and the first half of the nineteenth centuries contained the greater portion of a period of
extraordinary activity in Scotland. It was a period of prodigious
thought, prodigious work, prodigious discoveries. It was integ-
rated with what was going on in other countries in Europe and
abroad, yet in Scotland there was a particular intensity, as
though Scottish ways and methods and abilities were especi-

17

ally suited to the needs of the time. Very many of the technics of the modern world were fathered and nursed in this Golden Age of Scottish endeavour. Men of talent, with more than a sprinkling of men of genius, appeared in a diversity of fields – geology, astronomy, meteorology, natural history, medicine, surgery, in philosophy and mathematics, in the academic world, in workshops, and in back parlours where many ingenious devices were contrived.

Those who created were sustained by the belief that the miracle of mechanical power would solve the problems of mankind. They were unaware of the 'dark Satanic Mills' that were to rise after them; they had no idea that they were preparing the transformation of their country into desolate rural areas and mass metropolitan populations of hungry diseased multitudes.

Hopeful, eager energy was expended in all directions, and in all manner of activity – a special wheel, the principle of latent heat, discoveries about the circulation of the blood, a new outlook on the universe. Adam Smith wrote his *Wealth of Nations*. In philosophy Hume capsized the structure of thought that had been built over hundreds of years. He laid the foundation not only of subsequent philosophical thought but also of analytical psychology. Kant, who was stirred to write his *Critique of Pure Reason* in response, said that Hume 'woke him from his dogmatic slumbers'.

Looking back at the period, from mid-century to mid-century, one gets the impression of tumultuous activity. One is tempted to list a string of names as they come to mind, out of sequence, in no special order. The names, the discoveries, the years themselves, become mingled with steam and shale and coal and electricity, with anaesthetics, antiseptics, with poems and treatises and paintings. In the field of chemistry and physics alone there is a record of men that in itself demonstrates the progress of science – Black, Martine, Graham, Dewar, Playfair, Ramsay, Young, Beilby, Brewster, Swan, Clerk Maxwell, Lord Kelvin.

William Murdock who, like James Boswell, was born in Auchinleck, was the first man to light his home with coal gas. He did this in 1792. He also devised the first oscillating steam engine. Electricity – which by then was doing parlour tricks – followed in the next century. Clerk Maxwell ('Dafty' to his schoolboy friends) discovered the electromagnetic field. At the age of fifteen he had sent a paper to the Royal Society of Edinburgh. In 1847 Professor Simpson discovered chloroform in Queen Street, Edinburgh, during a hilarious evening when his friends, willing experimenters, collapsed unconscious under his dining-room table.

James Nasmyth, member of a family that had a 'corner' in Scottish landscape painting, so many painters did it produce, invented the steam-hammer that bears his name. He had other inventions, and drew plans for a submersible ship in which the Admiralty showed no interest. A book of his had the fascinating title, *The Moon Considered as a Planet, a World, and a Satellite.*

The gigantic appetite for work and discovery was itself the most astonishing aspect of the age. Because the emphasis was technical and abstract, rather than artistic, the period has received less attention than it merits. What it produced has largely been accepted unthinkingly in our modern life. But though the fruits of the period were, eventually, telephones and wireless and modern surgery, and half a hundred other things, there was at the time an equal devotion to all aspects of life. Poets, theologians, philosophers, economists, surgeons, engineers, argued and talked and worked together. They were creating a new age, and were aware of it, just as they were fully aware of the background to their own brilliance – the filthiness and disease of the towns, the naked coalminers, men and women, spending most of the day underground, the poverty of the country workers, the bigoted narrowness of religion.

Professor James Hutton is probably the foremost example of a man creating a new science out of nothing but a tradition of uncompromising thinking. He was born in Edinburgh in 1726 and became the 'father of modern geology'. He was educated at the Royal High School in Edinburgh and then attended the Arts and Medical Faculties in Edinburgh University. Afterwards he went abroad. When he returned to Edinburgh he was more attracted by research in chemistry than by the practice of a medicine that was, in the 1740s, still crude and unattractive to his exploratory mind. He inherited a farm and after further travels he set himself up as a scientific farmer. His chemical knowledge was directed to the soil and through this he turned to the land and its formation. At that time it was accepted that God had created the world in six days. Attempts had been made to explain 'scientifically' the features of the earth, but only in terms that fitted with the Mosaic teaching of the Bible.

At the age of fifty-nine, in 1785, Hutton presented his paper *Theory of the Earth*, to the Royal Society in Edinburgh. To men who believed the age of the earth was exact and measurable in a few thousand years, he offered, with the neatness of an inductive argument, his ideas of the immensity of time and the true nature of the world. He showed the process of erosion and the building up of new land masses under the oceans. It was an intellectual *tour de force*. But then, so was Hume's *Treatise on Human Nature*, so was the *Wealth of Nations*. So indeed was Watt's steam engine . . .

The invention of the steam engine opened up new possibilities for commerce. The Scots had experimented with tramways before, and in due course it was a Scot who put the flange on wheels so that machine traction could be mounted on rails.

The tramways had a long history. The monks of Midlothian, who had hewn coal since the Middle Ages, had used crude trams to take the coal the short distance from the mines to the sea. (In 1745 General Cope had his battle lines at Prestonpans intersected by a tram-road or wagon-way. The rails were of wood and led from the Tranent coal pits to the harbour at Cockenzie. It is the wooden rails that give us the word: the Scandinavian *tram*, or *trum*, is a tree cut lengthwise into logs.)

About 1800 the Scottish engineer, Thomas Telford, became interested in tramways as an alternative to canals. He was the son of an Eskdale shepherd. He built canals in England, the Caledonian Canal, and the Gotha canal in Sweden. The major monument to his work is the suspension bridge over the Menai Strait between Anglesey and Wales.

He advocated the use of 'iron railways' in 'countries whose surfaces are rugged'. The horse was the locomotive power he proposed. Before the steam engine was fitted to rails the Lothians and the Tweed valley were surveyed for many railroad schemes, worked out in cost to the last penny, with estimated profits and percentage returns on capital.

It is for his roads that Telford is best known. Until the first half of the eighteenth century miserable road conditions had made trade almost impossible by land. In 1750 a journey between Edinburgh and Glasgow was 'an arduous undertaking at any season of the year. It could only be performed on foot or on horseback, and during the winter it was a matter of the utmost difficulty . . . not more than ten or a dozen carriages of any sort – carts included – passed in a year.' The distance was forty miles.

Telford did the civil engineering to transform the roads of Scotland and England – and Russia, too, for that matter – and Macadam invented a type of smooth, durable surface. (Macadam was eventually appointed surveyor general of metropolitan roads and granted £10,000.) Many years later, in 1887, Dunlop re-invented the pneumatic tyre. (It was a Scottish doctor who devised the way of impregnating a cloth with rubber, an invention subsequently used by Mackintosh for his raincoats.)

Dunlop is an example of the great number of Scots who made discoveries in matters quite outside their normal business. He was a veterinary surgeon. When he died he was running a drapery business in Dublin.

Nasmyth, of the steam-hammer, was an example of the practical man produced by an artistic family, just as, in the contrary way, the Stevenson family of civil engineers and lighthouse builders, produced Robert Louis Stevenson. The balance between science and the arts was real, as though the Scots refused to have life arbitrarily divided into compartments. Life was to be seen whole, and the artist and the scientist were two aspects of the same person. (R. L. Stevenson's least-known work is, probably, his paper on *The Thermal Influences of Forests*. De Quincey, during his long residence in Edinburgh, must have been under the same dual influence when he wrote his *Logic of Political Economy*.)

Sir Walter Scott and his cronies may have turned an almost blind eye to technical development, but it was in an unconscious reaction to it that they re-explored the past and erected the New Romanticism which was to delight Europe, already excited by the 'Ossian' literature, the creation of another Scot.

The whole conception of modern shipping and shipbuilding was created when the stern-paddler, the *Charlotte Dundas*, built by Symington, was sent on her trials on the Forth and Clyde Canal, and then moved to Lochwinnoch because it was feared the canal banks would be damaged by that unparalleled occurrence, the wash of a steamship . . .

That this blossoming of talents could take place at all, in so many different ways, was due of course to the age providing many of the ideas and materials. It was also possible because Scotland was ready for it. Though the parliamentary union with England was a great setback, almost a fatal *mésalliance*, there was a long heritage of European culture on which to draw . . .

Though the full flowering was over by the 1850s the same type of comprehension and endeavour continued to show itself – in Hugh Miller, in Sir James Frazer, Sir Arthur Keith, Lord Boyd Orr. It was Alexander Bell who invented the telephone; James Baird who invented television; Sir Alexander Fleming who discovered penicillin.

Is there something particularly Scottish in these Scotsmen, and in what they did? Take a group on whom the crown of genius sits not too uneasily – Hutton, Robert Burns, Adam Smith, Hume, Frazer. It is difficult to avoid the conclusion that their minds had one quality in common – a perception of 'universality'.

To analyse beyond that may be dangerous. Yet one must ask why this should be, consistently, generation after generation, the stamp of Scottish genius. The lesser men made their numerous discoveries. The giants were chasing the universe as a boy chases a ball. 'To hold infinity in the palm of a hand' is almost too easy a way of describing the attitude of mind which seeks the final shape of things through the traditional application to detail. It is a metaphysical attitude, and that may be its Scottishness. Scratch a Scotsman and you find a preacher. There was a necessity to work hard at the job on hand, to master the detail: this was a bred-in-the-bones austerity of purpose, the 'character' handed down from father to son in sour farms on windy hills. But specialization was shunned except as a path to a fuller understanding of the whole.

Something was derived – and here one treads warily – from Scottish Presbyterianism, or perhaps the Scottish Church was itself moulded by the same attitude but without the generosity and tolerance of genius. One is led through a religion which postulated a personal god (noting the intellectual pride and power of a people who denied any other person the right to stand between themselves and their divinity), to a metaphysi-

22

cal attitude of mind which penetrated the blind depths beyond knowledge and dogmatic faith.

Napier, who lived before this period, was a Scottish mystic who discovered logarithms. Hume was accused of atheism. Burns satirized the church and preached human values. The scientists amongst them came to irrefutable scientific conclusions – yet making few dogmas, always leaving the next page clear for direct controversion. The goal was never knowledge itself, nor even a limited understanding, but wisdom, an apprehension incorporating religion and philosophy and morality and the freedom of humanity. Whether the approach was by test-tube or by poetic stanza they were all travelling the same way.

NEIL McCALLUM, *It's an Old Scottish Custom* (1951)

John Logie Baird

When it rained past Dumbarton Rock
You skipped Classics for a motorbike exploration

Of the Clyde's slow Raj. In sodden memsahibs' gardens
Hydrangeas unfurled into fibre-optics.

A dominie lochgellied you once
For pronouncing 'Eelensburgh' like those wild, untouchable
    tinks

Who, if they could see your biker's career from today's
Long distance, would snigger. A socialist most famous for

Inventing an undersock, screened from douce cousins,
Under bamboos at a small jam factory

Near Port of Spain you achieved television
And paid for it. At the trials a boy called Reith

Risen from your old class shook hands, then wrote you off.
You worked. When World War II ended

Baird equipment broadcast victory in the Savoy
But not one diner said cheerio when you faded,

An obsolete wallah, edited out, still beaming,
One hand outstretched across those Clydelike waves.

ROBERT CRAWFORD, *A Scottish Assembly* (1990)

It was quite by chance that I opened the 1933 edition of the Medical Directory at page 1236. It was by chance, by the fortuitous pull of certain small muscles of the eye – called, I think, the superior or inferior recti – that I happened to notice, near the top of the page, the words Glasgow and Aberdeen and Edinburgh. But chance having opened the door, curiosity stepped inside and hung up his hat: to be plain and straightforward, as current use prefers, I counted the number of doctors who, having graduated in a Scottish university, were now practising in England. There were twelve; and the total number of names on the page was twenty-six.

The immediate inference, however, was unjustifiable. It was too early to conclude that out of every thirteen doctors in England, six were Scots: because graduates of a Scottish university are not necessarily Scots by birth or blood – Edinburgh is notoriously attractive to exotics – and because other pages of the Directory might show a very different ratio.

I turned, again by chance, to page 488. It contained thirty-two names, of which eight were those of Scots, or Scottish graduates, practising in England. This brought the proportion down to one in four. I made a similar calculation on page 726, and found a ratio of seven to nineteen. But on page 924 it became alarmingly four to one: four Scots to one Englishman. This page, however, was a catalogue of Macdonalds: there was no room for English names among these descendants of the mountain clan, these survivors of the Penal Acts: and reading their brave patronymics I forgot for a while that I was hunting a ratio, and began to make in my mind pretty pictures of social evolution. For the grandfathers of many of these gentlemen whose names lay before me – and whose Austin motor-cars were everywhere aggravating the traffic problem, whose wives, at that very moment, were arranging fine flowers in their drawing-rooms – their grandfathers, I say, had been poor men in a plaid, with a black hillside for their morning view and a handful of meal for their dinner, and their grandfathers' great-grandfathers had fought at Inverlochy under the Great Marquis, and died no doubt, like MacTavish in the song, with a dirk in their bowels. But their grandsons, whose names I was studying, had put away their skean dhus, and carrying bistoury

24

and forceps instead, were bleeding their English neighbours more profitably than anyone since the Black Douglas.

England, or so it seemed from the evidence before me, was for Scots, or at any rate for Scottish doctors, a land of opportunity, a happy Canaan where panel patients grew in every tree. I returned to my statistics and came to the conclusion – though I am no actuary – that our surgeons and physicians had amply revenged Prince Charles Edward's retreat from Derby.

ERIC LINKLATER, *The Lion and the Unicorn* (1935)

. . . *And the Auld Enemy*

That Scotland is a part of the United Kingdom is an almost inevitable accident; at the same time, the unity of the English and the Scots should never be assumed. It was Sir Walter Scott who pointed out that the Scots and the English had fought three hundred and fourteen major battles against one another before their union; this kind of historical animosity does not disappear overnight. The fact remains that the two countries are altogether distinct in temperament and manner, and their conjunction, although it is by now a working one, has never been resolved to the satisfaction of either . . .

Of all the grievances nursed by the Scots, none is greater than the fact that the English apparently do not bother to hate back. Still, some of my English friends have owned up to an anti-Scottish disposition. 'What really gets me down,' said one businessman in the City, 'is this incredible myth – created undoubtedly by Scots – of their own reliability, their good sense, their business shrewdness. It used to be said in the City that a Scots accent was worth an extra thousand pounds a year. The Scots sound literally too good to be true, and they are, at that.'

ALASTAIR REID, *The New Yorker* (1964)

'Pull Yourself Together'

I

I really don't know what would happen if we Scots were more generally 'decent'. Decency being, I suppose, a good thing, it would be a good thing if we were more decent. But, somehow, I think I should regret so tremendous a transformation. I should regret it because we would lose, along with the acquisition of decency, so many qualities that are a part of not being decent. We would lose, for instance, our capacity for going to extremes in so much that we do and feel and are. You have said that 'the good Englishman is, somehow or other, typical'. How right you are. Goodness is the norm of the English character. It is not (I cannot help thanking goodness) the norm of the Scottish character. The best people I have ever met in my life have come from Scotland: so have the most detestable.

MORAY McLAREN to James Bridie,
A Small Stir (1949)

II

Do *you* appreciate tact? When Lord Rosebery's tenant-farmer took a big spoonful of his *surprise* and blurted out, 'Pudding's froze!' the ex-premier took a spoonful himself and remarked, 'By Jove, so it is.' Lord Rosebery was a Scotsman. Sam Johnson would have explained. Which of these would have put the farmer at his ease and guarded him against the abominable sniggerings of his fellow guests? Which would have been tactful and which sensitive? Eh? Pull yourself together.

JAMES BRIDIE to Moray McLaren,
A Small Stir (1949)

III

A great deal of what is called Scottish sentiment *is* funny. To anybody who knows the people who indulge in it, Wallacethebruceism, Charlieoverthewaterism, Puirrabbieburnsism, Bonniebonniebanksism, Myainfolkism and Laymedoonandeeism, those not very various forms of Scottish Sentiment, are very comical indeed. The Scot himself, greeting heartily beneath his bonnie briar bush, has been known to smile through his tears . . .

JAMES BRIDIE to Moray McLaren,
A Small Stir (1949)

IV

He was a profoundly religious man to whom it never occurred to doubt the essential tenets of the Christian religion, nor of certain political views which he held, and in which he was brought up. Nevertheless this did not prevent him from indulging in, even delighting in the most fantastic somersaults of speculation on the minutiae of his religious and political convictions. This used to infuriate his English and German friends. He spoke German well. They could never make up their minds whether these fireworks or mental gymnastics were the fruit of Celtic lightheartedness or Scottish Lowland pedantry. At any rate they were inoffensive to their stolidly held convictions. I do not think that they ever doubted his sincerity. It was his method of expressing it that maddened them. It delighted me: for I love to see a mind playing with a trivial point, just as I love to see a kitten playing with a ping pong ball. Delighted though I was, I shared the Saxon and Teutonic doubt as to the source of this nimble pedantry. My relative was half pure Highland and half Edinburgh stock. Whence came this flippant seriousness?

It should not be supposed that the irritation and anger was all on one side in these discussions with his Southern theological and political friends. He was as maddened by their matter of factness, their straight unparenthetical argument as they were by his agility. They crashed straightforwardly up the trunk of the tree of any argument, heedless of what they left behind on the way, or what they damaged. He, monkey like, could not forbear to explore each branch, each twig of every tree until he got to the top triumphantly. It infuriated him to hear their laughter at his often useless meticulousness which they dismissed as pedantry. For over half his life he was sightless. It may be that his curiosity about things of the mind was exaggerated by his blindness. I think it merely brought out and underlined a national trait which for lack of a better word I will call Scottish mental bisexuality.

It is a commonplace to label the various nations of Europe according to sex. Despite the most reckless generalizations and exceptions, there is a good deal in this habit. Whatever you may say, I affirm that the English are the most male nation in Europe, the French the most feminine. We are a curious blend of the two; and you will often find that blend in the one person. My elderly relative was the best example I have ever come across. The unswerving logicality of his mind was masculine. The capricious and instinctive way he used his logic was feminine – and particularly irritating to his English friends, who could not but recognize the calibre of his brain, but were put off by the movements of that brain. Their method (and it used to irritate him to the point of fury) of showing their own dislike of his mental agility was to burst into guffaws of laughter.

MORAY McLAREN to James Bridie,
A Small Stir (1949)

Scotland

It was a day peculiar to this piece of the planet,
when larks rose on long thin strings of singing
and the air shifted with the shimmer of actual angels.
Greenness entered the body. The grasses
shivered with presences, and sunlight
stayed like a halo on hair and heather and hills.
Walking into town, I saw, in a radiant raincoat,
the woman from the fish-shop. 'What a day it is!'
cried I, like a sunstruck madman.
And what did she have to say for it?
Her brow grew bleak, her ancestors raged in their graves
as she spoke with their ancient misery:
'We'll pay for it, we'll pay for it, we'll pay for it!'

ALASTAIR REID, *Weathering* (1978)

My Father's House

The dining room, never used except as an ancillary larder, a cool place in which to set jellies and store meat, eggs and fish for the cat, is unchanged in essentials since I first came here in 1945. This room has the air of formal disuse characteristic of the Scots company room of its period. It was assembled long before I was born and is now almost an informal museum of north-east Scots twenties style, heirlooms and memorabilia.

There is a Brussels carpet; a table of brightly varnished, heavily grained yellow pine built by a long-dead local joiner; wallpaper with cowed brown flowers; a mirrored sideboard piled with souvenir china, plastic bowls, flowers made of wood chips bought from whining tinkers, paper bags containing outmoded hats, a number of plastic dolls in blonde wigs and kilts brought back as giftlets for my now deceased aunt by cronies who tripped off to other parts of Scotland for wee holidays.

There is a glass-fronted cabinet where my great-grandmother's tea service is stored, stately shapes of white china teapot and slopbasin – clearly a better class of goods was available in the town in the 1950s than it is today. My father says she was a schoolteacher and used to ride to work in Banff, across the Deveron, on a little pony. Banff, a small, granite, seventeenth-century town so obscure that letters directed to it are sometimes sent to Banff, Alberta, in error.

I tentatively identify this great-grandmother as the one whose antique sepia photograph on the wall shows her, good God, in a long cloak, wimple and modified steeple hat – and not as if it were fancy dress, either, but her normal apparel, a little touch of the Aberdeen witches. (In 1636, rope to bind witches at Banff cost eight shillings, a lot of money in those days.) But this lady has the stern face of a kirk-goer. There's the picture of a distant uncle who was killed while working on a railroad in Canada. Other family photographs, no longer identifiable, are curiously poignant. Who the hell were they? Why are they not remembered?

There are several pictures in heavy frames on the walls. Two are reproductions in oils of stags in depopulated Highland glens, school of 'The Stag at Bay'. There are charcoal sketches of similar scenes in all the bedrooms, the house is crammed with stags, there's even a little stag, made of lead, on top of the massive clock in the master bedroom. But there isn't a landscape that could harbour a stag within a hundred miles of this place. It's a purely emblematic Scottishness, this scenery of crags, spruce, glens, tumbling waterfalls, untenanted except for deer, post-clearance landscapes, in which man is most present in his resonating absences.

Clearly this family was once heavily into the mythology of Scotland. I keep trying to interest my father in the history of his people, now he's gone back to them at last. I sent him John Prebble's books about Culloden and the Highland clearances.

But he's cast them aside after a preliminary, dutiful browse. He says they're too bloody depressing.

During the whole of his fifty years down South, he never showed any interest at all in his own foreignness. None of your St Andrew's Societies and Burns Nights, those folkmoots of the middle-class Scots expatriate. There's a joke he's still fond of, though. Jock goes down South for an interview and, on his return, is asked: 'Did you meet any Englishmen, Jock?' 'Och, no; I only met heads of departments.' A self-defensive joke. Like the sort of Jewish joke told by Jews. And back he went, eventually. Back home.

ANGELA CARTER, *Nothing Sacred* (1982)

Scottish Contradictions

'There is a storm coming that shall try your foundation. Scotland
must be rid of Scotland before the delivery come.'
James Renwick, on the scaffold in 1668.

I would argue that there remains one, and only one, contradiction in Scottish society which is fundamental. This is the old contradiction between self-assertion, and self-distrust.

It would of course be easy to propose many other contradictions. We live in a rich country and yet are poor; we appear to have the means for self-sufficiency, in terms of resources and land, and yet are economically dependent. We consider the further diffusion of political authority, within Scotland as within Britain, as an almost unquestionable good, however we interpret the content of the word 'devolution', and yet Scotland is a country regionalized, fragmented and divided by geography and tradition to a degree which I find frightening enough already.

But I believe that many Scottish contradictions can be discussed within the broad self-assertion/self-distrust paradox. Take for example the mystery of a people almost extravagantly devoted to the events of its own past, and at the same time so amazingly indifferent to preserving the monuments of that past. When Glasgow destroys a medieval university to build a goods yard, or when Edinburgh University blows its monstrous

30

and still expanding crater of devastation in the midst of the seventeenth- and eighteenth-century buildings of the South Side, we would appear to be confronting a society which prefers its past good and dead and even dematerialized into myth. The antiquarianism of Walter Scott, who would certainly have fought against both acts of official vandalism, was none the less of this nature. Scottish history was only safe for the historian or novelist to approach and touch when it was certain that the beast's limbs, the Cameronian tradition, for example, had finally lost the power of movement. Only then could *Old Mortality* be written, even-handedly sanctifying the brave men on either side at Bothwell Brig. Live Scottish history was to be feared. People might act upon it, imperilling the stable order of the present. The battlefield must be tastefully landscaped, a place for peaceful self-congratulation without partisanship except that of the most harmless and sentimental kind. Self-assertion, and self-distrust . . .

Our country is very individualist, but not very democratic. Self-distrust has focused on the possibility of self-government, as if national feeling and pride were – in a contradictory manner – private emotions which had no place in the public domain. The Scottish versions of history seem to oscillate between extolling the virtues of passive suffering and glorifying moments of volcanic, almost involuntary violence. Where are the episodes in which the Scottish people, by holding together and labouring patiently and wisely, achieved something?

We are beginning to escape from the great contradiction now. But self-government, even independence, cannot normalize Scotland by themselves. They must lead on to a cultural revolution, a society in which the people rebel, easily and good-humouredly, every day of their lives. Then, and not when we are rid of ourselves, will the delivery come.

NEAL ASCHERSON, *Games with Shadows* (1988)

Escueto

It was not long ago that my friend John Coleman pointed out to me the Spanish word *escueto*, deriving from the Latin *scotus*, a

31

Scot. In present Spanish usage, it means 'spare', 'undecorated', 'stark'; but when we eventually looked it up in Corominas' etymological dictionary we found that Corominas had an extensive commentary on it, remarking at one point: '[the word] seems to have been applied to men who travelled freely, impelled by the practice of going on pilgrimages, very common among the Scots'; and he gives the meanings of 'free', 'uncomplicated', 'unemployed', and 'without luggage'. The pilgrims obviously travelled light, probably with a small sack of oatmeal for sustenance. The word absorbed me, for it is clearly a *Spanish* notion, or translation, of the Scottish character – a view from outside, which chooses to interpret Scottish frugality as a freedom rather than a restraint.

ALASTAIR REID, *Whereabouts* (1987)

St Andrew's Nights

So resounding has been the success of St Andrew's nights in places like Singapore and Buenos Aires that in recent years even Scots at home have started, rather half-heartedly, to celebrate the occasion. Since few of the homeland Scots have any clear idea of who the fisherman saint was or what he stood for, these festivals have been rather tame and obviously activated by the Scottish Office, an institution with a boundless enthusiasm for temperate patriotism.

Up to the moment of writing, those Scots north of the fifty-fifth parallel have failed to cheer themselves hoarse in honour of St Andrew. (This may be because the building in which the Scottish end of the Scottish Office is located is called St Andrew's House. Why the fishery section in the Scottish Office should have been given this distinction is rather a mystery. It may be that Scots cannot help feeling that St Andrew's Day – which also happens to be Sir Winston Churchill's birthday – is really just a house party.)

St Andrew's Day in the scattered outposts of the Empire is very different. From remote creeks in the steaming jungle, from cattle stations on the Pampas, from far and near Scots converge joyously on the nearest staging point and stage a monumental jamboree in honour of their favourite saint. They even do this in Paris, France, and in Chicago, Illinois. At these occasions tartan is displayed in rich and sometimes incongruous profusion and the bagpipes skirl furiously. Scots are past-masters in the art of propaganda, and they see to it that neither the eye nor the ear is neglected.

One school of thought holds it that these celebrations are deliberately organized as provocative and challenging gestures. On this theory they are engineered to demonstrate Scottish supremacy. There is no disputing that they are enormously popular and are frequented by persons who have no Scots blood at all in their veins. Some time ago I met a Scot who was on leave from some undisclosed jungle. To his horror he discovered that St Andrew's Day had never been celebrated in his locality. He immediately started issuing invitations. Out of a total neighbouring population of 250 Europeans, 160 had attended. An Englishman who had accepted his invitation was so stung that he set about arranging a St George's Day the following year. It had been attended by seven people, all of them Englishmen.

WILFRED TAYLOR, Scot Free (1953)

Smeddum

She'd had nine of a family in her time, Mistress Menzies, and brought the nine of them up, forbye – some near by the scruff of the neck, you would say. They were sniftering and weakly, two-three of the bairns, sniftering in their cradles to get into their coffins; but she'd shake them to life, and dose them with salts and feed them up till they couldn't but live. And she'd plonk one down – finishing the wiping of the creature's neb or the unco dosing of an ill bit stomach or the binding of a broken head – with a look on her face as much as to say *Die on me now and see what you'll get!*

from LEWIS GRASSIC GIBBON, 'Smeddum' (1934)

On Football

Is emotional exposure at football matches peculiar to the otherwise buttoned-up Scot, do you think?

A.S.: I believe it's a Scottish device, yes. But I don't think it's solely a Scottish thing. You don't notice it so much in the English because they have a greater variety of outlets for their emotional condition. Scotland lives in the grip of a dream. The original dream was of a kingdom of heaven on earth, a serious attempt to produce a total theocracy. The failure of that attempt, it's my conviction, has left a psychic fault in the Scottish character. They're prone, at the drop of a whisky bottle, to commit themselves to perfection, to Eden in a way, an Eden that they've never inhabited. At football they believe, as they stand there on the terracing, that they're going to see football played of the purest essence, that the game's suddenly going to be irreducibly perfect. They remain dissatisfied with anything less than this, and they remain hopelessly, endlessly optimistic that it will happen the next day. This is what gives the Scottish fans their unique qualities as a football-supporting nation, and to some extent gives Scottish players their unique qualities. They're all engrossed in this dream of perfection. Three–two at Wembley . . . you know, Scotland was much better than that. The accurate score was about 4 or 5–1. But the Scots weren't interested in scoring goals. They wanted to do these wee, totally infantile, things, like Eddie McCreadie would get the ball and run up, and Baxter would shout, 'Mine.' McCreadie would seem to be going to pass to him, then stop the ball and walk away. Baxter would then walk over and get it, literally. There's a degree of puerility about this that can be disapproved of. But what the players were saying was: normally we'd have beaten you, but today we're beating you so far away that you won't bother even going for that ball. I think there's no such thing in the English psychic mentality. They're a nation who've done innumerable things and whose national identity has been adequately expressed. The Scottish national identity has been expressed by going off to build bridges across rivers in India and things like that, supplementary things, incoherent things, and, by definition, in the end unsatisfying. There is no national achievement that Scots can both draw upon and contribute to. Football seems to me, in a very fragmented way, to be the one possibility.

from an interview with ALAN SHARP,
Scottish International (1972)

Fi'baw in the Street

Shote! here's the poliss,
the Gayfield poliss,
   an thull pi'iz in the nick fir
   pleyan fi'baw in the street!
Yin o thum's a faw'y
like a muckle foazie taw'y,
   bi' the ither's lang and skinnylike,
   wi umburrelly feet.
Ach, awaw, says Tammy Curtis,
fir thir baith owre blate ti hurt iz,
   thir a glaikit pair o Teuchters
   an as Hielant as a peat.
Shote! thayr thir comin
wi the hurdygurdy wummin
   tha' we coupit wi her puggy
   pleyan fi'baw in the street.

Sae wir aff by Cockie-Dudgeons an
   the Sandies and the Coup,
and wir owre a dizzen fences tha'
   the coppers canny loup,
and wir in an ou' o backgreens an
   wir dreepan muckel dikes,
an we tear ir claes on railins
   full o nesty irin spikes.
An aw the time the skinnylinky
   copper's a' ir heels,
though the faw'y's deid ir deean,
   this yin seems ti rin on wheels:
noo he's stickit on a railin wi
   his helmet on a spike,
noo he's up an owre an rinnan, did
   ye iver see the like?

Bi' we stour awa ti Puddocky
   (that's doon by Logie Green)
and wir roon by Beaverhaw whayr
   deil a beaver's iver seen;

noo wir aff wi buitts and stockins
   and wir wadin roon a fence
(i' sticks oot inty the wa'er, bi'
   tha's nithin if ye've sense)
syne we cooshy doon thegither
   jist like choockies wi a hen
in a bonny wee-bit bunky-hole
   tha' bobbies dinna ken.
Bi' ma knees is skint and bluddan,
   an ma breeks they want the seat,
jings! ye git mair nir ye're eftir,
   pleyan fi'baw in the street.

ROBERT GARIOCH,
Complete Poetical Works (1983)

Philargyrie

I

Another thing there is that fixeth a grievous scandal upon that
nation in matter of *philargyrie* or love of money and it is this:
there hath been in London and repairing to it for these many
yeers together, a knot of Scotish bankers, collybists[1] or
coinecoursers,[2] of traffickers in merchandise to and againe and
of men of other professions who by hook and crook, *fas et nefas,*[3]
slight and might, all being as fish their net could catch, having
feathered their nests to some purpose, look so idolatrously
upon their Dagon of wealth and so closely, like the earth's dull
center, hug all unto themselves, that for no respect of vertue,
honor, kinred, patriotism or whatever else, be it never so
recommendable, will they depart from so much as one single
peny, whose emission doth not, without any hazard of loss, in a
very short time superlucrate beyond all conscience an
additionall increase to the heap of that stock which they so
much adore; which churlish and tenacious humor hath made
many that were not acquainted with any else of that country to
imagine all their compatriots infected with the same leprosie
of a wretched peevishness whereof those *quomodocunquizing*[4]
clusterfists and rapacious varlets have given of late such canni-
bal-like proofs by their inhumanity and obdurate carriage
towards some whose shoos' strings they are not worthy to unty;

that were it not that a more able pen than mine will assuredly not faile to jerk them on all sides, in case, by their better demeanor for the future, they endeavor not to wipe off the blot wherewith their native country, by their sordid avarice and miserable baseness, hath been so foully stained, I would at this very instant blaze them out in their names and surnames, not-withstanding the vizard of Presbyterian zeal wherewith they maske themselves, that like so many wolves, foxes or Athenian Timons, they might in all time coming be debarred the benefit of any honest conversation.

Thus is it perceptible how usual it is, from the irregularity of a few to conclude an universal defection, and that the whole is faulty because a part is not right; there being in it a fallacy of induction, as if because this, that and the other are both greedy and dissembling, that therefore all other their countrymen are such, which will no wayes follow, if any one of these others be free from those vices; for that one particular negative, by the rules of contradictory opposites, will destroy an universal affir-mative; and of such there are many thousands in that nation who are neither greedy nor dissemblers.

SIR THOMAS URQUHART,
Ekskybalauron ('The Jewel') (1652)

[1] usurers; [2] money-changers; [3] right and wrong; [4] indiscriminate money-making

II

Several gentlemen of good account and other of his familiar acquaintance having many times very seriously expostulated with him why he did so implacably demean himself towards me, and with such irreconcilability of rancour that nothing could seem to please him that was consistent with my weal, his answers most readily were these: 'I have (see ye?) many daugh-ters (see ye?) to provide portions for (see ye?) and that (see ye now?) cannot be done (see ye?) without money; the interest (see ye?) of what I lent (see ye?) had it been termly payed (see ye?) would have afforded me (see ye now?) several stocks for new interests; I have (see ye?) apprized lands (see ye?) for these sums (see ye?) borrowed from me (see ye now?), and (see ye?) the legal time being expired (see ye now?), is it not just (see ye?) and equitable (see ye?) that I have possession (see ye?) of these my lands (see ye?) according to my undoubted right (see ye now?)?' With these overwords of 'see ye' and 'see ye now', as if they had been no less material than the Psalmist's *Selah* and *Higgaion Selah*, did he usually nauseate the ears of his hearers when his tongue was in the career of uttering anything concerning me; who always thought that he had very good reason to make use of such like expressions, 'do you see' and 'do you see now' because there being but little candour in his meaning whatever he did or spoke was under some colour.

SIR THOMAS URQUHART, *Logopandecteision* (1653)

III

'Yes,' said the broker after lunch, 'the only man who ever did me was a Scotsman, and in doing me he made me.' He paused, and we all listened. 'I'd just started on my own, and things were slack. A few orders here and there. In those days we had to watch our stamps. Well, I had one queer client, or rather he wasn't a client. His name was James Ian McQuilternach – a queer sort of name. But it wasn't only his name that was queer. The man himself was queer. Not that I ever saw him, but you could tell he was queer by his letters. In fact they weren't letters. That was the queer thing about them.'

'Post cards?' I suggested.

'No,' said our host, looking round the table, 'they were not post cards, and they weren't telegrams. I'll tell you what they were – they were menus from restaurants of the cheaper sort, old luggage labels – why, now I remember he once even used a label steamed off a jam jar. Yes, McQuilternach was a queer fellow.

'Were they stamped? Of course they were stamped, or I wouldn't have got them. On one side a halfpenny postage stamp and my address, on t'other his inquiries. No stationery expenses. Pen and ink provided by the post office.

'Oh, his inquiries were sensible enough. Was there room for capital appreciation in West Rands? What was the return on G.W. Fives compared to Midland Fours? Why were Tins depressed? Were Textile Possibilities fully discounted? That sort of thing. Interested in everything, was McQuilternach.

'Any orders? That's what I wanted to know. There were no

orders. So I told my clerk that we couldn't waste time, paper and stamps on the fellow. I said his next request was to be brought to me, so that I'd write him myself and tell him we weren't a Carnegie free library.

'His next arrived all right – the damned thing, written on the cardboard circular cover of a jam jar. What d'ye say? Was it the same jam jar? How the devil do I know? Anyway this time it looked like business. He had come into ten thousand pounds and wanted to invest it in ten securities, having in mind safety, geographical position, dividends, and room for appreciation. What did I suggest, and would I give my reasons, likewise all-in cost, stamps, brokerage, and total income less income-tax, separately stated for each? Of course I thought he was a rich crank. Work! You people don't know what work is. You think it's something that grows on a tree.'

'We do,' said I, 'and you have every reason to be proud of yourself.' But the broker ignored the soft answer that usually brings on wrath, and continued his tale.

'That evening I carted home the office-books of reference. Borrowed a portmanteau to hold them. Taxi, then tips to porters. Cab at the other end. For five whole days and nights I worked at McQuilternach's income. Got it up to six hundred and fifty-nine pounds seventeen shillings and threepence. And that was pre-war, remember. Then I posted my reply, condensed on to five sheets of paper. Nicely typed, too.

'What happened? Nothing. At least nothing for a week or so. Then a man showed me a paper. He said it contained an excellent set of investments. It did. The paper had offered a prize of two hundred pounds for the best list of investments. McQuilternach had won the prize. He deserved it. His selections couldn't be beaten.

'How did that do me good? Well, I went round to the paper and made a row. Of course they were very sorry and only laughed. They'd paid McQuilternach. They couldn't publish my name as a broker, but they did put in a paragraph about what a certain broker thought of their competition. A lot of people wrote to the paper for the broker's name and their letters were sent to me. Then we began to get busy. And now I must be going. Where's that waiter? . . .'

HALLIDAY SUTHERLAND, *The Arches of the Years* (1933)

Hugh MacDiarmid Will Now Say
a Few Words . . .

My aim all along has been (in Ezra Pound's term) the most drastic *desuetization* of Scottish life and letters, and, in particular, the de-Tibetanization of the Highlands and Islands, and getting rid of the whole gang of high mucky-mucks, famous fatheads, old wives of both sexes, stuffed shirts, hollow men with headpieces stuffed with straw, bird-wits, lookers-under-beds, trained seals, creeping Jesuses, Scots Wha Ha'evers, village idiots, policemen, leaders of white-mouse factions and noted connoisseurs of bread and butter, glorified gangsters, and what 'Billy' Phelps calls Medlar Novelists (the medlar being a fruit that becomes rotten before it is ripe), Commercial Calvinists, makers of 'noises like a turnip', and all the touts and toadies and lickspittles of the English Ascendancy, and their infernal womenfolk, and all their skunkoil skulduggery. (I have said a good deal about the submersion, under inferior types, of the true Scotsman. Having mentioned womenfolk, I must say here that the race of true Scotswomen, iron women, hardy, indomitable, humorous, gay, shrewd women with an amazing sense of values, seems to be facing extinction too in today's Scotland.)

HUGH MacDIARMID, *Lucky Poet* (1943)

LAND OF THE NAKED KNEE

Before the Union [the kilt] was considered by nine Scotchmen out of ten as the dress of a thief.

LORD MacAULAY, *History of England* (1849–61)

Pour l'amour, oui, mais pour la guerre, non.

GENERAL JOFFRE

La Garde Ecossaise du Corps du Roi

A few of the facts in the history of the Scots troops employed by France bring it closer home than any generalization can; for instance, after other incidents of a like character, M. Michel quotes from D'Auton's Chronicle, how, in a contest with the Spaniards in Calabria, in 1503, the banner-bearer, William Turnbull, was found dead with the staff in his arms and the flag gripped in his teeth, with a little cluster of his countrymen round him, killed at their posts, 'et si un Ecossais était mort d'un côté, un Espagnol ou deux l'étaient de l'autre'. The moral drawn from this incident by the old chronicler is, that the expression long proverbial in France, 'Fier comme un Ecossais', was because the Scots 'aimaient mieux "mourir pour honneur garder, que vivre en honte, reprochez de tache de lascheté".'

J. H. BURTON, *The Scot Abroad* (1864)

Bergschotten

'Grand-looking fellows all of them,' said the Germans. 'And did you ever see such horses, such splendour of equipment, regardless of expense? Not to mention the "Bergschotten" with their bagpipes, sporrans, kilt, and exotic costume and ways. Out of all whom Ferdinand got a great deal of first-rate fighting.'

The brigade of Maxwell particularly distinguished itself in the battle of Warburg (1760). They did some excellent practice with the bayonet, muskets, and cannon, 'obstinate as bears'. But what pleased Prince Ferdinand most was the dashing bravery of the Highlanders under their colonel, Robert Murray Keith. He ordered even more regiments to be raised in Perth, Inverness, Ross, and Sutherland. In non-military circles of Germany, however, the notions entertained of the 'Bergschotten' were still as singular as when the curious woodcut appeared at Stettin in 1627. Says the *Vienna Gazette* of 1762: 'The Highlanders are in dress, temper, and custom altogether different from the rest of the inhabitants of Great Britain. They are caught in the mountains when young, and they still run with incredible swiftness. The soldiers are of small stature and mostly either old or very young. They show an extraordinary love for their officers, who are all handsome and young. Their good endowments, proving the innocence of nature before being corrupted by example and prejudice, make us hope that their King's laudable though late endeavours to bring them up in the principles of Christianity will be crowned with success.'

TH. A. FISCHER, *The Scots in Germany* (1902)

Brave Skirts

Half Scotland sniggered, and the other half scowled, when in letters to the *Scotsman* and the *Glasgow Herald*, I put forward my suggestion that prisoners in Scottish jails be allowed to wear kilts, as their national birthright, if such was their wish. Those sniggerers and scowlers may well snigger more moronically and scowl more impatiently when I now confess that I donned my own first kilt, at the age of seven and a half, not with pride and joy, but with reluctance and anguish; and also that for the rest of my life I never buckled one on without feeling something of the grief and shame with which James IV, unhappy parricide, must have put on his penitential shirt of iron.

Puritanic and parochial Scots, you murdered my young and beautiful mother. As one of you, I must share the blame.

My mother bought the kilt from a second-hand clothes dealer called Lumhat Broon. It had once belonged to a boy whose father was a director of Stewart's of Gantock, the shipbuilding company for which my 'father' (the honourable good-hearted champion quoiter John Lamont, whose name is on my birth certificate) worked as a joiner, and my maternal grandfather, Donald McGilvray, as chief pay-clerk. The tartan was the dress McLeod.

She had seen the kilt in the window, beside the tile hat; but she had not gone into the shop to buy it, she had gone in to avoid Mrs Maitland and Mrs Blanie who were coming along the street. She had been so agitated when asking Lumhat to show us the kilt that I was too worried to object.

In the house, with this yellow and black kilt spread out over her lilac lap, my mother, twenty-six years old, pale-cheeked and red-haired, urged me, with a passion I thought extravagant and unfair, to put it on.

I kept muttering dourly: 'They'd a' ca' me a jessie.'

I had seen boys in kilts before, toffs from the villa'd West End, as remote from us in tenemented Lomond Street as the whites in South Africa are from the blacks.

Her delicate hand gripped the cameo brooch at her breast, so tightly that I could see her knuckles turn white.

More than sixty years later that brooch lies before me on the table, yellowish with age. I think of the peaty water of Puddock Loch, and shudder.

'You'd look like a prince, Fergie,' she whispered. 'As you should.'

I considered the consequences of obliging her. My eyes went skelly with apprehension.

'Jock Dempster wad lift it up,' I groaned.

Suddenly she was in tears again. I could do or say nothing to comfort her. I didn't know her well. She had been away too long; and, as I had tried to hint, ever so tactfully, she was a bit too beautiful, too perfumed, and too haughty for Lomond Street, and for me.

She had come too unexpectedly. I needed longer than three days to fit her into my life.

'And if he did you would give him a right good kick on the shin, wouldn't you? Have you got my red hair for nothing?'

Too embarrassed to compare our hair, I studied my boots. As

weapons they were formidable, with their tackets. I had the courage too to use them. But it wouldn't do any good. Anybody I kicked for laughing would howl with pain all right, but then everybody else would laugh all the more. Fergie Lamont in a kilt would be funny, Fergie Lamont in a kilt in a fury would be funnier still.

The trouble was, though I found her contempt for other people's opinions of her exciting, I also found it alarming. That walk with her had been a pleasure and an agony.

Through in the kitchen our canary Rob Roy burst into song, but only very briefly.

It was my mother who had bought him years ago, and when she had gone away he had missed her. So my father had told me; but when I had mentioned it to Miss Montgomery, my penny-buff teacher, she had been shocked. 'No, Fergus. Canaries only miss other canaries. If that. Besides.' She too disapproved of what my mother had done, and like all the rest wasn't going to tell what it was.

My mother's tears frightened me. I had seen women weeping before, but for reasons easily understood; when someone had died, if the rent couldn't be paid, if a husband had been brutal. These tears of my mother's had some cause more terrible and desolating than death or poverty or cruelty.

'Whit was it you did?' I whispered, once again. 'Why did you go away? Why is everybody so angry?'

Her scent reminded me of the roses in my grandfather's garden. Other boys' mothers smelled of pipeclay, scrubbing brushes, baby's milk, parozone, and black lead. She spoke too in a more ladylike way than any of my teachers. I would have liked very much to be able to brag about her to my friends, but I couldn't, there were too many things to be settled first; and I just couldn't see who was going to settle them.

'Oh, something terrible,' she murmured.

I wasn't sure whether or not she was joking.

'But whit?'

'Some day they'll tell you. But do you know what I want you to do now? I want you to put on this braw kilt and go up the brae with me to see your grandfather.'

I blew out my cheeks in the loudest, most incredulous gasp I could manage.

Once, seated on his knee, I had boldly asked my grandfather

where she was and when she was coming back. A tall stern man with a black beard, he had replied in the same calm voice he always used, whether reading bits out of the Bible or discussing his roses. 'She is in hell, Fergus, and no one ever comes back from there.'

I had had a hard job not to grin, because a few days before one of my best friends, Smout McTavish, had shouted to Miss Cochrane to go to hell. She had already given him two of the tawse for getting his sums wrong, and he had thought that was enough. She had dragged him to the headmaster who had given him two more for swearing. The joke was, Smout was one of the few boys in our district who seldom swore.

Inside his beard my grandfather's mouth had gone as hard as railway lines. 'When he's no' pleased,' Jim Blanie had once whispered, 'your grandfather looks like Goad.'

'I don't think he wants to see you,' I said, cautiously.

'But if you come with me, Fergus, and ask him for me, maybe he will.'

I was sure he wouldn't, but I felt I ought to oblige her.

'Whit will I wear under it?' I asked.

Few of us in Lomond Street wore underpants.

'Soldiers don't wear anything under their kilts.'

I wondered how she knew. But even if it was true, soldiers just had Boers shooting at them, they didn't have Jock Dempster or Rab McIntyre come whooping out of a close to snatch up their kilts and show their bums to lassies.

'I could take my barrow and gether dung.'

She laughed.

'Weel, he said I should. He needs it for his roses.'

'I'm sorry, Fergie. You gether dung if you want to.'

'It's my grandfather wants it, no' me. I've got nae roses.'

She hugged me then, laughing and weeping at the same time.

'Whatever happens, Fergie, wherever I go, I'll always remember my wee kiltie gathering dung for his grandfather's roses.'

'You said you wouldnae go away again.'

'Ah, but you see, Fergie, I thought I could stand it here, as long as I had you. It's only you I've missed. But I don't think I can stand it.'

I knew it was really my father she couldn't stand. (Let me in

45

the meantime call John Lamont that.) Since she had come back, three days ago, she had hardly spoken to him. He had been very quiet too, though once he had shouted at her. In our room-and-kitchen with the lavatory outside on the stairs privacy was never easy. She had slept with me in the room. My father had stood outside the door for a long time, sighing. She had sighed too.

No neighbours had called to say they were glad she was back, not even the Strathglasses or the Kerrs who lived on our landing. Everybody seemed sorry for me, instead of being pleased. My Aunt Bella had seized me by the jersey in the street and demanded that I go and stay with her. I had indignantly refused, though I liked my Uncle Tam and his pigeons. Aunt Bella was the one who, after my grandfather, hated my mother the most.

'If you go away again,' I said, 'take me wi' you.'

She considered it for half a minute, a long time.

'We'll see, Fergie. Let's try on the kilt, shall we?'

'Oh, a' right.'

With a groan I took off my breeks. I placed them where they would be quickly available if I lost my nerve.

Eagerly she wrapt the kilt round me.

To my relief it was too long.

'Kneel,' she said.

'Hae I to pray?'

'I doubt if that would help much, Fergie. Soldiers kneel, you see, to find out what's the right length. The edge should just touch the ground.'

When I knelt the kilt lay in folds on the floor.

'That's easy mended.' She tugged the waist up to my neck almost.

'I can hardly breathe.'

She buckled it there.

'Your jersey will cover it. Look. What a pity you've not got a tweed jacket and a sporran and green stockings.'

'I'm glad I havenae.'

'Don't be silly. You look braw.'

I thought I looked a terrible jessie. They were sure to laugh at me. Except Smout, maybe. He would be too ashamed of the holes in his breeks. To hide them he stood against walls or lampposts or dustbins or even big dogs.

Looking in the mirror, my mother put on her feathered hat, lilac in colour to match her costume. She dabbed scent behind her ears. I liked its smell, but I suspected it was one of the things about her that angered the women of our street. I wished she hadn't put it on, but I would have died rather than beg her not to.

She noticed my anxiety. 'Well, if we're to be gathering dung we'll need something nice to drown the smell.'

Where had she been, I wondered, miserably, that she hadn't learned there was nothing nasty about the smell of horses' dung, even when it was fresh?

ROBIN JENKINS, *Fergus Lamont* (1979)

The Executive Kilt

In the matter of images, the kilt looms large. And no wonder when one recalls how the whisky-exporters spread it through the world. Before 1914 Haig used to send through the Berlin streets a kilted Highlander in a 'trap' drawn by Shetland ponies to advertise their beverage; and the Dewars in London had an enormous illuminated kilted and bearded Highlander, whose kilt and sporran and beard – Timothy Shy of the old *News Chronicle* once termed a sporran a 'lapsed beard' – swung rhythmically as he lifted his elbow to quaff another dram. Also the 'Scoatch coamic' of the music halls has been an embarrassment to quite a lot of the more staid lawyerly Elder-of-the-Kirk types, who sedulously have their trousers pressed.

DOUGLAS YOUNG, *Scotland* (1970)

'We're Daft'

When I was young there was a ball. And the ladies wore long dresses with tartan sashes and the gentlemen wore funny velvet jackets with diamond-shaped silver buttons, a lace hankie at their throat, leather 'sannies', the kilt (natch) and tartan hose-tops with a dagger stuck down the side. Is that what a Scotsman looks like? I found out later when I was the busiest man on the West Coast wedding circuit that you could hire all that stuff. It came in a flat brown case from Keogh and Savage and since no knickers were included you had to presume that it was true what they say about Scotsmen. I hate country dancing but I always wear the tammy at Wembley. We're daft. The whole lot o' us.

BILL BRYDEN, ''Member 'at?' in ed. Trevor Royle, *Jock Tamson's Bairns* (1977)

Haunted by Time

The Mark of the Scot

For that is the mark of the Scot of all classes: that he stands in an attitude towards the past unthinkable to Englishmen, and remembers and cherishes the memory of his forebears, good or bad; and there burns alive in him a sense of identity with the dead even to the twentieth generation.

R. L. STEVENSON, *Weir of Hermiston* (1896)

'Stone'

We drove through the night. I awoke, as I always do, as we crossed the border. I have never outgrown that. The first small towns, with bannock in the windows and hosiery shops with the word spelt out in red and white stockings, the ugly villas with names tooled into the keystone – 'Ardrishaig', 'Kinphail', 'Sgreadan'; even the foodstuffs have celtic names – 'Glenwheat', 'Tobermac Fish Bits'. No other country has fallen so hard for its own image in the funfair mirror. Tartan rock, and a Scottie dog for every pot. But it is to me the only serious place to be. The road opens out into rearing country after the border, and the coarse grass and blue roads shiver under the grudging, then hospitable, sun. Nowhere dirties the air quicker than Scotland with all its swearing, drinking, cigarettes and dying factories. The gas towers over Grangemouth hold sulphur orange and a copper green up into the sky like brushes full of poster colour. But there is more air to dirty than in the rest of Britain, and each morning is new, the old day having cleared its throat and gone during the short night of the north.

Past the green flocking hills, always between the walls of dry stones which are clapped together at the top like hands, and past big harled houses with too little window and slipping turrets at their shoulder, and with not flowers but green vegetables on the south walls. If any of it were to disappear, I would still see it, for I see, of course, with sentimental eyes. What would another make of it? I am partial.

The car snicked between the Crook Inn and its walled garden on the other side of the road. The gate into the garden, against the freshly colouring sky, was flat as a nursery frieze, two woolly lambs flanked by two shepherds' crooks, white flat iron, white as milk and wool. There are those words used by tourists to Scotland – 'beauty spot', suggesting contrivance and falseness. The Lowlands have nothing of vain beauty though; they are protective, gentle, reliable, nurse to the rakeheaven grande-dame of the Highlands. Those mountains put on black and diamonds at night. Down here in the Lowlands, there is a shawl of mist in the country and a good rabbit fur of fag-ash over the towns. We may omit the Lion of Glasgow and the Unicorn of Edinburgh. Each of those is singular.

Stone lies between the two, and is approached by an irregular drive. To arrive, it is necessary to pass the house, which is entered from the side. It has two fronts and two climates. In the douce summer I live in every room; in winter the wind makes the eastern face of the house too brusque for papers and too cold for sitting. In the winter I have found flowers, matured to their fruit, left from the autumn, in ice, held in the vase like Fabergé's gemmy berries in crystal. Asleep in one of these rooms, you might put out a hand in sleep and in the morning find it gone quite white. The only way to foil the cold is to be in love, and even that is not sure. The house is plain. It is not squinched or pepperpotty, it recollects no French alliance. It is of grey stone, unfaced, and the stone is black when it is wet. There are hills to the west and hills to the east, but they are small for hills and the house is big for a house. It has twenty-seven windows on each side, three rows of nine, their glass of the type which spins all light that hits it. It tells the sky to itself. In the sills of the windows tortoiseshell butterflies hatch too soon and need daily rescuing. There is an attic room where the flies go to die. It fills your hair with noise. To east and west there are porticos, that to the west with a pointed pediment, to the east with a curved pediment. These are supported by unfluted columns to the east, fluted to the west. The columns are Doric. There is no suggestion of romantic vegetable matter anywhere in the architecture of the house. It looks as it sounds, stone.

When the sun rises, it fills the arc of the eastern pediment and the tubes of the columns with light. The smoothness of the portico looks pale against the grey house, and larger, as though it were another house itself. These steps end in a terrace. The terrace is lapped by a lawn shaped like an almond. The man who built the house had lost his heart to India, and found there rich compensation for this loss. The tip of the almond drops to a ha-ha. Cowslips grow in spring at its ashlar foot. A long field of leaning trees moves out into the heather. What the wind began, the trees' disease has completed. Scotland seems to favour brushy trees, hazel and rowan and gorse, over the English givers of contemplation and stealthy veiling shade.

CANDIA McWILLIAM, *A Case of Knives* (1988)

Mist in Menteith

Some say the name Menteith meant a peat moss in Gaelic, and certainly peat mosses fill a third of the whole vale. However that may be, its chiefest attribute is mist. Shadows in summer play on the faces of the hills, and snow in winter spreads a cold carpet over the brown moss; but the mist stays the longest with us, and under it the semi-Highland, semi-Lowland valley puts on its most familiar air.

When billowing waves wreathe round the hills, and by degrees encroach upon the low, flat moors, they shroud the district from the world, as if they wished to keep it from all prying eyes, safe and inviolate. Summer and spring and winter all have their charms, either when the faint green of the baulked vegetation of the north breaks out, tender yet vivid, or when the bees buzz in the heather in the long days of the short, nightless summer, or when the streams run noiselessly under the shroud of ice in a hard frost. The autumn brings the rain, soaking and blurring everything. Leaves blotch and blacken, then fall swirling down on to the sodden earth.

On trees and stones, from fences, from the feals upon the tops of dykes, a beady moisture oozes, making them look as if they had been frosted. When all is ready for them, the mists sweep down and cover everything; from the interior of the darkness comes the cries of wild ducks, of herons as they sit upon the trees, and of geese passing overhead. Inside the wreaths of mist another world seems to have come into existence, something distinct from and antagonistic to mankind. When the mist once descends, blotting out the familiar features of the landscape, leaving perhaps the Rock of Stirling floating in the air, the three black trees upon the bare rock of the Fairy Hill growing from nothing, or the peak of the Cobbler, seeming to peer above enormous mountain ranges, though in reality nothing more vast than the long shoulder of Ben Lomond intervenes, the change has come that gives Menteith its special character.

There are mists all the world over, and in Scotland in particular; mists circling round the Western Islands, filling the glens and boiling in the corries of the hills; mists that creep out to sea or in towards the land from seawards, threatening and dreadful-looking; but none like ours, so impalpable and strange, and yet so fitting to our low, flat mosses with our encircling hills. In older days they sheltered the marauders from the north, who in their gloom fell on the valley as if they had sprung from the night, plundered and burned and harried, and then retreated under cover of the mist, back to their fastnesses.

R. B. CUNNINGHAME GRAHAM, *A Hatchment* (1913)

Scotch Mist

Inversnaid, 3 July – Last night seemed to close in clear, and even at midnight it was still light enough to read; but this morning rose on us misty and chill, with spattering showers of rain. Clouds momentarily settled and shifted on the hill-tops, shutting us in even more completely than these steep and rugged green walls would be sure to do, even in the clearest weather. Often these clouds came down and enveloped us in a drizzle, or rather a shower, of such minute drops that they had not weight enough to fall. This, I suppose, was a genuine

Scotch mist; and as such it is well enough to have experienced
it, though I would willingly never see it again.

NATHANIEL HAWTHORNE, *The English Notebooks* (1870)

Inversnaid

This darksome burn, horseback brown,
His rollrock highroad roaring down,
In coop and in comb the fleece of his foam
Flutes and low to the lake falls home.

And windpuff-bonnet of fáwn-fróth
Turns and twindles over the broth
Of a pool so pitchblack, féll-frówning,
It rounds and rounds Despair to drowning.

Degged with dew, dappled with dew
Are the groins of the braes that the brook treads through,
Wiry heathpacks, flitches of fern,
And the beadbonny ash that sits over the burn.

What would the world be, once bereft
Of wet and wildness? Let them be left,
O let them be left, wildness and wet;
Long live the weeds and the wilderness yet.

GERARD MANLEY HOPKINS (1844–89)

A House on the Kyles of Bute

Merlewood had been my father's father's house. It was built by
one of the Clydeside ironmasters to accommodate his Victorian
family – wife, children, governess, nanny, cook, chauffeur, coy
servant girls brought up from the city. There were eight bedrooms and an attic of rooms, and two turrets, and a scaled-
down portico à la Balmoral, and steeped corbie-stanes on the
gables, and a flagpole to fly the Union Jack or the Saltire. The
building had weathered very slowly, bald grey sandstone
against the blue Atlantic sea-skies, the bracken hill behind, the

rhododendron bushes studded with purple, pink and white heads.

We spent every summer there, and an occasional Easter or September weekend. A ritual developed.

My parents drove the hundred miles or so from Glasgow.

The day before, the rest of us would sail up from the Broomielaw on the steamer.

We would stand watching at the rails for a first glimpse of Merlewood. On overcast days the chimneys would be smoking, in sunshine the windows shone like mirrors.

Merlewood was waiting: and it was as if – I would think – I only had to see it again to become the 'other' version of myself.

As the distance to the shore grew less and less I had the sensation of sailing into last summer, and the one before, and the one before that.

We nudged against the pier; the holding ropes were thrown, and the gangways were hoisted up to the gates.

Our feet clattered over the soft, salty, echoing wood.

Trunks and cases were loaded into a Humber taxi, not the pony trap of my father's time.

Gregor and Rhona and I would start walking, as we always walked, while Kirsty and Sandy and Angus bundled themselves into the Humber.

Tighnabruaich grass was springy with moss. The sun dazzled off the sea. Wavelets slapped about the rock in the bay, standing in line with the house. The red road was always redder than I remembered. Bees big as halfpennies stuck to garden walls. The Scoulers had this year's new model of Daimler. Rhona walked as our mother walked, with a woman's rolling hips. The steamer's hooter blew. The taxi was disappearing out of sight along the coast track, spreading a balloon of white dust behind it.

The real summer had begun . . .

Merlewood became someone else's (a hairdresser with a chain of salons bought it: my mother specifically asked us not to tell her who the new owner was, and what 'sort of person'), then it was re-sold in inflation days and the house was divided and the property put on the market as time-sharing accommodation.

The steamers only ran to Tighnabruaich on nostalgia cruises. I went on one once, with Rhona. It lashed with rain that day, but as we sailed up the Kyles of Bute we doggedly stood at the rails for a first sight of Blair's Ferry, then Kames, then

Tighnabruaich. We mistook another house for Merlewood, and then we saw it. The garden was missing the evergreens and most of the rhododendron bushes; it looked naked, and functional and very modern. Someone in a yellow kagoul and sou'wester was walking a dog. The rock in the bay hadn't been claimed yet, as we'd always told ourselves we were going to do: we would row out and christen it with one of our father's bottles and an Arthur Ransome name, and fly the Saltire. The thought of the blood-smears must have been in both our minds.

The upstairs tea-room had gone from the pier, the room was empty. The slippery boards under our feet were very worn and in the gaps the sea sternly churned beneath us. We bought a postcard and sent it to our mother, now resident in a private hotel in Budleigh Salterton. We searched for a post box and eventually found one, in a mossy wall.

The red road with its pot-holes and puddles of rain water was redder than I remembered. It was raining too hard for us to spot any droning bees. Under a golf umbrella we walked along as far as the boatyard, which seemed – oddly, in these doldrum days – to be doing good business.

We imagined how the postcard would be received; my mother's favourite time of the day was the topping-up hour before dinner, and we saw her handing it to favoured fellow-guests over a snifter. In Zanzibar she'd shown her svelte international friends her family's postcards from Scotland and (so she would tell us) they had envied her. Life goes round in a circle, I said to Rhona, and she agreed with me, in a slightly strained voice she'd had all day.

We looked in at Merlewood from the gates. The creeper on the south wall of the house had been taken down – by the builders or on the hairdresser's instructions – and double-glazing fitted to the windows.

We only had an hour between landing and setting sail again. Rhona said she thought we'd done something 'useful' with our day, but I couldn't think quite what.

I felt we'd travelled to a place which had any number of realities, as many as there had been people to live there and days to be lived. But more than that, though, reality blurs – and imagination does a magician's trick on events that may have happened or not happened.

'The past is like a prism,' I said. 'All those reflecting surfaces.'

Rhona looked backwards over the rails, to what was being left behind in the rain.

'But it's *not* empty, a prism, is it?' she said, thinking matters out *her* way. 'It's solid. A thing, it exists.'

I couldn't think how I should reply, if there really was an answer – or a question.

from RONALD FRAME, 'Merlewood',
A Long Weekend with Marcel Proust (1984)

Views

From one of my favourite vantage-spots for a great scene? But where are Scotland's finest views to be found? I would not be a Borderer if I did not rank high among them the summit of Hart Fell in the Southern Uplands, whence nineteen counties are to be seen, extending from the blue distance of the Cheviots, the Cumberland hills, the Lowthers and Blacklarg; and all around stretches the billowy sea of the green hills of Tweeddale and the Forest. Below lies Blackshope ravine, dark and awesome. Guarding the parent hill are Whirly Gill, Cold Grain, Arthur's Seat, Swatte Fell, and razor-shaped Saddle Yoke, fit companions all for Bodesbeck and its Brownie and other local tales of tragedy and romance. To the east lies 'dark Loch Skene', the mountain lake, source of the Grey Mare's Tail cascade, and visions rise as we ponder the names of Chapelhope and Riskinhope, where Renwick, youngest and last of Scotland's martyr sons, ministered to the hunted remnant for the last time, his 'fair rapt countenance with spiritual fire transfigured'; of Birkhill, Dob's Linn, the 'Covenanters' Lookout'; and the old bridle-track by Penistone Knowe to Ettrick Kirk and Yarrow's story. Silent and lonely, it still remains, yet vibrant with the hidden pulse of history and personality. And to the westward is Tweed's Well, where in a meadow the first fountain of silvery Tweed rises from 'its own unseen unfailing spring', still bubbling up through sand and pebbles, but altered in shape from what it was when as a lad Dr John Brown peered into its depths and saw 'on a gentle swelling like a hill of pure white sand, a delicate column, rising and falling and shifting in graceful measures as if governed by a music of its own'. Or, again, that view when you gain the top of the Mam Ratagan Road and glimpse the Atlantic and the Coolins of Skye, while behind you lies Loch Duich with its guardians the Five Sisters of Kintail. Or that view with the golden sands of Arisaig in the foreground, the sun playing on the dancing waters, and the Isles of the Hebrides beyond 'dim unto very dreaminess'. Or from Elgol across Loch Scavaig to the Coolin Mountains, where every peak and shattered crag, and all the naked black rocks, stand out clearly. Or from the Cathkin Braes over Glasgow to the Arrochar and Crianlarich mountains forty miles away. Or from Middle Eildon Hill, near Melrose, Sir Walter Scott's best view-point, of which he said: 'I can stand on Eildon Hill and point out forty-three places famous in war and verse.' Or from the summit of Tinto Hill, whence in good weather you can identify Skiddaw in England seventy miles away, Lochnager ninety miles to the north, and Knocklard in Ireland 100 miles distant. Or the majestic panorama of 'the roof of Scotland' from the summit of Bideam Nam Bien, the highest peak of Argyll. Or from the Ranfurly Castle Golf Club, at Bridge of Weir, which affords, it is claimed, the best view in the west. From the indicator on the wall near the 16th tee, the eye travels round from the Cowal hills to the Luss and Arrochar Hills, Ben Lomond, the Crianlarich peaks, Ben Venue, and Ben Ledi and the nearer Campsies. Even the giant Ben Cruachan beyond Loch Awe can be seen; and visitors may try to pronounce all the names on the chart – Cruach Bhuide, Sgarach Mor, Mullach Coir A'Choire and Creagan Leinibh, and the rest. Preponderantly concerned with materials directly experienced. Digging and delving in the Scottish environment with unflagging zeal and vitality. Not merely recording appearances with a skilful technique or photographing the various appearances of my country; my aim always to get at meanings, to know Scotland, and to design compact structures communicating the poetry and magnificence, the irony, the humour, the shabbiness, the tragedy, and, not least, the social significance of my chosen materials.

HUGH MacDIARMID, Lucky Poet (1943)

Everywhere in Orkney there is the sense of age, the dark backward and abysm. The islands have been inhabited for a very long time, from before the day of the plough.

The Norsemen came 1200 years ago to a place that was already populous with fishermen, herdsmen, farmers; a clever ingenious folk who built 'brochs' along sea coasts and lochs to defend themselves against sea raiders, or perhaps to dominate a subject population. These primitive castles presented a high blank circular wall to any besiegers. In the open courtyard inside the broch were wells, quernstones, stores of fish and cheese and grain, animals, people able to withstand a long siege. Between the double walls a stone stairway, with galleries, led to the top, from where the defenders could pour savage fire and stone on the enemy below.

But the broch-builders were themselves invaders. The silent vanished races stretch back beyond them, laid in barrows and howes under the green waves of time. Not a spring, but a plough somewhere, turns up another relic.

The first Orkney peoples can only be seen darkly, a few figures on a moorland against the sky, between twilight and night. They are beyond the reach of legend even. Archaeologists describe a Mediterranean folk who committed themselves to the sea. They steered their boats through the Straits and northwards, keeping close inland (for they could not trust such frail vessels far out, with their precious cargo of tribal symbols and secrets, stock, seed, nubile girls), all the way up the coastline of Spain and France. Instinctively, like all voyagers, they veered west, until they rounded the Scillies. Still they sailed north into the widening light – they would have planned their journey for the summer – past Wales and Man, the southern coast of Scotland, the many Hebrides. Beyond the savage bulk of Cape Wrath there was empty ocean, until in a summer dawn they saw the Orkneys like sleeping whales. There they made landfall. It seemed a likely place, secure from whatever dynastic tyranny or famine or plague or population pressure they had fled from. The sounds and seas about the islands swarmed with fish, the hills with birds and hares. They hauled their boats into the shelter of Rackwick, Yesnaby, Skaill, Aikerness.

Hardly a thing is known about these first Orkneymen (if they were the first Orkneymen) apart from the monuments they left behind them, the huge stones of Maeshowe and Brodgar, and the pastoral village of Skara Brae in the west. History can tell nothing; not a word or a name comes out of the silence – there

are a few ambiguous scratches on a wall at Skara Brae. We wander clueless through immense tracts of time. Imagination stirs about a scattered string of bone beads found in Skara Brae. Did the girl have no time for adornment when a westerly gale choked the doors with sand; or did sea raiders tear them from her neck? . . . The Skara Brae dwellers had lost the skills and mysteries of agriculture; they were shepherds and fishermen of a primitive kind. The sand sifted through doors and roofs, and soon their village was a blank; until another nineteenth-century gale laid bare an arrangement of stones.

GEORGE MacKAY BROWN, *An Orkney Tapestry* (1969)

Childhood

Long time he lay upon the sunny hill,
    To his father's house below securely bound.
Far off the silent, changing sound was still,
    With the black islands lying thick around.

He knew each separate height, each vaguer hue,
   Where the massed isles more distant rolled away;
But though all ran together in his view,
   He knew that unseen straits between them lay.

Sometimes he wondered what new shores were there:
   In thought he saw the still light on the sand,
The shallow water clear in tranquil air,
   And walked through it in joy from strand to strand.

Oft o'er the sound a ship so slow would pass
   That in the black hills' gloom it seemed to lie;
The evening sound was smooth like sunken glass,
   And time seemed finished ere the ship passed by.

Grey tiny rocks slept round him where he lay,
   Moveless as they; more still when evening came.
The grasses threw straight shadows far away,
   And from the house his mother called his name.

EDWIN MUIR, *Collected Poems* (1963)

Crossing the Border

I sit with my back to the engine, watching
the landscape pouring away out of my eyes.
I think I know where I'm going and have
some choice in the matter.

I think, too, that this was a country
of bog-trotters, moss-troopers,
fired ricks and roof-trees in the black night – glinting
on tossed horns and red blades.
I think of lives
bubbling into the harsh grass.

What difference now?
I sit with my back to the future, watching
time pouring away into the past. I sit, being helplessly
lugged backwards

through the Debatable Lands of history, listening
to the execrations, the scattered cries, the
falling of roof-trees
in the lamentable dark.

NORMAN MacCAIG, *Collected Poems* (1990)

In Galloway

In Galloway the drystane dykes that curl
like smoke over the shoulder of the hill
are built with holes
through which sky shows and spindrift birls,
so the wind is baffled but not barred
lest drifting snow smoors a sheltering herd.

There is an art in framing holes
and in the space between the stones.
Structures pared to the bone –
the line that pleases by what's not there
or drydykes laced across the whirling air.

ANDREW GREIG, *Surviving Passages* (1982)

Boyhood Research

This journey, tentative at first, consisting of little sallies and
retreats, with no conscious aim beyond satisfying the hunting
instinct, became in the end a thrilling exploration into the
source of the river and the source of himself.

And also into the source of his forebears back beyond the
dawn of history. It was remarkable how the races that had gone
to his making had each left its signature on the river bank;
often over and over, as children on gates and walls scrawl the
names of those amongst them who are 'courting'.

On one side of the harbour mouth the place-name was
Gaelic, on the other side it was Norse. Where the lower valley
broadened out to flat, fertile land the name was Norse, but the
braes behind it were Gaelic. A mile up the river where the main

stream was joined by its first real tributary, the promontory overlooking the meeting of the waters was crowned by the ruins of a broch that must have been the principal stronghold of the glen when the Picts, or perhaps some earlier people, were in their heyday.

And all these elements of race still existed along the banks of the river, not only visibly in the appearance of the folk themselves, but invisibly in the stones and earth. The 'influence' continued, sometimes so subtly that Kenn had more than once been surprised into a quick heartbeat by the very stillness of certain ancient spots, as though the spots had absorbed in some mysterious way not only the thought but the very being of the dark men of prehistory.

It required no very great effort to reconstruct what had happened in the comparatively recent times of the Norse invasions, round about AD 800. There were pictures of the longships of the Vikings in the school readers. Round the familiar Head, these longships had come with their banks of rowers. The folk had gathered but were afraid of the terrible fighting men, for fearsome stories had been told round the peat fires of swinging iron axes and flashing swords. On the edge of the surf the battle would have been desperate but short. Often there would have been no battle at all, the peaceful pastoral folk hurriedly retiring inland and driving their livestock before them. From their fastnesses they could harry at their will. Anyway, the Norse occupied the flat lands along the lower reaches of the river. The names of their homesteads are in valuation roll and feu charter to this day. But beyond the Broch, no Norse name is known.

A story could have been made of all this for the scholars, but in Kenn's time no teacher ever attempted it. The Vikings were a people like the Celts or the Picts, concerning whom a few facts had to be memorized. But the facts were really very difficult to memorize, because they had no bearing on anything tangible. They were sounds in the empty spaces of history. The Saxons and the Romans were different because so many facts had to be learned about them that they gathered a certain bustling reality. And then there were stories about them, too, human stories, like the one about Alfred burning the cakes or Nero burning Rome. One could see Alfred and laugh and like him. He was the man one would follow on a desperate adventure.

But no Gael or Viking or Pict was ever drawn as humanly as

Alfred, and Kenn in his boyhood had certainly no glimmering of an idea of how these three had filled his own glen with peaceful and violent history, with cunning tunes for the chanter, and odd laughable twists of thought, with courage for the sea. And yet in some unaccountable way he seemed to be aware of the living essence of this history without having been explicitly taught it.

He knows this is difficult to maintain, and is ready to admit that a long-forgotten word, a chance phrase – like 'the little folk' – may have been sufficient to set his imagination going. But yet he thinks it goes deeper than this. He knows he has been the subject of 'influences', the nature of which could never have been imparted. And he knows finally that these have given him moments of such exquisite panic, of such sheer delight, that they make by comparison many of the crises of his after-life moments of blunt endurance or of gross joy.

And knowing this, he would like to stop the thickening of his mind, to hunt back into that lost land, where Alfred and Nero, for all that they could be understood, were foreigners to his blood. The mind that secretly quickened before a broch, before a little path going up through a birch wood, to presences not looked at over the shoulder, possessed a magic that it seems more than a pity to have lost. For it was never deliberately induced. It was often feared, and sometimes hated. It was intensely real.

Kenn has a feeling that if he could recapture this he would recapture not merely the old primordial goodness of life but its moments of absolute ecstasy, an ecstasy so different from what is ordinarily associated with the word that its eye, if it had one, would be wild and cold and watchful as the eye of the gull on the cliff-top. Though that is a cold image, conveying only the suggestion of a first momentary aspect, of the initial thrill – before translation takes place.

Can he recapture this moment and the subsequent ecstasy? Is it possible in mature years to thin the lenses of the eye, to get the impulses and responses acting as they acted in boyhood? Has knowledge 'explained' the youthful wonder, and lethargy killed it?

Kenn knows what he is searching for here, and no amount of worldly scepticism or hint of sentimental credulity can affect his purpose. The physicist deals with too much invisible evidence to be put off by a visible attitude.

The adventures of boyhood were adventures towards the source, towards the ultimate loneliness of moor and mountainside . . .

NEIL GUNN, *Highland River* (1937)

Saint Andrews

Saint Andrews seems to be a place eminently adapted to study and education, being situated in a populous, yet a cheap country, and exposing the minds and manners of young men neither to the levity and dissoluteness of a capital city, nor to the gross luxury of a town of commerce, places naturally unpropitious to learning; in one the desire of knowledge easily gives way to the love of pleasure, and in the other, is in danger of yielding to the love of money.

SAMUEL JOHNSON, *A Journey to the Western Islands* (1775)

After what Dr Johnson has said of St Andrews, which he had long wished to see, as our oldest university, and the seat of our Primate in the days of episcopacy, I can say little. Since the publication of Dr Johnson's book, I find that he has been censured for not seeing here the ancient chapel of *St Rule*, a curious piece of sacred architecture. But this was neither his fault nor mine. We were both of us abundantly desirous of surveying such sort of antiquities: but neither of us knew of this. I am afraid the censure must fall on those who did not tell us of it. In every place, where there is any thing worthy of observation, there should be a short printed directory for strangers, such as we find in all the towns of Italy, and in some of the towns in England. I was told that there is a manuscript account of St Andrews, by Martin, secretary to Archbishop Sharp; and that one Douglas has published a small account of it. I inquired at a bookseller's, but could not get it. Dr Johnson's veneration for the Hierarchy is well known. There is no wonder then, that he was affected with a strong indignation, while he beheld the ruins of religious magnificence. I happened to ask where John Knox was buried. Dr Johnson burst out, 'I hope in the highway. I have been looking at his reformations.'

JAMES BOSWELL, *Journal of a Tour to the Hebrides* (1786)

We went and saw Colonel Nairne's garden and grotto. Here was a fine old plane tree. Unluckily the colonel said, there was but this and another large tree in the county. This assertion was an excellent cue for Dr Johnson, who laughed enormously, calling to me to hear it. He had expatiated to me on the nakedness of that part of Scotland which he had seen. His 'Journey' has been violently abused, for what he has said upon this subject. But let it be considered, that, when Dr Johnson talks of trees, he means trees of good size, such as he was accustomed to see in England; and of these there are certainly very few upon the *eastern coast* of Scotland. Besides, he said, that he meant to give only a map of the road; and let any traveller observe how many trees, which deserve the name, he can see from the road from Berwick to Aberdeen. Had Dr Johnson said, 'there are *no* trees' upon this line, he would have said what is colloquially true; because, by no trees, in common speech, we mean few.

When he is particular in counting, he may be attacked. I know not how Colonel Nairne came to say there were but *two* large trees in the county of Fife. I did not perceive that he smiled. There are certainly not a great many; but I could have shewn him more than two at *Balmuto*, from whence my ancestors came, and which now belongs to a branch of my family.

JAMES BOSWELL, *Journal of a Tour to the Hebrides* (1786)

From the bank of the Tweed to St Andrews I had never seen a single tree, which I did not believe to have grown up far within the present century. Now and then about a gentleman's house stands a small plantation, which in Scotch is called a *policy*, but of these there are few, and those few are all very young. The variety of sun and shade is here utterly unknown. There is no tree for either shelter or timber. The oak and the thorn is equally a stranger, and the whole country is extended in uniform nakedness, except that in the road between *Kirkaldy* and *Cowpar*, I passed for a few yards between two hedges. A tree might be a show in Scotland as a horse in Venice. At St Andrews Mr Boswell found only one, and recommended it to my notice; I told him that it was rough and low, or looked as if I thought so. This, said he, is nothing to another a few miles off. I was still less delighted to hear that another tree was not to be seen nearer. Nay, said a gentleman that stood by, I know but of this and that tree in the county.

SAMUEL JOHNSON, *A Journey to the Western Islands* (1775)

The Best Pompeii

There is no place in this country over which the Genius of Antiquity lingers so impressively. The architectural wrecks that have been spared are in themselves too far gone. They are literally ruins, or rather the ruins of ruins. Few of them have left even their outlines more than discoverable. But this improves the mysteriousness of the fragments . . .

And the associations of ancient venerableness which belongs so peculiarly to St Andrews are less disturbed by the

67

repugnance of later ages than in any place that I can think of, where the claims of antiquity are opposed to those of living convenience. The colleges which, though young in comparison with the cathedral, the tower, and the castle, are coeval with the age of the Reformation, instead of interfering with the sentiment of the place, bring down the evidence of its learning into a nearer period, and prolong the appropriate feeling . . .

It is the asylum of repose – a city of refuge for those who cannot live in the country, but wish for as little town as possible. And all this in unison with the ruins, the still surviving edifices, the academical institutions, and the past history of the place. On the whole, it is the best Pompeii in Scotland. If the professors and the youths be not studious and learned, it must be their own fault. They have everything to excite their ambition – books, tranquillity, and old inspiration. And if anything more were wanting, they have it in their extensive links, their singular rocks, and their miles of the most admirable, hard, dry sand. There cannot be better sea walks.

LORD COCKBURN, *Circuit Journeys* (1888)

Overwhelmed

. . . And in Edinburgh, where the past is so strong, and the memory of Scottish history is perpetually reminding you, if you are a Scotsman, that this was once a capital, the half-meaninglessness of Scottish life overwhelms you more strongly than anywhere else. The Scots have always been an unhappy people; their history is a varying record of heroism, treachery, persistent bloodshed, perpetual feuds, and long-winded and sanguine arguments ending in such ludicrous sackends as Bothwell Brig. But they were once discontentedly unhappy, and they are now, at least the better off of them, almost contentedly so. And this acceptance of the sordid third or fourth best, imported from every side, is what oppresses one so much as one walks down their streets.

EDWIN MUIR, *Scottish Journey* (1935)

Nothing but Heather

Thistles, Heather, Bog Myrtle, Blaeberries

An easy way to make an Irishman angry is to tell him there is no such plant as the Shamrock. The statement, however, is disingenuous, the truth being that there are several Shamrocks, at least several plants with trefoil leaves that have gone by that name. The heraldic Fleur-de-lys is also a mysterious plant; nowadays it is usually identified with the Iris, but Alphonse Karr is not sure that it is a plant and not a bunch of lance-heads, or even bees. The Welshman's plant is the Leek, but some would make out it is the Daffodil. A Thistle has long been the national flower of Scotland; Dunbar wrote *The Thistle and the Rose* for James IV's wedding with the English princess; but which of the many Thistles it is, no one knows.

The distinction has been claimed for Melancholy Thistle, a plant of northern pastures with large magenta blooms and leaves that show their white undersides to the wind. The name might seem against it, but Culpeper says its name belies its nature; a decoction of it makes a man not melancholy, but merry as a cricket; Modern Writers may laugh, as he wisely remarks, *Let them laugh that win!* The plant, however, is without prickles, and so may be ruled out of account. Milk Thistle, on the other hand, is well-armed. If Mary Queen of Scots, imprisoned in the castle, saw it growing on Dumbarton Rock, one of its haunts, she may have supposed it was the national flower. That might not have prevented her from eating it, for like its relation, the Globe Artichoke, it was much used as food. Most Thistles indeed are considered nutritious; donkeys eat them, and, as Sam Weller says, 'no man never see a dead donkey'. Yet Milk Thistle is unlikely to be the national flower, for while it has curious white markings, due, it is said, to milk dropped from the Virgin Mary's breast, no such markings appear on the badge. Probably it is Spear Thistle that most Scotsmen regard as their national flower. The farmer, it is true, slashes off its heads, but we could not expect that hardworking man to be as patriotic as a Knight of the Thistle. Yet Spear Thistle does not altogether correspond with the badge, and those who have studied the matter are generally agreed that the plant in question is the Cotton Thistle, sometimes indeed called Scotch Thistle. It is a handsome plant of which Scotsmen should be proud. Unfortunately it is not a true Thistle, nor is it native to the North; the only Scotch Thistle I have seen in Scotland grew in a flower-pot at Stirling station.

Heather might have been a better national flower, but it does not lend itself to artistic treatment. Thumping his staff on the ground to emphasize his words, Scott said to Washington Irving, 'If I did not see the heather, at least once a year, *I think I should die!*' The remark was of course rhetorical, for how could he avoid seeing it a hundred times a year? When Tennyson told Carlyle he would like to see the splendours of the Brazilian forests before he died, his friend answered, 'The scraggiest bit of heath in Scotland is more to me than all the forests of Brazil.' A Scotsman takes a sentimental, almost a proprietary interest in Heather. When as a child I crossed the border into Cumberland, I felt indignant to see it growing in England. Yet Heather, like the Scots Pine, will grow almost anywhere, though it is not fond of chalk and limestone hills. Even now I feel a certain indignation when it is called Ling by English people. Who ever heard of White Ling? There would be no luck about the house if we brought home a sprig of White Ling. Ling is the name of a coarse fish, and it ought to be enough that two plants have the same name as shellfish, Periwinkle and Cockle. If the words Heather and heathen are connected, meaning the plant and people that live on heaths, Dr Johnson would of course have agreed that the name was appropriate at least in Scotland. It is used loosely, for Bell and Cross-leaved Heath are also called Heather, but every Scotsman knows to what plant Hudson refers when he says:

> Over all the revelations of the glory of flowers I have experienced in this land I hold my first sight of heather on the Scottish moors in August.

We cannot fail to see the Heather's flowers, for with remarkable thrift it clings to them long after they are withered and grey; but Bog Myrtle's rusty inflorescence is not so often seen, for, appearing before the leaves – natural in a wind-pollinated plant – it is soon gone to seed. As no plant has a more haunting scent, I half grudge it to England, though there, I admit, it has a pleasant name, Sweet Gale. Yet I scarcely believe it grows in England, for even in the New Forest, when I crush its leaves and close my eyes, the scent transports me to a Highland glen. Blaeberry grows in drier places; early in autumn, scared by the thought of drought, it may drop its leaves to restrict the loss of moisture, and so present a stringy appearance. But in May or June it is a beautiful plant; its urn-shaped flowers having no need to hang and blush in the way they do. I cannot grudge it to England; it is too abundant on southern hills, where it goes by such names as Bilberry, Whinberry and Whortleberry. In any case I have a grievance against it. Climbing towards the summit of the Cobbler one July day, I was hot and thirsty, but the sun, hotter and thirstier, had been before me and drunk the runnels dry. Lying flat in a bed of Blaeberries I thrust handfuls of the purple fruit into my mouth, and, greatly refreshed, gained the summit. An hour or so later, having descended from the hill, I was walking along the road that runs round the head of the loch to Arrochar. Meeting people who smiled pleasantly to me, I smiled pleasantly to them. But they seemed unusually pleasant, and I began to wonder what was wrong. Though I knew it was nothing about my dress, for I always climb mountains in my ordinary clothes, I adjusted my tie. Their pleasantness became at last unbearable, and I darted into the Arrochar hotel. 'Who have you been kissing today?' asked the barman. 'Blaeberries,' I replied, seeing in the mirror at his back the large purple stain on my mouth.

ANDREW YOUNG (1885–1971), *A Prospect of Flowers* (1945)

'Nothing but Heather!'

Scotland small? Our multiform, our infinite Scotland *small*?
Only as a patch of hillside may be a cliché corner
To a fool who cries 'Nothing but heather!' where in
    September another
Sitting there and resting and gazing round
Sees not only the heather but blaeberries
With bright green leaves and leaves already turned scarlet
Hiding ripe blue berries; and amongst the sage-green leaves
Of the bog-myrtle the golden flowers of the tormentil
    shining;
And on the small bare places, where the little Blackface
    sheep
Found grazing, milkworts blue as summer skies;
And down in neglected peat-hags, not worked
Within living memory, sphagnum moss in pastel shades
Of yellow, green, and pink; sundew and butterwort
Waiting with wide-open sticky leaves for their tiny winged
    prey;
And nodding harebells vying in their colour
With the blue butterflies that poise themselves delicately
    upon them;
And stunted rowans with harsh dry leaves of glorious colour.
'Nothing but heather!' – How marvellously descriptive! And
    incomplete!

HUGH MacDIARMID, 'Direadh',
The Complete Poems, vol. 2 (1978)

Land and Lairds

The land united those it nourished. Dandie Dinmont felt quite
at home with Counsellor Pleydell, and Cuddie Headrigg sat,
although below the salt, at the same table as the laird of
Milnwood. A friendly independence and a man-to-man recognition of each other's qualities warmed the relations of the
Laird with the Laird's Jock. Only in the Lowlands of Scotland
could there exist that peculiar blend of loyalty and informality
– and macabre humour – enshrined in the anecdote of the
laird's man who was to be hanged. The unfortunate man was

lingering in his cottage when the laird strolled down to watch the ceremony; the goodwife entertained the laird with light conversation for some minutes, but her man, not unnaturally, still hesitated to emerge and meet his fate. At last the woman turned and cried through the doorway, 'Come awa', Jamie – come awa' to your hangin', and dinna vex the laird!'

The entwined strands of loyalty to the land and loyalty to the blood make up the history of the Lowland families. They clung to the land and the land clung to them. It was not only the great earldoms, like Crawford and Rothes and Erroll, that passed down through families whose origins were almost prehistoric. Families like Balfour of Balfour, Haig of Bemersyde, MacDowall of Garthland, Scrymgeour-Wedderburn of Wedderburn, and Swinton of Swinton have roots that lie far back beyond the Ragman Roll [i.e. before 1296], and have remained as landmarks in the changing scene of Scotland, their fortunes rising and falling with their country's. Some, like the great house of Douglas, began in a little upland valley and spread till their branches and alliances covered whole shires. Others, like Buccleuch and Cassillis, grew and consolidated themselves in smaller, solider units till they became little tyrants in their own districts, waging small wars of their own and lording it over neighbouring families equally old but less dynamic: it was not for nothing that the Earls of Cassillis were nicknamed 'the kings of Carrick' or that one Buchanan of Arnprior styled himself 'king of Kippen'.

JAMES FERGUSSON, Lowland Lairds (1949)

Dung and Darg

It is worth remembering that the word manure originally meant working with the hands, manœuvre. To manure was to hold, to cultivate, to improve. So manured land, in the old sense, was not earth treated with farm-yard dung or purchased chemicals; it was earth larded with the sweat of human labour. Much of Aberdeenshire was thus manured by years of draining marsh and cutting the reeds and the bushes. The climate, it is true, usually mitigates perspiration, but the grapple was intense. Townsmen often think of a farm as something natural; there is nothing more contrived, nothing more artificial, especially in parts of Scotland. Take the Aberdeenshire map and look at the farm-names. The word moss is very frequent. So is the word bog. The mire had to be fought and beaten. Scrapehard is typical; so are Boggendinny, Crannabog, and Slackbog; Windyhills, Stoneyfield, Mosside, Heathery Banks – so they sing their song of the land that was salvaged from the swamp or conquered for a crop by riving the stone from the earth, the heather from the hill.

IVOR BROWN, *Summer in Scotland* (1952)

In December

I watch the dung-cart stumble by
  Leading the harvest to the fields,
That from cow-byre and stall and sty
  The farmstead in the winter yields.

Like shocks in a reaped field of rye
   The small black heaps of lively dung
Sprinkled in the grass-meadow lie
   Licking the air with smoky tongue.

This is Earth's food that man piles up
   And with his fork will thrust on her,
And Earth will lie and slowly sup
   With her moist mouth through half the year.

ANDREW YOUNG, The Poetical Works (1985)

Farmer's Wife

Yonner, ay,
It's Jean hersel'!
Wa' oot by
Wi' the orra[1] pail!

Meenlicht skailin[2]
Owre her hair,
Siller-bricht,
As she trauchles[3] there

Wi' thochts in her min'
Gey ill te ken![4]
A lass lang syne[5]
Wi' the wale[6] o' men.

Danced at King's
Took a gweed degree
Kent maist things
But what she'd be –

Work-worn wife
At Futtratsprot!
A fairm-toon life,
The scunner[7] o't!

J. C. MILNE, Poems (1963)

[1] scrap; [2] spilling; [3] makes her way wearily; [4] hard to fathom; [5] long ago; [6] pick; [7] disgust

The Praise of Ploughmen

Ye lads and lasses a' draw near,
I'm sure it will delight your ear,
And as for me I'll no be sweir
   To sing the praise o' ploughmen.
The very King that wears the crown,
The brethren of the sacred gown,
The Dukes and Lords of high renown,
   Depend upon the ploughmen.

The gardener he cries out wi' speed,
I'm sure I was the first man made,
And I was learned the gardener trade
   Before there was a ploughman.
Oh, gardener, lad, it's true you say;
But how long gardener did you stay?
I'm sure it was just scarce a day
   Ere ye became a ploughman.

The blacksmith he says, I hear news,
Do I not make your iron ploughs,
And fit the coulter for its use,
   Or there would be nae ploughmen?
Oh, blacksmith, we must allow
That you can make an iron plough,
But you would ne'er got that to do
   If it were not for the ploughmen.

The mason he cries, Ho, ho, fie,
Do I not build your castles high
The wind and rain for to defy,
   Far better than the ploughman?
Oh, mason, ye may build a house,
And fit it for its proper use,
But from the King unto the mouse
   Depends upon the ploughmen.

The miller he speaks out wi' glee –
Do I not sit at the mill e'e,
And grind the corn food for thee
   Far better than the ploughman?
Oh, miller, ye maun haud yer jaw,
And sit and look at your mill wa',
And see if dust frae it would fa'
   If it were not for the ploughmen.

The souter he cries out, Hurrah,
Do I not make boots and shoes richt braw
For to defend baith frost and snaw
   That's worn by the ploughmen?
You may mak' boots and shoes wi' speed,
Wi' last and leather, birse and thread,
But where's the meal for to mak' breid,
   If it were not for the ploughmen?

The tailor he cries out wi' haste –
I pray of this don't make a jest;
Oh, I can make coat, trews, and vest
   Far better than a ploughman.
Oh, tailor, ye may mak' braw clothes,
But where's the meal for to be brose?
Ye might close up baith mouth and nose,
   If it were not for the ploughmen.

Success the ploughmen's wages crown;
Let ploughmen's wages ne'er come down,
And plenty in Scotland aye abound,
   By labour of the ploughmen.
For the very King that wears the crown,
The brethren o' the sacred gown,
The Dukes and Lords of high renown,
   Depend upon the ploughmen.

JOHN ANDERSON (mid-19th century),
in ed. John Ord, *Bothy Songs and Ballads* (1930)

Fife Farm Names

Ladernie, Lother, Lathones,
Minziemill, Seggiehill,
Pittormie stands alone;
When you see the lichts o Dersiemair
Ye're at the gates o Dron,
Ye'll hear the cock at Middlefiddy
Cryin' Kilmaron.

ANON

Gardens and Gardeners

I

The most typical of the components of the Scottish estate is the walled garden. It is true that these exist in all parts of the British Isles, but nowhere in such numbers as in Scotland; nor is the use to which the kitchen garden is placed exactly the same in other parts of the country, except, perhaps, in the extreme north of England.

Through all the changes which have taken place in gardens and horticulture the walled garden has very largely kept its character and differs little from the original conception in the middle of the eighteenth century. It is still a very pleasant mixture of flowers, fruit and vegetables, a compact area enjoyed by the whole household and under the watchful eye of the gardener. Our forebears paid much attention to the kitchen garden, an attention worthy of respect which is still paid in Scotland . . .

E. H. M. COX, *A History of Gardening in Scotland* (1935)

II

He played off his wit against Scotland with a good-humoured pleasantry, which gave me, though no bigot to national prejudices, an opportunity for a little contest with him. I having said that England was obliged to us for gardeners, almost all their good gardeners being Scotchmen. *Johnson*: 'Why, Sir, that is because gardening is much more necessary amongst you than with us, which makes so many of your people learn it. It is *all* gardening with you. Things which grow wild here, must be cultivated with great care in Scotland. Pray now (throwing himself back in his chair, and laughing), are you ever able to bring the *sloe* to perfection?'

JAMES BOSWELL, *Life of Johnson* (1791)

Shiant Islands

I dare say many of my listeners have an idea of the Hebrides as bleak and colourless and windswept. I wish they could see the flowers on my islands – tracts of yellow irises with forget-me-nots and kingcups and ragged-robins, honeysuckle and dog-roses in crevices of the rocks, campion in every shade of pink and crimson as vigorous as garden stocks, silver-weed and milkwort and thyme and heather, bog-asphodel and cotton-grass, bog-violets and red rattle and – but that's enough.

text of a radio talk by
SIR COMPTON MacKENZIE (1928)

Highland Cattle

Today I saw about twenty Highland cattle following a cart of hay across a field. They were drawn out in a line, and with their shaggy dun coats and long horns had a soft wild beauty that held the eye. I have seen them frequently throughout the winter and have often marvelled at their hardihood. Delicately they would nose the snow away and pick up moss or withered grass with fastidious lips. They were never indoors at any time. More than once, late at night, with the small burn a solid sheet of ice, I have heard a rustling beyond the hedge, and on peering through have watched them standing there quietly, eating the twigs of some felled trees. In the frosted moonlight, as they turned their heads towards me, a sense of dumb fellowship could be felt in a strange stillness of endurance.

How truly a product of their environment, how naturally they fit into the native scheme of things! Their milk is rich, and connoisseurs have said of their flesh that it is the sweetest of all. It was not only tragic, it was uneconomic when the Highlands were cleared of crofters and their hardy cattle together with all the wealth of shieling life, in butter and cheese, in song and story, to make wastes for sheep. In the old economy they knew that the land goes sour under sheep, and so kept heart and sweetness in it with their cattle.

The tufts of shaggy hair hanging down over their eyes may make them look rather ferocious, but they are the gentlest of beasts – except, let it be remembered, when it is the case of a mother and a young calf. Then, as I have heard East Coast people say, 'thae highlanders are treacherous'. And, in fact, I do know of a man who was lucky enough to get through a fence in time from the charge of one of the timid score that I saw following the hay-cart. But the calf was only two days old and the man had gone between it and its mother – never a wise proceeding in the case of any breed of cattle, or even, for that matter, of (what we deem) the most important mammal of all.

NEIL GUNN, *Highland Pack* (1949)

When they'd scythed roads in the five fields of corn and wheat it was time to get the binder out and start cutting. Telfer drove the tractor with Willie on the binder seat, his hand on the lever that raised the mowing arm when they turned round on the corners, his eyes on the teeth that whipped twine round the sheaves, on the lookout for a break in the string. Corn fell forwards over the mower teeth on to an endless canvas belt that carried it to the middle of the binder. It was carried up one side of the triangle-shaped machinery and down the other, tied sheaves dropping out every yard or so.

It took a while to get into the way of stooking again. Dunky remembered how stiff he'd been the summer before. The weather forecast said it would be fine for most of August, not that you could rely on the forecast, but if it was they wouldn't have to rush the whole harvest through in a panic in case it rained. The year before had been wet and when there was a couple of fine days Craig had them working in the fields till it was dark.

Stooking was a plodding job. You picked up a sheaf by grabbing the corn just above the string round its middle. The sheaf didn't weigh much. You walked forward to the next one and picked it up with your right hand. One of you would start the stook by propping the heads of two sheaves together, like a Red Indian wigwam, short stalks on the inside so that it would stand in the wind. You bunged your two sheaves down in line with the first two, the ears at the top of each sheaf pushed together, the base close to the first two. When there were five pairs of sheaves leaning against each other the stook was finished. You walked on and picked up more sheaves and began another stook. The new stubble cracked under your boots. In some places there was thick green grass and clover shoving up among the stubble, in others, where it was drier, you walked on earth. Sometimes you came on a sheaf the binder had dropped without twine, then you had to take a handful of stalks and knot them round the sheaf, a job that needed a strong hand.

McCann and McPhail and Rafferty and himself stooked until Telfer and Willie had cut the whole field. Then they'd join in till all the sheaves were up, you didn't want to cut another field ahead of the stookers in case it turned to rain and sheaves went rotten lying on their sides. Corn was easier than wheat, it was soft and you could stook with your bare arms, even stripped to the waist, the sweat running off your brow, the sun on your back. They started about eight, having to walk or bike to the field. They had their break at half-nine, then the dew had gone and Willie and Telfer could start cutting again. He biked home for his dinner at half-twelve and was back again by half-one, his afternoon piece in the gas-mask case. It was harder bending down after dinner, with your belly full and your eyes wanting to go to sleep. By afternoon break you were starving again. They'd sit against a stook and grunt with stiffness as they ate their pieces. Then it would be up again, going round and round the field, never-ending rows of lying sheaves, your back so sore you couldn't think of anything but the next sheaf, the tips of your fingers beginning to smart from the hard straws. Around five o'clock Craig would come down to the field – God knew where he spent the rest of his time – and have a look at the sky and a look at his boots and a squint at his workers and then tell Willie whether you were doing overtime or not. If you were you went on at it till eight or nine o'clock, still going round the field, the six of you bending and picking up, banging sheaves together, walking forward, bending and picking up, another stook finished, another to start, each man with a different style of working, some always doing a wee bit more than others, Willie liking to place the first two sheaves, keeping his hands buried in the ears of corn till the next two were placed at their side, making sure the stook was steady, eye on the sky when there was a moment to look up, would it rain by morning, were they well ahead, had they fallen behind?

On the second morning you were so stiff you swore you wouldn't be able to bend to lift a sheaf to save your life. Your back was raw with sunburn. You felt giddy and sick and ruptured but nobody told you to have a rest, you started with the others and panted with the stiffness in your back and your shoulders and your legs and soon you didn't notice the stiffness any more.

People came up the road to watch the harvest, it always attracted them, women with prams, men on the panel, men on the burroo. That made it more enjoyable, somehow, as though you had an audience. By the second day you were used to it again.

GORDON WILLIAMS, *From Scenes Like These* (1968)

There were scores upon scores of animals and birds I knew far better then than I now know the domestic cat, which is the only specimen of the 'lower animals' of which I see much in the lean days upon which I have fallen – and not only I; a wholesale alienation and reduction of mankind to familiarity only with their own 'miserable matter', as if it were a second and far more drastic and irrevocable expulsion from the Garden of Eden. My eye may, perhaps, still seek out and recognize and appreciate a dozen or so wild flowers in the course of a year, but my memory recalls – with a freshness and a fullness of detail with which such living specimens cannot vie at all – hundreds I have not seen for over thirty years. My poetry is full of these memories – of a clump of mimulus 'shining like a dog's eyes with all the world a bone'; of the quick changes in the Esk that in a little stretch would far outrun all the divers thoughts of Man since Time began; of the way in which, as boys, with bits of looking-glass we used to make the sun jump round and round about us; of

> . . . the thunder-plump,
> The moss-boil on the moor, the white-topped tide,
> A tow-gun frae the boon-tree,

the orchid that smells like cherry-pie; 'the common buds o' thrift', the sun 'when its rays in the grey lift (sky) blinter like honesty'; an old land whose 'hillsides lirk like elephant skins as we gang by!'; of the 'last dark reid crawberries under the firs'; of 'a great fish *contra nando incrementum*'; of 'the way a wild duck when she hears the thunder dances to her own Port a Beul'; of charms of goldfinches on the thistles and hardheads, a cock siskin singing in a spruce, crossbills busy with the rowans, a big crop of beechmast attracting countless bramblings we'll hear 'breezing' before they leave for the North again, a group of hungry waxwings stripping a briar of its hips in less time than it takes to write these words; a yellow-browed warbler; four grey shrikes; milk-wort and bog-cotton; corbie oats and corcolet and doulie water 'that like sheepeik seeps through the duffie peats'; sundew and butterwort.

HUGH MacDIARMID, *Lucky Poet* (1943)

Milk-Wort and Bog-Cotton

To Seumas O'Sullivan

Cwa' een like milk-wort and bog-cotton hair!
I love you, earth, in this mood best o' a'
When the shy spirit like a laich wind moves
And frae the lift nae shadow can fa'
Since there's nocht left to thraw a shadow there
Owre een like milk-wort and milk-white cotton hair.

Wad that nae leaf upon anither wheeled
A shadow either and nae root need dern
In sacrifice to let sic beauty be!
But deep surroondin' darkness I discern
Is aye the price o' licht. Wad licht revealed
Naething but you, and nicht nocht else concealed.

HUGH MacDIARMID

The Wild Goose

They were coming towards me – and passed almost overhead, making for the firth, a haunt of greylags. I suspected poachers (as it turned out, I was right) and wondered if they had got any. The birds above had fallen into an arrow formation, even if it tended to waver a trifle – and no wonder. I was watching them very carefully for any sign of a hit but could detect none. The distance a wounded bird will fly is often very remarkable. They were now well away towards the firth and going strong, when one of them spoke.

Let me say that up in this crofting world sounds carry an incredible distance on a still day, even farther than they carry over sea-water in the quiet of the night, as if the gentle slope of the ground were a vast sounding-board. (So it seems, anyhow, when half a mile away I can hear feminine farewells at a croft door.) I mention this because the voice of the goose was not loud; it was quiet but anxious. It was the anxiety in the voice that held me. I have heard flying geese talking among themselves too often in too many places, in daylight and moonlight, not to know the general tone of their discourse. Sometimes that anxious note will creep in when the whole gaggle grows uncertain in its flight, as though some lusty young fellow were disputing the old man's sense of direction among the hills. At such a moment, the formation will break and swirl as if these sure creatures of the wild were no more than a mass of plantation rooks. Not that the old man pays much attention: he steers a point or two north and heads on for he knows the way, and the last you see of them they are tailing in behind him on either side. Now though the many voices during the mix-up may sound anxious, they are also disputatious, if not indeed querulous.

But this voice was not uplifted, it was quiet. In such a voice a young man might say to his fellows: 'I'm done, boys; I can't go any farther.'

At once the others answered. For it was clearly and entirely the wrong place to give in. They yattered to him and their voices were strangely liquid and sweet and urgent.

I waited with a feeling of absolute suspense. The conversation continued for a few moments, then one of the geese left the formation. I saw him dropping away, then turning into the wind as he came down to land in a wide, slow, beautiful curve. As he passed from view, his flight was still so sure that he might himself have been a leader who had unexpectedly come upon some paradisal loch or firth.

But the others did not follow. They continued straight on their way without the slightest suggestion of hesitation or deviation. Indeed their long necks seemed outthrust more ardently than ever. But their voices lifted a little, and though I have always been a trifle uncomfortable over the attribution of human feelings to bird or beast, it struck me in that moment with a clear conviction of certainty that they were crying their hail and farewell.

When the gardener appeared I told her what had happened and we set off down the slopes, through hedge and fence and watercourse, to find the greylag. It is only at such a time that you realize how intricately broken-up may be a hillside which from a distance looks smooth enough. The gardener was beginning to have vague doubts, and I was wondering myself if the bird had waddled into some cover, when I saw at the upper edge of a small field what looked like any other grey stone. But there was a whiteness of one part that no weathered stone has on our hillside.

The goose was quite dead and, judging from how it lay, I knew that it had fallen the last few yards like a stone. There were three drops of blood on the white and the body was warm.

It weighed just on seven and a half pounds. Subsequent examination showed that at least two pellets of shot had penetrated through the very deep flesh of the breast right to the bone.

It must have flown nearly a mile before that conversation took place which has remained so clearly in my mind.

NEIL GUNN, *Highland Pack* (1949)

Eagle

The Child Stolen from the Harvest-field

An eagle, circling high.
The swaddled child
Lay in the bronze
Shadow of a barley stook.
The mother,
Bronze-throated, bent and gathered and bound.
The eagle
Hovered, stooped, threshed.
The child hung
Hooked in talons, dragged
Up blue steps of sky
To a burning nest
In a crag of Coolag hill.

The harvest mother
Followed. She changed
Burnish for blue wind,
Bleeding hands. She
Lifted the boy like an egg
From the broken
Circles of beak and claw and scream.

She brought him down
To her nest of crib and milk.
She kissed him.
She lit the lamp.
She rocked the cradle. She sang.

Old grand-da muttered
Through the gray
Spittle and smoke of his pipe,
'Better for the boy, maybe
That freedom of rock and cloud,
A guest
In the house of the king of birds –
Not what must come,
Ten thousand brutish days
Yoked with clay and sea-slime.'

GEORGE MacKAY BROWN,
The Wreck of the Archangel (1989)

The Monster

The great topic of 1933 was the Loch Ness Monster. The monster boom began with a series of circumstantial reports from residents and visitors to the loch. An A.A. scout claimed to have seen a serpent-like shape in the water; other reports suggested that the monster was a gigantic bearded eel. Yet when a big-game hunter went north to investigate, he found a spoor in the shingle by the side of the loch. Serpents and eels do not leave spoors; which discredited the local theories. The Natural History Museum then gave its opinion that the spoor resembled that of a hippopotamus. Sir Arthur Keith, the scientist, decided that the monster might be a legged reptile, but he suspected that it was an illusion and that the case was one for psychologists rather than zoologists. Others suspected a practical joke. Despite such doubts the monster's fame attracted thousands of summer tourists. The Catholic monks of Fort Augustus on the loch side had most of them seen the monster, and the Father Superior had been aware of its existence for some years.

Theories multiplied, and so did efforts to trace the monster. A local ghilly declared that it was an old blind salmon. The most commonly accepted theory was that it was some sort of whale that had entered the loch when small and could not get back to the sea. But if so, on what would it subsist? Someone then tried to detect its presence with hydrophones; someone else reported having seen it cross the road with a sheep in its mouth. An old woman disappeared and her body was later discovered on the moors; she was said to have been carried off. Mutilated carcases of sheep were found on the shores of the loch, and the tooth-marks in them were pronounced to be the monster's. Someone said that it might be a walrus; but rather smudgy photographs which appeared in London newspapers bore out the whale theory. The Royal Scottish Museum suggested that it was a large tunny or shark come into the loch from the sea. A film was made, 'The Secret of the Loch', which showed occasional glimpses of dark shapes on the water's surface, but nothing to swear by; however, the proceeds of the film endowed a bed for divers at Greenwich Hospital. The monster was equally a gift to the foreign Press. A Japanese paper said that it was roaming over the great heaths where Macbeth saw the weird sisters. On April Fool's Day, 1936, the *Berliner Illustrierte Zeitung* announced that the monster had been captured and was now on exhibition at Edinburgh; and reproduced photographs of it by a 'famous Scottish zoologist, Professor MacKeenkool'. Yet the monster was not seen again, and interest in it gradually died down.

ROBERT GRAVES AND ALAN HODGE,
The Long Weekend (1940)

Heron

It stands in water, wrapped in heron. It makes
An absolute exclusion of everything else
By disappearing in itself, yet is the presence
Of hidden pools and secret, reedy lakes.
It twirls small fish from the bright water flakes.

(Glog goes the small fish down.) With lifted head
And no shoulders at all, it periscopes round –
Steps, like an aunty, forward – gives itself shoulders
And vanishes, a shilling in a pound,
Making no sight as other things make no sound.

Until, releasing its own spring, it fills
The air with heron, finds its height and goes,
A spear between two clouds. A cliff receives it
And it is gargoyle. All around it hills
Stand in the sea; wind from a brown sail spills.

NORMAN MacCAIG,
Collected Poems (1990)

Cities and Towns

Considering its size, Scotland is overweighted with cities . . .
Glasgow is larger in the Scottish scale than London is in the
English, while, in the same proportion, Edinburgh, Dundee
and Aberdeen are swollen giants as compared with, say, Bir-
mingham, Leeds and Bristol within the English economy. The
size of the cities is the most obvious symptom of the hopeless
lack of balance in Scottish life. The influence of the cities is too
great.

It can be said at once that there is not a Scottish city but differs spiritually from the three others in the most marked
degree. You could hardly pass at random through a concourse
of human beings and pick out four individuals more strongly
assorted. We look for well-marked character in the Scot, and
we know that he can present one or two, or even three, characters – Highland or Lowland or some curious blend of these in
their infinite permutations and combinations – but if the stu-
dent would quickly grasp the outlines of a complicated system,
he would do worse than confine himself to an intensive study
of the Scot as he exhibits himself in his four most populous
centres. If it be observed that there is no Highland town of size,
the answer must be that Glasgow is that: a fact which strangely
complicates and adds to the interest of that community.

GEORGE BLAKE, *The Heart of Scotland* (1934)

'The Clyde Made Glasgow and
Glasgow Made the Clyde'

He took a bulky folder, the biggest of all his 'bits and pieces', and laid it in front of him on the table with a sigh of satisfaction. On the front of the folder, typed on a piece of white paper and stuck on, was the motto 'Rutherglen's wee roon red lums reek briskly.' Beneath that was a reproduction of the City of Glasgow's coat-of-arms with its tree, its bird, its fish and its bell. Beneath that again was typed a little piece of doggerel verse which is known to all Glasgow school children.

> This is the tree that never grew,
> This is the bird that never flew,
> This is the fish that never swam,
> This is the bell that never rang.

On the coat-of-arms there were printed the words *Let Glasgow Flourish*. Mat sat and looked at it for a while, then he printed the word *Lord* in front of it and the words *by the preaching of the Word* after it, and restored the modern truncated motto to its old length and meaning.

Lord, Let Glasgow Flourish by the Preaching of the Word.

As he made the addition he smiled wryly to himself as if at some private joke. Then he muttered to himself in supplication, with ironic fervency, 'Lord, let Glasgow flourish by the preaching of the Word,' and opened the folder, exposing the first neatly typed page.

The manuscript began with the words *'The Clyde made Glasgow and Glasgow made the Clyde.'* It had been some time since he had opened the folder, though he had thought of it often with a warm feeling. As he read what he had written he was rather surprised that he only remembered it slightly. The words came to him now as almost new and he read on, curious to know what he had written these years ago. The typescript continued: *'For many centuries there were fishermen's huts around the spot where the old Molendinar burn flowed into the Clyde, where the shallows of the Clyde occurred, where the travellers crossed who made their way from the North-west parts of Scotland down to the South. Some authorities have it that this place where St Mungo, or to give him his proper Celtic name St Kentigern, built his little church was given the*

Gaelic name Gles Chu, meaning "the dear green place", and that the present name of Glasgow is a corruption of those two Gaelic words. The dear green place – as it must have been. Even late into the Eighteenth Century when the modern city that is Glasgow had begun to grow it was talked about as "the most beautiful little town in all Britain". In the Sixth Century St Mungo had built a mission there, building it like any inn or hostelry at the most likely place to catch the customers, or converts, at the spot where the drovers or travellers would pause before crossing the ford. Being on the West coast of Scotland its connections were with the Celtic Christian culture in Ireland and so it became an ecclesiastical town. In the Fifteenth Century a University was built and Glasgow remained a religious centre until the European Reformation when it acquired with vengeance the Protestant ethic and its natives turned their hands with much zeal to worldly things. These same natives had always been pugnacious; the Romans in an earlier day had found them an intolerable nuisance; and in the Tenth Century they maintained their reputation for pugnacity by knocking spots off the Danes down on the Ayrshire coast. Thereafter they mixed almost solely with people of their own racial type. During the Industrial Revolution when Glasgow suffered a great influx of people it was from Ireland and the West Highlands of Scotland that the people came so that even today the characteristic Glasgow type is short, stocky and dark like his very remote Celtic-Iberian forebears.

'When St Mungo fished in the Clyde from his leaky coracle the source of the river was a different one from that of today. The old rhyme goes,

> *"The Tweed, the Annan, and the Clyde,*
> *A' rin oot o' ae hillside",*

and this is not now the case. It is probable that, as some people claim, a farmer led the original Clyde burn, which rose away back in the hills, along a ditch and into the Elvan and thus on South into the Solway. This to prevent the burn from flooding his fields.'

Beside this sentence Mat marked the word *'avulsion'*. As he printed the word in the margin he felt a strange kind of satisfaction. Then he went on reading his manuscript.

'It happened that about the same time the Glasgow merchants were howking at the river bed further downstream in order to make the deep channel which allowed Glasgow to become the great sea port which nature intended it to be.'

Again in the margin beside this sentence Mat printed

another word, in alternative forms *'alluvion'* and *'alluvium'*. Then he added the sentence: *'And thus the wiseacres are confirmed in their saying that Glasgow and the Clyde were mutually responsible for one another's being.'* He found the idea that the river had been tamed, or 'domesticated', for the sake of all this husbandry, that the big river had become something of a human artifact, he found this idea exciting and satisfying.

ARCHIE HIND, The Dear Green Place (1966)

Blows

Two other memories sometimes returned while I was working in that office, but now my familiarity with George and the lorry-boys made them less horrible. The first was of a summer evening when I was walking down the Salt Market and came upon a crowd at the end of a close. A muscular, red-haired woman with her arms bare to the shoulder was battering the face of a little, shrinking man and screaming, 'It's him that led me away when I was a young lassie, the b—! It's him that put me on the streets, the b—! I might have been a respectable woman if it hadna been for him, the b—!' The little man shrank against the wall with his hands over his face. He did not seem to have put them there for protection, but merely out of shame, so that no one might recognize the long-lost seducer of this woman. He looked forlorn and shabby and old; I felt sorry for him, and did not believe what the woman was saying: he did not look like a seducer. I do not know how it ended, for the thud of the big, red-haired fist on the man's face sickened me. The crowd looked on without interfering.

The other memory was of a dull winter Saturday afternoon in Crown Street, another slum. I had been to see some doctor. Again I came on a crowd. Two young men were standing in the centre of it, and one of them, who looked serious and respectable and not particularly angry, raised his fist slowly every now and then, and, as if objectively, hit the other man, who stood in silence and never tried to defend himself. At last an older man said, 'Why dinna you let the chap alane? He hasna hurt you.' But the serious young man replied, 'I ken he hasna hurt me, but I'm gaun tae hurt him!' And with a watchful look round him he raised his fist again. I did not want to see any more; but the scene and particularly the words of the serious young man – the other having said nothing at all – took hold of my mind as if they were an answer to some question which, without my knowing it, had been troubling me: perhaps Johnnie's slow and painful death, during which, without being able to return a single blow, he had been battered so pitilessly. In both these memories there was the quality of Scottish Calvinism: the serious young man's reply had the unanswerable, arbitrary logic of predestination; and the encounter of the red-haired woman with her seducer, when both were so greatly changed that their original sin might have been committed in another world, and yet lived on, there in that slum, was a sordid image of fate as Calvin saw it. Somewhere in these two incidents there was a virtue of a dreary kind, behind the flaunted depravity: a recognition of logic and reality.

EDWIN MUIR, *An Autobiography* (1954)

O Glasgow

And this short postscript deals with you, O Glasgow, city without beauty, city of noise and commerce, city of factories and wharves, harbour for wares of all kinds. What am I to say about you? Is there then any beauty in factories, docks and warehouses, cranes in the harbour, towers of steel-works, flocks of gasometers, clattering cartloads of goods, tall chimneys and thunderous steam-hammers, structures of girders and iron, buoys in the water and mountains of coal? I, miserable sinner, think and see that all these things are very beautiful and picturesque and monumental; but the life which is born from this is neither beautiful nor picturesque, but it is deserted by the breath of God, crude and grimy and sticky, noisy, reeking and oppressive, disorderly and burdensome, more burdensome than hunger and more disorderly than squalor; and there sank upon me the weariness of myriads, and I fled, O Glasgow, for I had no courage to behold and compare.

KAREL ČAPEK, *Letters from England,* trans. Paul Selver (1925)

Personifications

Glasgow is one of the few places in Scotland which defy personification. To image Edinburgh as a disappointed spinster, with a hare-lip and inhibitions, is at least to approximate as closely to the truth as to image the Prime Mover as a Levantine Semite. So with Dundee, a frowsy fisher-wife addicted to gin and infanticide, Aberdeen a thin-lipped peasant-woman who has borne eleven and buried nine. But no Scottish image of personification may display, even distortedly, the essential Glasgow. One might go further afield, to the tortured imaginings of the Asiatic mind, to find her likeness – many-armed Siva with the waistlet of skulls, or Xipe of Ancient America, whose priest skinned the victim alive, and then clad himself in the victim's skin . . . But one doubts anthropomorphic representation at all. The monster of Loch Ness is probably the lost soul of Glasgow, in scales and horns, disporting itself in the Highlands after evacuating finally and completely its mother-corpse.

LEWIS GRASSIC GIBBON, 'Glasgow',
in *Scottish Scene* (1934)

A Glasgow Cemetery

[Cementerio de la ciudad]

Walls with gaping railings, and behind them
black earth holding no grass and no trees,
only wooden benches where the old folk
sit in silence in the long afternoons.
All round are houses, shops are near,
children play through the streets. The trains pass
close by the side of the graves. The people are poor.

Rain has soaked the rags that hang in windows:
patches on the grey tenement face.
Blotted already are the In Memoriams
cut on these tombs two centuries ago
over the dead who have now no friends to forget
    them.
Huddled the dead are, hidden. Yet when the sun
    shines and June comes
even old buried bones must feel some June-day touch.

No leaf here, no bird. Stone only, and earth.
Hell is like this? – Pain without forgetfulness,
clamour and wretchedness, huge cold without hope.
No place for death to sleep in silence. It is always
life that among the very graves roves like a whore
plying her trade under the unstirring stars.

Dusk comes down out of a cloudy sky;
smoke from the factories floats off, lost
soon in grey dust; voices are heard from the pub;
then one passing train
shudders and echoes loud like a black trumpet-blast.

Not the last judgement yet: sleep, if you can,
sleep on, anonymous dead, in your long calm.
God too perhaps forgets you, not just man.

LUIS CERNUDA, trans. Edwin Morgan,
in Rites of Passage (1976)

Charles Rennie Mackintosh

The Scotland Street school is in the western part of the Gorbals, and it was designed, like most board schools of the time, as a single, tall, gaunt slab. But whereas the London board schools, good in their way, trimmed their tops with Dutch gables, Mackintosh realized that frills were not enough. He built a plain central block and flanked it with two enormous glazed staircases, one for boys, one for girls – ten years before Gropius's famous staircase at the Cologne exhibition, thirty years before the motif became *de rigueur* among the white young things of the nineteen-thirties. Originality is not necessarily a mark of genius, but Mackintosh was never merely original: the deeper significance of these towers is the way in which they showed that the only way to humanize such a building was to exploit its scale, not to deny it. Mean entrances in the bottom of a cliff-like front would have simply screwed home the facts of authority: the huge staircases make the block comprehensible, articulate it and relate it to little people – going up to the top becomes a game, not a kind of purgatory. And the iron railings in front are lightened by a motif so fanciful that they can never have symbolized the usual restriction of the playground wall. The architect, in fact, was here playing a game along with the children. Incidentally, if a section of the railings was removed and exhibited at the Institute of Contemporary Arts, people would wonder who the promising young sculptor was.

Single-handed, Mackintosh invented in one way or another almost the whole vocabulary of the modern movement.

IAN NAIRN, *Britain's Changing Towns*, (1967)

Imagine Glasgow

One morning Thaw and McAlpin went into the Cowcaddens, a poor district behind the ridge where the art school stood. They sketched in an asphalt playpark till small persistent boys ('Whit are ye writing, mister? Are ye writing a photo of that building, mister? Will ye write *my* photo, mister?') drove them up a cobbled street to the canal. They crossed the shallow arch of a wooden bridge and climbed past some warehouses to the top of a threadbare green hill. They stood under an electric pylon and looked across the city centre. The wind which stirred the skirts of their coats was shifting mounds of grey clouds eastward along the valley. Travelling patches of sunlight went from ridge to ridge, making a hump of tenements gleam against the dark towers of the city chambers, silhouetting the cupolas of the Royal infirmary against the tomb-glittering spine of the Necropolis. 'Glasgow is a magnificent city,' said McAlpin. 'Why do we hardly ever notice that?' 'Because nobody imagines living here,' said Thaw. McAlpin lit a cigarette and said, 'If you want to explain that I'll certainly listen.'

'Then think of Florence, Paris, London, New York. Nobody visiting them for the first time is a stranger because he's already visited them in paintings, novels, history books and films. But if a city hasn't been used by an artist not even the inhabitants live there imaginatively. What is Glasgow to most of us? A house, the place we work, a football park or golf course, some pubs and connecting streets. That's all. No, I'm wrong, there's also the cinema and library. And when our imagination needs exercise we use these to visit London, Paris, Rome under the Caesars, the American West at the turn of the century, anywhere but here and now. Imaginatively Glasgow exists as a music-hall song and a few bad novels. That's all we've given to the world outside. It's all we've given to ourselves.'

'I thought we had exported other things – ships and machinery, for instance.'

'Oh, yes, we were once the world's foremost makers of several useful things. When this century began we had the best organized labour force in the United States of Britain. And we had John McLean, the only Scottish schoolteacher to tell his students what was being done to them. He organized the housewives' rent strike, here, on Clydeside, which made the government stop the landlords getting extra money for the duration of World War One. That's more than most prime ministers have managed to do. Lenin thought the British revolution would start in Glasgow. It didn't. During the general strike a red flag flew on the city chambers over there, a crowd derailed a tramcar, the army sent tanks into George Square; but nobody was hurt much. Nobody was killed, except by bad pay, bad housing, bad feeding. McLean was killed by bad housing and bad feeding, in Barlinnie Jail. So in the thirties, with a quarter of the male workforce unemployed here, the only violent men were Protestant and Catholic gangs who slashed each other with razors. Well, it is easier to fight your neighbours than fight a bad government. And it gave excitement to hopeless lives, before World War Two started. So Glasgow never got into the history books, except as a statistic, and if it vanished tomorrow our output of ships and carpets and lavatory pans would be replaced in months by grateful men working overtime in England, Germany and Japan. Of course our industries still keep nearly half of Scotland living round here. They let us exist. But who, nowadays, is glad just to exist?'

ALASDAIR GRAY, *Lanark* (1981)

A Navy Immortal

It was in a sense a procession that he witnessed, the high tragic pageant of the Clyde. Yard after yard passed by, the berths empty, the grass growing about the sinking keel-blocks. He remembered how, in the brave days, there would be scores of ships ready for the launching along this reach, their sterns hanging over the tide, and how the men at work on them on high stagings would turn from the job and tug off their caps and cheer the new ship setting out to sea. And now only the gaunt dumb poles and groups of men workless, watching in silence the mocking passage of the vessel. It was bitter to know that they knew – that almost every man among them was an artist in one of the arts that go to the building of a ship; that every feature of the *Estramadura* would come under an expert and loving scrutiny, that her passing would remind them of the joy of work, and tell them how many among them would never work again. It appalled Leslie Pagan that not a cheer came from those watching groups.

It was a tragedy beyond economics. It was not that so many homes lacked bread and butter. It was that a tradition, a skill, a glory, a passion, was visibly in decay, and all the acquired and inherited loveliness of artistry rotting along the banks of the stream.

Into himself he counted and named the yards they passed. The number and variety stirred him to wonder, now that he had ceased to take them for granted. His mental eye moving backwards up the river, he saw the historic place at Govan, Henderson's of Meadowside at the mouth of the Kelvin, and the long stretch of Fairfield on the southern bank opposite. There came Stephen's of Linthouse next, and Clydeholm facing it across the narrow yellow ditch of the ship-channel. From thence down river the range along the northern bank was almost continuous for miles – Connell, Inglis, Blythswood and the rest: so many that he could hardly remember their order. He was distracted for a moment to professionalism by the lean grey forms of destroyers building for a foreign power in the sheds of a yard that had dramatically deserted Thames for Clyde. Then he lost himself again in the grim majesty of the parade. There came John Brown's, stretching along half a mile of waterfront at Clydebank, the monstrous red hull of Number 534 looming in its abandonment like a monument to the glory departed; as if shipbuilding man had tried to do too much and had been defeated by the mightiness of his own conception. Then came, seeming to point the moral, the vast desolation of Beardmore's at Dalmuir, cradle of the mightiest battleships and now a scrap-heap, empty and silent forever, the great gantry over the basin proclaiming stagnation and an end.

GEORGE BLAKE, *The Shipbuilders* (1935)

Greenock lies along the Clyde littoral and is built up on to the hills behind. Thus it is a long lateral town and the streets rise steeply and provide open view of the river and the Argyllshire hills. In the winter there is snow on them and in the summer their great tawny flanks are charred occasionally by heather fires. They are seen across an expanse of roofs and chimneys, the slates dull purple scales and the ridges presided by clumps of lums, cans churning and smoke pennons flying. The buildings are of sandstone block, greybuffs and occasional reds, and are erected in monolithic tenements, achieving their only rhythm in the flowing lines enforced by the land.

During the day the town channels mind and eye swiftly out to the river and the hills, constantly transcending self by the dynamics of its construction. It is only in the evenings, and especially in the autumnal early nights, that it states itself. Then the sky takes on a steely blue clarity and against this in edges of unbearable blue black the buildings inflict themselves, the simplicity of outline fantasticated by the chimney abstractions, castles, chess problems, graveside gatherings, with the smoke in slow upgoing to the enormous empty sky.

At this time there is a heroism in the shapes and the colours, an elemental starkness which attains archetype, a town looking across a river at hills. The river flows, the hills abide and the town ponders these images of evanescence and antiquity, while above, with the disinterest of the truly eternal, the sky endures.

ALAN SHARP, *A Green Tree in Gedde* (1965)

Tenements

I

It is so ludicrous to imagine anybody actually building the things that I have always assumed that Glasgow's tenements have just always been there. Nobody could have put them up deliberately . . .

Most of them run to four storeys, built in rectangles to enclose the back courts. The back courts are divided by brick walls and brick-built wash-houses built for climbing over. It was on one of these that I made my first acquaintance with the terror that lurks in the big city. I would be four years old at the time, a perilous age in Glasgow because in order to live a full rich life at four, you have to attach yourself to the bigger fry and they can always run faster and jump higher than you can. So I was at the tail end of the line one night on the run along the top of the back court wall in Gallowgate and on to the high wash-houses of Cubie Street, and I was good and far behind when I arrived at one of the obstacles of the course.

There was a turn in the wall, and in order to finish the run you had to dreep to the ground, stand on a dustbin to get astride the next bit of wall and then home to the roofs. The instant I lowered myself to dreep I knew it was too far. It was too dark to see the ground below, but I had heard enough about people breaking both legs. I had heard practically nothing else, in fact, from the time I could walk. But by this time I was hanging by my fingers and I couldn't climb back up either. I shouted, but nothing happened, so I screamed, and I had a good vibrant scream in those days. A Glasgow back court on a dark Tuesday night is the loneliest place in the world.

Some time later my sister Johanne, sitting in the house a hundred yards away and two storeys up, recognized the screams and bolted out to save me. She had to prise my fingers off the top of the wall before she could pick me down.

Danger and death were always familiar acquaintances. A few weeks later the boy downstairs, Tommy Mulholland, was playing on his rocking-horse on the first-floor landing when the whole thing overturned and carried him down a flight in a oner. It never seemed to cure him of riding facing the stairs, though it may seem odd that he was riding a rocking-horse on the landing at all.

The explanation is that the close in Glasgow is not just a hole in a building but a way of life. The close leads directly from the street to the back court, and the staircase to the flats above starts in the middle of it; and there is always something going on – somebody is always washing it or writing on the walls or hiding in it or giving a yell to test the echo.

After they wash it, the women give the stone flags a finish of wet pipeclay that dries bold and white and shows every footprint. Then, round the edges, they add a freehand border design drawn in pipeclay; sometimes a running loop like blanket-stitch, sometimes more tortuous key patterns, always mathematically accurate. It's a symptom of the unquenchable folk memory, or something, derived from long-buried Celtic eternity and fertility symbols.

By day the close and the stairs rang with the old cries and chants of Glasgow. Sonny Hillhouse (Sonny would be about twenty years old) always obliged with his own version of the popular hits on his way upstairs. I can still hear him:

> 'Am I wasting my time,
> By smoking Woodbine
> And wheezing the way that I do . . .'

Or another Gallowgate favourite:

> 'If you should see a big fat wummin
> Staunin' at the coarner bummin'
> That's my Mammy . . .'

Some cheery housewife on the top landing would join in the chorus with encouraging shouts of 'Nark it!' or 'Shut yer noisy jaw!'

CLIFFORD HANLEY, *Dancing in the Streets* (1958)

II

Looking on with the architect at the completion of a new tenement of workmen's dwellings in the High Street of Old Edinburgh, a block modest enough, of course, yet with some advances in hygiene and aspect over what had been before available, a workman of the neighbourhood tapped one of us on the shoulder: 'Pity you haven't a hundred working-men that understand what you're about there!' 'You mean building their own homes?' 'Ay, that's it! By Jove! wouldn't they go down the street!' 'You mean their working efficiency would be increased?' 'Rather!'

This happened more than twenty years ago; and there are still few signs of the hundred Edinburgh working-men. Their marked individuality – in their leaders indeed an outstanding intellectuality – their mastery of (and by) abstract politics has long raised them far above sharing the petty local interests of us

103

city improvers or town planners, who occupy our minds and hands with concrete trifles like homes and gardens, and pleasanter streets – all very well, no doubt, but which only your slow concrete-minded German really cares for. Houses and gardens, streets and squares? No, no. Whole city wards even are too small. 'Constituencies' are the very smallest units really worth recognizing, and these only at election times, when they heckle their rival candidates to tatters more sharply than Government or Opposition will afterwards do. Measures of national, imperial magnitude are not less shrewdly discussed; for among such groups of workmen one used to hear – doubtless may still hear – talk as good and clear, as shrewd and trenchant, as one gets in club or committee, in college or debate, in learned society or salon. In all cities probably the skilled artisan's opinion is far less behind that of 'the intellectuals' than these suppose; and, in Edinburgh at least, it is too often the intellectuals who fall behind. Yet after all this high and serious converse, our Scots workmen retire to their homes – no, their houses – no, not houses. There is no word which can convey to ordinary old-fashioned English readers – who still cling to the national idea on which they were brought up, of homes as separate houses, of each family with its own bit of ground, at least its yard, however small – the full content and savour which our Scottish cities – Historic Edinburgh, Great Glasgow, Bonnie Dundee, and minor ones, with burghs without number – manage to condense and to express in their, in one sense, high tradition of 'Working-class Tenements'. Inspiring name! These are inhabited by the majority of the Scottish people: more than half the whole population, in fact, are in one- and two-room tenements – a state of things unparalleled in Europe or America, in fact, in the history of civilization. To realize these Scottish conditions with any measure of town-planning concreteness the English reader must build up for himself a model, if indoors, with small packing-cases up to the ceiling; or, if he be rustic enough still to possess an adequate backyard, small one- and two-chambered coops and hutches would be the thing, if he could get but enough – piled storey above storey, four, five, and six, to keep within modern regulations – around a single lofty spiral ladder. Old tenements, of course, are far higher; indeed the sky-scraper became as characteristic of Old Edinburgh, especially after the Revolution of 1688, as they have now become of New York – and with analogous effect on land-values, and consequent difficulty of escaping from them, and from their multiplication elsewhere.

Yet this Scotland is the nation which, up to the beginning of the Industrial Age, was, save Norway, the most rustic and the most stalwart in Europe. It is now the most urban; and how far deteriorated it is happily not here our present duty to inquire.

Into the complex question of historic and contemporary conditions which have thus brought it about – that the most educated, and politically the most 'advanced', of British workmen are the worst housed in Britain, or anywhere else – we cannot here enter. We can merely refer to our 'Civic Survey of Edinburgh', and kindred studies, assume the facts, and add to them one more: that when, as of course now and then of late years, some little Housing discussion is raised in Scotland, the tenements, and even their one- and two-roomed components, still find no lack of advocates, and these among all classes! Not only do individuals speak in their defence, but even local pride is aroused. The fact is, we rather look down upon small brick houses: we admire our lofty piles of stone: we still use their historic and legal name of 'Lands'. Finally, the whole matter is put upon what are really high metaphysical grounds (which 'the practical man' is ever so liable to wander into). We are made to feel a certain fitness in these things, a certain established harmony; in fact a sort of foreordination of Scotsmen for tenements, and of tenements for Scotsmen. Upon these towering heights of national destiny, therefore, the economic verdict is easy to give, and hard to refuse – that 'we can afford nothing better'. Economic explanations are added by some, and political explanations of these by others: none of them sufficient. But without this abstract and philosophical turn, in fact this at bottom theological dignity of argument, the proposition – that the printers and masons of Edinburgh, the shipbuilders and engineers of Glasgow, all admittedly second to none in their production, are to be in their economic consumption second to all, and that permanently – would be realized in all its flagrant absurdity.

PATRICK GEDDES, *Cities in Evolution* (1915)

105

from *Auld Reikie, A Poem*

Auld Reikie! wale o' ilka town
That Scotland kens beneath the moon;
Whare couthy chiels at e'ening meet
Their bizzing craigs and mou's to weet:
And blythly gar auld Care gae bye
Wi' blinkit and wi' bleering eye:
O'er lang frae thee the Muse has been
Sae frisky on the simmer's green,
Whan flowers and gowans wont to glent
In bonny blinks upo' the bent;
But now the leaves a yellow die,
Peel'd frae the branches, quickly fly;
And now frae nouther bush nor brier
The spreckl'd mavis greets your ear;
Nor bonny blackbird skims and roves
To seek his love in yonder groves.

Then, Reikie, welcome! Thou canst charm
Unfleggit by the year's alarm;
Not Boreas, that sae snelly blows,
Dare here pap in his angry nose:
Thanks to our dads, whase biggin stands
A shelter to surrounding lands . . .
Prepare, and gently lead the way
To simmer canty, braw and gay;
Edina's sons mair eithly share
Her spices and her dainties rare,
Than he that's never yet been call'd
Aff frae his plaidie or his fauld . . .

Now Night, that's cunzied chief for fun,
Is wi' her usual rites begun;
Thro' ilka gate the torches blaze,
And globes send out their blinking rays.
The usefu' cadie plies in street,
To bide the profits o' his feet;
For by thir lads Auld Reikie's fock
Ken but a sample, o' the stock
O' thieves, that nightly wad oppress,
And make baith goods and gear the less.

Near him the lazy chairman stands,
And wats na how to turn his hands,
Till some daft birky, ranting fu',
Has matters somewhere else to do;
The chairman willing, gi'es his light
To deeds o' darkness and o' night . . .

Frae joyous tavern, reeling drunk,
Wi' fiery phizz, and ein half sunk,
Behald the bruiser, fae to a'
That in the reek o' gardies fa':
Close by his side, a feckless race
O' macaronies shew their face,
And think they're free frae skaith or harm,
While pith befriends their leaders arm:
Yet fearfu' aften o' their maught,
They quatt the glory o' the faught
To this same warrior wha led
Thae heroes to bright honour's bed;
And aft the hack o' honour shines
In bruiser's face wi' broken lines:
Of them sad tales he tells anon,
Whan ramble and whan fighting's done;
And, like Hectorian, ne'er impairs
The brag and glory o' his sairs.

Whan feet in dirty gutters plash,
And fock to wale their fitstaps fash;
At night the macaroni drunk,
In pools or gutters aftimes sunk:
Hegh! what a fright he now appears,
Whan he his corpse dejected rears!
Look at that head, and think if there
The pomet slaister'd up his hair!

ROBERT FERGUSSON (1750–74)

I always liked Scotland as an idea, but now, as a reality, I like it
far better . . .

. . . and who indeed that has once seen Edinburgh, with its
couchant crag-lion, but must see it again in dreams waking or
sleeping? My dear Sir, do not think I blaspheme when I tell you
that your Great London as compared to Dun-Edin 'mine own
romantic town' is as prose compared to poetry, or as a great
rumbling, rambling, heavy Epic – compared to a lyric, bright,
brief, clear and vital as a flash of lightning. You have nothing
like Scott's Monument, or, if you had that and all the glories of
architecture assembled together, you have nothing like
Arthur's Seat, and above all you have not the Scotch National
Character – and it is that grand character after all which gives
the land its true charm, its true greatness.

CHARLOTTE BRONTË, letter, 20 July 1850

Nothing that sticks up without smoking seems to me to look ill
in Edinburgh.

LORD COCKBURN, *Examination of the Trials for Sedition*
which have Hitherto Occurred in Scotland (1888)

Edinburgh

Edinburgh pays cruelly for her high seat in one of the vilest
climates under heaven. She is liable to be beaten upon by all
the winds that blow, to be drenched with rain, to be buried in
cold sea fogs out of the east, and powdered with the snow as it
comes flying southward from the Highland hills. The weather
is raw and boisterous in winter, shifty and ungenial in summer, and a downright meteorological purgatory in the spring.
The delicate die early, and I, as a survivor, among bleak winds
and pumping rain, have been sometimes tempted to envy them
their fate. For all who love shelter and the blessings of the sun,
who hate dark weather and perpetual tilting against squalls,
there could scarcely be found a more unhomely and harassing

place of residence. Many such aspire angrily after that Somewhere-else of the imagination, where all troubles are supposed to end. They lean over the great bridge which joins the New Town with the Old – that windiest spot, or high altar, in this northern temple of the winds – and watch the trains smoking out from under them and vanishing into the tunnel on a voyage to brighter skies. Happy the passengers who shake off the dust of Edinburgh, and have heard for the last time the cry of the east wind among her chimney-tops! And yet the place establishes an interest in people's hearts; go where they will, they find no city of the same distinction; go where they will, they take a pride in their old home.

R. L. STEVENSON, 'Edinburgh' (1878)

The Perambulator in Edinburgh

Edinburgh is a city from which you look down on distant lighthouses and out on green bare hills. Her houses are built of a hard grey stone cut at her doors with barely a front of brick or painted plaster to break her rocklike monotony; so that in a distant first impression you are reminded less of man's handiwork than of a re-arrangement of Nature. Natural images crowd in the mind as one remembers Edinburgh. Most of her roads rush headlong downhill like salmon rivers. To the east her choppy waves of tenements surge out to the hills to recoil, in the backwash of St Leonard's cottages and sheds, from the face of Salisbury Crags; and to the nor'-east she throws a long grey wave of terrace round Calton Hill, and leaves a jetsam of grey monuments on the summit.

Walking along Princes Street, you see the gay tulip parterres on the garden ridge set against the plum bloom which the valley yields to the wrinkled face of the great Castle rock, that piles itself up to the clouds as from a glen in Skye instead of in the main street of a capital city engraved by tramway cars. As you look up to the Castle, all you see on the long neck between the Old Town houses and the Castle port are a few small trees and a spiky monument or two; although you know that there are acres of houses beyond, you do not see a chimney, and the Castle and its approach seem as isolated as if the open country

109

lay on the far side. Farther west again, there advance the distant woods of Corstorphine, like Macduff's army marching on the Castle, reminding you by their mass of foliage that a poverty of trees is a characteristic of the city that contributes to its general impression of clean, wind-swept austerity.

Then, if you turn away to stir your limbs against the northern cold, you are made aware of another of Edinburgh's characteristics – the great skies that are always in your sight. To take leave from a friend who walks north from Princes Street is to see him impressively walking straight into the clouds, and to come up any of the northern streets is to find the Castle and the Old Town high before you in the sky. 'Princes Street is only hauf a street', as another Glasgow critic well said, but he might have said it too of Queen Street and of many another. Wide gardens with small trees and the great sky bending overhead is the burden of an impression you receive again and again with added pleasure. Nor is it long before you succumb to the singular fascination lent to all this spaciousness of the New Town by the contrasting gaunt perpendicular Gothic of the old.

Wandering there among the close-set labyrinths of that stony forest one arrives at many view-points, but best of all are those of the Castle walls. Below you lies Auld Reekie, black-ened and dried, an immortal herring, 'smeeked' for hundreds of years and cured in the sun till – one may add for those who remember their Smollett – all or nearly all her famous savours have been carried away on the airs of heaven. To the north you behold the whole fall of the country behind the green dome and the spires and chimneys of the New Town; the land spreading out in this Pisgah sight, rich with fields, mansions, avenues, harbours and ships, the dark floor of the Firth, the Fife villages smoking on their plains – a distant Kingdom indeed – and the eye draws up to the fastnesses of the Ochil and the Lomond Hills and the blue pyramid of Largo Law. Sometimes in the cold spring days, when the land lies grey before you, a pale light suddenly spreads like a meaning over the prospect, and distant spires and glinting roofs raise their heads, and then as quickly sink back into the universal greyness, and all you reap for your watching is that a shower begins to break over Kirkcaldy, and that they are stepping new masts (they shine vividly) on that barque at Leith. He is king for a day who sits thus on his Castle Wall and surveys this wide champaign below. Not only from the Castle, but from many an office and study window you may enjoy these great views. In no other city in the kingdom can a man sit thus at his affairs and catch Nature busy at her processes over so vast a panorama. When rainbows arch him he sees clearly in whose field they have their ending, and can determine whose by right are their pots of gold . . .

Travellers have generally agreed that Edinburgh has a strong resemblance to Athens, and the inhabitants have apparently been willing to humour them by planting happy adaptations and variations of Athenian buildings on prominent places and cutting down tall trees. Thus some see the Royal High School on Calton Hill as the Temple of Theseus; Dugald Stewart the philosopher and Robert Burns the poet are both commemo-rated by adaptations of the choragic monument to Lysicrates; the observatory on Calton Hill is the Temple of the Winds. Most pointed of all the resemblances, there stands on the top of Calton Hill the Parthenon itself, reduced presumably by the onslaught of the Scots weather to a peristyle. But Nature's reproductions are even more convincing. From the spur of the Pentlands immediately above Colinton the resemblance of the view to that from the bottom of Mount Anchesmus is said to be undeniable. Bulessus is the Hill of Braid; the Castle Hill is the Acropolis; Lycabettus joined to Areopagus form the Calton Hill; and the Firth of Forth is the Ægean Sea. Inchkeith is, of course, Ægina, and the hills of the Peloponnesus rise in Fife . . .

A minister of the Gospel from the West Coast identified Edinburgh as an 'east-windy, west-endy city'. James Payn, who settled there in 1858 as editor of *Chambers's Journal,* made as much ado about its east wind as he did about the Edinburgh Sunday. In vain Robert Chambers assured him that the same isothermal band passed through Edinburgh and London.

'I know nothing about isothermal bands,' was Payn's reply, 'but I know that I never saw a four-wheeled cab blown upside down in London.'

JAMES BONE, *The Perambulator in Edinburgh* (1926)

The Land of Stone

And now to the north, to the north! County flits after county, in some of which the cows are lying down, in others of which they are standing up; in some places sheep are grazing, elsewhere horses and elsewhere only crows. Then comes into view the grey sea with rocks and marshes, the quickset hedges cease, and in place of them small stone walls range along. Small stone walls, stone villages, stone towns; beyond the river Tweed is the land of stone.

An English friend of mine was almost right when he declared Edinburgh to be the finest city in the world. It is a fine place, stonily grey and strange of aspect. Where in other cities a river flows, there a railway runs; on one side is the old town, on the other side the new one, with streets wider than anywhere else, every vista showing a statue or a church; and in the old town the houses are appallingly high, a thing which exists nowhere in England, and the washing is flaunted upon clothes-lines above the streets like the flags of all nations – and this also does not exist down in England; and there are dirty, red-headed children in the streets – this also does not exist down in England; and blacksmiths, carpenters and all sorts of fellows, this also does not exist in England; and strange little streets, wynds or closes, this also does not exist in England; and fat, dishevelled old women, this also does not exist in England. Here the people begin to be as in Naples or in Czechoslovakia. What a funny thing it is to see old houses here with chimneys on the gable, apparently instead of towers, as I have shown in my drawing. Such a thing exists nowhere in the world except at Edinburgh. And the city is situated on hills; you are hurrying along somewhere or other, and all at once beneath your feet you have a deep green chasm with a fine river below; you are taking a walk and all of a sudden there is another street located on a bridge above your head, as at Genoa; you are taking a walk, and you reach a perfectly circular open space, as at Paris. The whole time there is something for you to be surprised at. You make your way into the Parliament, and there whole troops of lawyers are rushing about in wigs with two tails behind, just like two hundred years ago. You go and have a look at the castle, which is situated so picturesquely on a vertical rock, and on your way you meet a whole band of pipers and a company of Highlanders; they have striped plaid trousers, and caps with ribbons, but the pipers have red and black skirts, and on them leather bags, and on their pipes they play a bleating and excit-ing song to the accompaniment of a whole band of drummers. The drumsticks are brandished above the heads of the drum-mers, they twist and leap up in a strange and savage dance; and the pipers bleat a war-song and march bare-kneed along the castle esplanade with the tripping step of ballet-girls. And bang, bang, the drumsticks twist more rapidly, are crossed, fly up, and suddenly this turns into a funeral march, the pipers whistle an endless and trailing melody, the Highlanders stand at attention, behind them the castle of the Scottish kings, and still farther behind them the whole blood-stained and dreadful history of this land. And bang, bang, the drumsticks dance a wild and wise dance overhead – here the music has remained a spectacle as in the earliest times; and the pipers lift themselves, as if with the impatience of a stallion they were dancing into battle.

Another land and other people. It is a province, but a monumental one; a poorer land, but a sturdy one; a russet and angular type of people, but the girls are prettier than down in England; beautiful and dirty-nosed children, a life ample and jolly in spite of all Calvinism. Upon my soul, I quite took a fancy to it; and to show how pleased I was I will give you as make-weight a strip of sea near Leith and Newhaven, a cold and steely sea, and blue sea-shells as a keepsake and a greeting from the fishing-smacks; and on top of that I will add for you the entire old-fashioned and picturesque town of Stirling with the castle of the Scottish kings. If you stand near the old cannon on the castle rampart, you hold in your hand the key to the Scottish mountains; suppose we went there and had a look at them?

In front of the castle a ballet-girl moves to and fro with a bayonet and a striped kilt; ten paces to the gate, then back, attention, present arms, order arms; the ballet-girl shakes her skirts and dances back again. In the south the battle-field of Robert Bruce, in the north the blue mountains; and below on the green meadow the river Forth twines as no river in the world twines; and I have drawn it so that everybody may see what a beautiful and gratifying river it is.

KAREL ČAPEK, *Letters from England*
(1925)

Old Edinburgh

Down the Canongate
down the Cowgate
go vermilion dreams
snake's tongues of bannerets
trumpets with words from their mouths
saying *Praise me, praise me.*

Up the Cowgate
up the Canongate
lice on the march
tar on the amputated stump
Hell speaking with the tongue of Heaven
a woman tied to the tail of a cart.

And history leans by a dark entry
with words from his mouth
that say *Pity me, pity me
but never forgive.*

NORMAN MacCAIG, *Collected Poems* (1990)

The Prows o' Reekie

O wad this braw hie-heapit toun
Sail aff like an enchanted ship,
Drift owre the warld's seas up and doun
And kiss wi' Venice lip to lip,
Or anchor into Naples Bay
A misty island far astray,
Or set her rock to Athens' wa',
Pillar to pillar, stane to stane,
The cruikit spell o' her backbane,
Yon shadow-mile o' spire and vane,
Wad ding them a'! Wad ding them a'!
Cadiz wad tine the admiralty
O' yonder emerod fair sea,
Gibraltar frown for frown exchange
Wi' Nigel's Crags at elbuck-range,
The rose-red banks o' Lisbon make
Mair room in Tagus for her sake.

A hoose is but a puppet-box
To keep life's images frae knocks,
But mannikins scrieve oot their sauls
Upon its craw-steps and its walls;
Whaur hae they writ them mair sublime
Than on yon gable-ends o' time?

LEWIS SPENCE, *Plumes of Time* (1926)

A Bad Miss

I drove to the Butchers along Princes Street, all beastly with snow, but my breath was taken away by the beauty of it. There is a deep fall of ground along one side where there was once a lake, then with one incredible lep up towers the crag – three hundred feet and the Castle and the ramparts all along the top. It was foggy, with sun struggling through and to see that thing hump its great shoulder into the haze was fine. You know I affect Scott – so would you if you once saw Edinburgh. It was almost overwhelming to think of all that has happened there –

However, to resume – before you are bored. Andrew [Lang] he received me so dacent and so pleasant, he's as nice a man in fayture as I ever seen before – He is indeed – a most correct and rather effeminate profile. No one else was in – He was as miserable about the snow as a cat, and huddled into a huge coat lined with sable. In state we drove up to the Castle by a long round, and how the horse got up that slippery hill I don't know. The Castle was very grand, snowy court yards with grey old walls and chapels and dining halls – most infinitely preferable to Frederiksborg. The view should have been noble, as it was one could only see Scott's monument – a very fine thing – and a very hazy town. My word, it is an awful thing to look over those parapets. The Black Watch was drilling in the outer court yard, very grand, and a piper went strutting like a turkey cock and skirling. It was wild – and I stood up by Mons Meg and was thrilled. Is it an insult to mention that Mons Meg is the huge historic old gun, and crouches like a she mastiff on the topmost crag, glaring forth over Edinburgh with the most concentrated defiance? You couldn't believe the expression of that gun. I asked Andrew L whether it was the same as Muckle-mouthed Meg, having vague memories of the name. He said in a dying gasp that Muckle-mouthed Meg was his great-great-grand-mother. That was a bad miss, but I preserved my head just enough to enquire what had become of the Muckle mouth. (I may add that his own is admirable.) He could only say with some slight embarrassment that it must have gone in the other line.

from letter dated 1895 in
Selected Letters of Somerville and Ross,
ed. GIFFORD LEWIS, (1989)

Edinburgh

Midnight

Glasgow is null,
Its suburbs shadows
And the Clyde a cloud.

Dundee is dust
And Aberdeen a shell.

But Edinburgh is a mad god's dream,
Fitful and dark,
Unseizable in Leith
And wildered by the Forth,
But irresistibly at last
Cleaving to sombre heights
Of passionate imagining
Till stonily,
From soaring battlements,
Earth eyes Eternity.

HUGH MacDIARMID,
The Complete Poems (1978)

What Images Return

A few years ago I was obliged to spend some weeks in the
North British Hotel in Edinburgh, isolated and saddened by
many things, while my father's last illness ran its course in the
Royal Infirmary. It was necessary for me to be within call. I do

not like the public rooms and plushy lounges of hotels anywhere in the world, I do not sit in them; and least of all in one's native city is it spiritually becoming to sit in the lounges of big hotels.

I spent most of my time in my room waiting for the hours of visiting my father to come round. I think at such times in one's life one tends to look out of the window oftener and longer than usual. I left my work and my books and spent my time at the window. It was a high, wide window, with an inside ledge, broad and long enough for me to sit in comfortably with my legs stretched out. The days before Easter were suddenly warm and sunny. From where I sat propped in the open window frame, I could look straight onto Arthur's Seat and the Salisbury Crags, its girdle. When I sat the other way round I could see part of the Old City, the east corner of Princes Street Gardens, and the black Castle Rock. In those days I experienced an inpouring of love for the place of my birth, which I am aware was psychologically connected with my love for my father and with the exiled sensation of occupying a hotel room which was really meant for strangers.

Edinburgh is the place that I, a constitutional exile, am essentially exiled from. I spent the first 18 years of my life, during the 1920s and 1930s, there. It was Edinburgh that bred within me the conditions of exiledom; and what have I been doing since then but moving from exile into exile? It has ceased to be a fate, it has become a calling.

My frequent visits to Edinburgh for a few weeks at a time throughout the years have been the visits of an exile in heart and mind – cautious, affectionate, critical. It is a place where I could not hope to be understood. The only sons and daughters of Edinburgh with whom I can find a common understanding are exiles like myself. By exiles I do not mean Edinburgh-born members of Caledonian Societies. I do not consort in fellowship with the Edinburgh natives abroad merely on the Edinburgh basis. It is precisely the Caledonian Society aspect of Edinburgh which cannot accommodate me as an adult person.

Nevertheless, it is the place where I was first understood. James Gillespie's Girls' School, set in solid state among the green meadows, showed an energetic faith in my literary life. I was the school's Poet and Dreamer, with appropriate perquisites and concessions. I took this for granted, and have never since quite accustomed myself to the world's indifference to art and the process of art, and to the special needs of the artist.

I have started the preceding paragraph with the word 'nevertheless' and am reminded how my whole education, in and out of school, seemed even then to pivot around this word. I was aware of its frequent use. My teachers used it a great deal. All grades of society constructed sentences bridged by 'nevertheless'. It would need a scientific study to ascertain whether the word was truly employed more frequently in Edinburgh at the time than anywhere else. It is my own instinct to associate the word, as the core of a thought-pattern, with Edinburgh particularly. I can see the lips of tough elderly women in musquash coats taking tea at MacVittie's, enunciating this word of final justification, I can see the exact gesture of head and chin and gleam of the eye that accompanied it. The sound was roughly 'niverthelace' and the emphasis was a heartfelt one. I believe myself to be fairly indoctrinated by the habit of thought which calls for this word. In fact I approve of the ceremonious accumulation of weather forecasts and barometer-readings that pronounce for a fine day, before letting rip on the statement: 'Nevertheless, it's raining.' I find that much of my literary composition is based on the nevertheless idea. I act upon it. It was on the nevertheless principle that I turned Catholic.

It is impossible to know how much one gets from one's early environment by way of a distinctive character, or whether for better or worse. I think the puritanical strain of the Edinburgh ethos is inescapable, but this is not necessarily a bad thing. In the south of England the puritanical virtues tend to be regarded as quaint eccentricities – industriousness, for instance, or a horror of debt. A polite reticence about sex is often mistaken for repressions. On the other hand, spiritual joy does not come in an easy consistent flow to the puritanically-nurtured soul. Myself, I have had to put up a psychological fight for my spiritual joy.

Most Edinburgh-born people, of my generation at least, must have been brought up with a sense of civic superiority. We were definitely given to understand that we were citizens of no mean city. In time, and with experience of other cities, one would have discovered the beautiful uniqueness of Edinburgh for oneself as the visitors do. But the physical features of the place surely had an effect as special as themselves on the outlook of the people. The Castle Rock is something, rising up as it does from prehistory between the formal grace of the New Town and the noble network of the Old. To have a great primitive black crag rising up in the middle of populated streets of commerce, stately squares and winding closes, is like the statement of an unmitigated fact preceded by 'nevertheless'. In my time the society existing around it generally regarded the government and bureaucracy of Whitehall as just a bit ridiculous. The influence of a place varies according to the individual. I imbibed, through no particular mentor, but just by breathing the informed air of the place, its haughty and remote anarchism. I can never now suffer from a shattered faith in politics and politicians, because I never had any.

When the shrill telephone in my hotel room woke me at four in the morning, and a nurse told me that my father was dead, I noticed, with that particular disconnected concentration of the fuddled mind, that the rock and its castle loomed as usual in the early light. I noted this, as if one might have expected otherwise.

MURIEL SPARK, 'What Images Return', in ed. Karl Miller, *Memoirs of a Modern Scotland* (1970)

Stirling

Edinburgh and Stirling are spinster sisters, who were both in their youth beloved by Scottish kings; but Stirling is the more wrinkled in feature, the more old-fashioned in attire, and not nearly so well to do in the world. She smacks more of the antique time, and wears the ornaments given her by royal lovers – sadly broken and worn now, and not calculated to yield much if brought to the hammer – more ostentatiously in the public eye than does Edinburgh. On the whole, perhaps, her stock of these red sandstone gew-gaws is the more numerous . . .

Stirling, like a huge brooch, clasps Highlands and Lowlands together.

ALEXANDER SMITH, *A Summer in Skye* (1865)

Perth

There should be Cities of Refuge. Hence the envy which it is said that Perth sometimes has of Dundee, is nearly inconceivable. One would have thought that there was no Perth man (out of the asylum) who would not have rejoiced in his unstained tranquillity, in the delightful heights that enclose him, – in his silvery Tay, – in the quiet beauty of his green and level Inches. Yet it is said that some of them actually long for steam engines on Kinnoul Hill, and docks, and factories, and the sweets of the Scouring burn. But I do not believe this. It is incredible. Long may both they and we be spared.

LORD COCKBURN, Journals (1874)

Yon Toun

1

Hae ye come in be yon toun
Ablow the craigie knowes?
Hae ye come in be yon toun
Whaur the clear water rows?

2

Birk and rodden[1] on the brae,
Hawthorn in the hauch;
And clear water churlin by
The elder and the sauch.[2]

3

At day-daw and at grey-fa'
The merry bells ding doun:
At day-daw and grey-fa'
There's music in yon toun.

4

Merle and mavie whistle clear;
And whan the hour is still
Haikers[3] owre the auld brig hear
The gowk[4] upon the hill.

5

Wha wudna bide in yon toun
Ablow the craigie knowes?
Wha wudna bide in yon toun
Whaur the clear water rows?

WILLIAM SOUTAR,
Poems of William Soutar: A New Selection,
ed. W. R. Aitken (1988)

¹ rowan; ² willow; ³ travellers; ⁴ cuckoo

Dundee

I

It is an East Coast town with a West Coast temperament. It is a big place without any distinguishing marks save its somewhat strange political history during recent years and certain other associations that do not, however, seem to have grown naturally out of its essence. It is something to have returned to Parliament within twenty years or so both Mr Winston Churchill and a Prohibitionist so austere as Mr Edwin Scrymgeour; and a reputation for the production of marmalade is not easily come by . . .

It stretches agreeably along a hillside above the estuary of the Tay. It has a history. It gave its name to a gallant soldier and a gallant song. In the Town Churches it has a building of the most unusual character, a great cruciform pile that, dominated by the sign Old Staple, houses three parish churches under one roof. And yet, once again, the modern Dundee does not exist at all on the strength of that past. One fancies that it would choose to be judged on the strength of what it is, a municipality up to date and 'improved' – even to the extent of the demolition of its oldest building. In short, the city might be said to have renounced its Scottish birthright and to have become in consequence what diplomacy calls a *heimatlos* alien: neither quite one thing nor the other.

GEORGE BLAKE, *The Heart of Scotland* (1934)

Nature intended Dundee to be a dignified and gracious city, for the site is one of the most magnificent in Europe. But as men have made it it stands today perhaps the completest monument in the entire continent of human folly, avarice, and selfishness; a perfect object-lesson in what results from the divorce of economic life from ethics. Dundee ought to have been the pride of Angus, living with, and within, the life of this old and beautiful and fertile province, the head of a richly individual provincial culture. Instead, Dundee was turned into a shambles of industrialism; and strikes one today merely as a tragic accident and a blight on a prepossessing landscape. Strictly speaking, Dundee is not a city; it is merely a monstrously overgrown small town. No total and unified conception governed its disorderly growth. It has scarcely a spacious street, or a dignified building. Its housing is a something monstrous, which can be seen and yet defies belief. Moreover, the conditions governing its chief and vital industry involved a peculiarly horrible circumstance, the preponderance of wretchedly badly-paid female labour. The results are tragically in evidence today. It is doubtful if there can be seen anywhere in the world so large a proportion of a population stunted, sickly, and deformed. And now, in Dundee earlier perhaps and more completely than anywhere, the process of capitalist industrialism has worked out to its logical and inevitable end; that which brought Dundee into existence as an industrial city is no longer able to maintain it even at the level of its one-time sordid and poverty-bound prosperity. Dundee is a great industrial derelict.

FIONN MAC COLLA, 'Angus and Mearns',
in ed. George Scott Moncrieff, *Scottish Country* (1935)

The Silver City

Yonder she sits beside the tranquil Dee,
Kindly yet cold, respectable and wise,
Sharp-tongued though civil, with wide-open eyes,
Dreaming of hills, yet urgent for the sea;
And still and on, she has her vanity,
Wears her grey mantle with a certain grace,

While sometimes there are roses on her face
To sweeten too austere simplicity.

She never taught her children fairy lore,
Yet they must go a-seeking crocks of gold
Afar throughout the earth;
And when their treasure in her lap they pour,
Her hands upon her knee do primly fold;
She smiles complacent that she gave them birth.

MARION ANGUS, *Sun and Candlelight* (1927)

Aberdeen in the 1930s

Here is an Aberdonian 'funny story':

> An Aberdonian died and gave instructions in his will that his
> body be cremated. This was done. The day after the cremation
> the widow heard a knock at the door. She opened it and saw a
> small message-boy standing on the doorstep holding out a pack-
> age towards her. 'What's this?' she enquired. 'Your husband,
> Mem,' said the boy, '– his ashes, you know.' Slowly the widow
> took the package in her hand. 'His ashes. Oh, ay. *But where's the
> dripping?'*

I choose this example deliberately as that of an Aberdonian
story insufficiently padded. You laugh, but (if you have any
imagination at all) you have a slight qualm. The grisliness
below the humour is insufficiently concealed. You can smell
the stench of that burning body, you can see the running
human fats – with a dish in appropriate position to collect
them . . . You see too closely in this instance the grinning skull
behind the large, jolly countenance of the laughing man; you
may suspect him, outside the flare of lights in the bar and the
help of alcohol, as one solemn and serious enough, uneasy,
haunted by an unending apprehension of life as a bleak
enough parade.

Bleakness, not meanness or jollity, is the keynote to
Aberdonian character, not so much lack of the graces or gra-
ciousness of existence as lack of colour in either of these. And
this is almost inevitable for anyone passing his nights and days

in The Silver City by the Sea. It is comparable to passing one's existence in a refrigerator. Aberdeen is built, largely and incredibly, of one of the most enduring and indestructible and appalling building-materials in use on our planet – grey granite . . .

LEWIS GRASSIC GIBBON,
'Aberdeen', *Scottish Scene* (1934)

A Per Se

Aiberdeen an' twal' mile roon,
Fife an' a' the lands aboot it,
Ta'en frae Scotland's runkled map
Little's left, an' wha will doot it?

Few at least 'at maitters ony,
Orra folk, it's easy seen,
Folk 'at dinna come frae bonny
Fife or canny Aiberdeen.

DAVID RORIE,
The Lum Hat Wantin' the Croon (1935)

Inverness

I

Inverness, a small town containing trout and Highlanders, is built entirely of pink granite.

KAREL ČAPEK

II

Set thus so beautifully among the hills and waters, Inverness demands citizens with a more gallant air than suits a purely lowland town. I would not say that all the people of Inverness walk about as if they were Jacobites at heart and secretly drink to Charles Edward; yet there are those who have a something, just as all highlanders have a something, though they do not always know what to do with it. For instance there are quite a few kilts around Inverness, some of them worn by gentlemen with rather anxious expressions, for the kilt is sometimes more than a garment: it can be a gesture and a protest, and a protest is not an assuring cover for the nakedness of the human body. But when it is worn as a gesture of pride and youth, the streets of Inverness light up and there is music on the hills.

J. R. ALLAN, *North-east Lowlands of Scotland* (1974)

Highlands and Islands

All But an Island

Scotland is not wholly surrounded by the sea – unfortunately. Nevertheless it is all but an island and in addition to its main land mass comprises not only a host of single islands of all sorts and sizes but the archipelagoes of the Hebrides, the Orkneys, and the Shetlands. It stands to reason that seafaring and fisheries and allied industries have always played a very large and important part in the life of Scotland although they do not bulk in anything like due proportion in the general conception of Scotland nor are they at all adequately reflected in its literature. What is true of the Scottish mainland is even truer of these three great exclaves. Little or nothing is popularly known of their island economies of crofting and fishing. The Hebrides enter into the general consciousness by way of a glamorous myth which has little or no relation to reality – so little indeed that the average Scotsman had no conception at all of the economic history, present conditions, and problems and potentialities of these islands. Indeed the vast majority could not name more than a few of them and I was amused a few years ago when my friend Compton Mackenzie bought the Shiant Isles to find how few supposedly well-educated Scots knew where they lay or had even heard of them before, a state of affairs paralleled, I found, by the general inability to understand what I meant by a line in one of my poems which deals with

'Fladda Chuain and the Ascrib Isles.'

HUGH MacDIARMID, 'The Sea', *Scottish Scene* (1934)

Shiant Islands

The Shiant Islands are not large. On the usual map of Scotland they look as if somebody had left three specks of black pepper in the middle of that uncomfortable stretch of sea between the Outer Isles and the mainland which is called the Minch and which has probably had more triumphs over the weakness of the human body than any other stretch of sea of similar size in the world. I was not trying to give my talk a coloured frontispiece when I called it 'The Enchanted Isles'. The epithet sounds too good to be true, but that is what 'Shiant' means. Perhaps ages and ages ago somebody baffled by the charm of these islands gave them this name in despair, like myself, of being able to communicate even faintly their incommunicable charm. Or perhaps the name is an echo of the ancient legend of the Blue Men who haunt the dangerous tidal rips and overfalls that guard the islands on either side. One of these nowadays is called the Stream of the Barking Dogs from the noise the waves make in their anger. Anyway, whatever the origin of the name, nobody who has stood on the highest point of the islands 540 feet above the dark green sea that washes the base of these stupendous cliffs and looked westward to the blue hills of Harris, or northward to the Atlantic rolling in between the Butt of Lewis and Cape Wrath, or eastward to where the mountain line of Sutherland and Ross runs indigo-dark along the horizon like a jagged saw, or southward to the fantastic luminous huddle of Skye and the misted peaks of Uist – nobody who has stood thus, swung between earth and heaven, could deny the magic of these islands.

text of a radio talk by SIR COMPTON MacKENZIE (1928)

The Outer Isles

The village was bounded on the east and west by two huge headlands that flung themselves into the Atlantic like two couching beasts cooling their dark bellies in the sea. The wide and shelterless bay that lay below the crofts was cleft by a long skerry at whose outermost end a rounded bastion of rock stood up above the stones. When the tide flowed in over the skerry, this thing looked like the citadel of a drowning city over whose roofs the water was beginning to rise. To the south we were guarded by a ridge of high hills and from the moors behind them the night leapt upon us in the winter time with the suddenness of an animal's leap. The village itself was built for the most part on two rocky ridges that rose gradually from the wide valley which separated them. From the centre of the valley the houses on either ridge could be seen clearly etched against the sky and their huddled forms appeared to stand on the lonely edge of the world. A river came tumbling down through the valley and poured itself into a great fresh-water loch which bordered so closely on the sea that only a few yards of soil kept the peace between them. There were no trees against which the wind could wrestle, to spend its crude strength before it shook the houses. So the winter landscape was bare and desolate, with nothing to hide the outlines of the naked earth; but it had the inexpressible, sad beauty which barrenness has everywhere, in nature and in man. And the barrenness did not last

129

long, for it only required the embrace of the spring to fill the dark earth with new life and new joy. But there was one measure of self-defence taken by the villagers against the colourless winters. Every conceivable piece of wood in the village was painted in bright and striking colours. Red windows peered out from under the golden straw that thatched the houses. Doors of flaming red caught the light of the sun on the top of each ridge and glared at each other across the shivering fields. The boats lay in a cluster at one end of the shore, splashed with shades of blue and white. Sometimes a red petticoat flew from a clothes-line, looking as if it had been dyed in blood, and red ploughs, painted afresh in preparation for the spring, leaned against gables and walls . . .

When there was no other form of pastime in the village there was always the *céilidh*. *Céilidh* is the Gaelic word for a visit, not for a 'social'. It is not, as is usually supposed, a continual recital of Gaelic songs relieved by interludes of long-winded Fenian sagas. It is much more human than that, because the primary things that interest country people are the events of their daily lives and the attractive gossip that arises therefrom. The islanders have as keen an appetite for gossip and scandal as peasants have in all parts of the world, and it is out of their gossip that their tales are born. For when news is scarce, as it often is in the Hebrides, the most trivial event becomes a sensation and when it has been mouthed by whole villages, it gradually takes on the dimensions of a legend. The result is that many islanders become half legendary characters before they die.

So it was in the village of which I speak. There were songs to be heard at a *céilidh* for the asking, and old men could tell tales of their own experiences that would hold the company spellbound for hours. But quite often the entire evening was given up to the lively gossip and conversation which the different seasons brought round. News travelled round the village like a gust of wind. If a child was born the garrulous midwife called in every house on the way home to announce the event, and in a twinkling it was known at the other end of the village. If any strangers arrived in the village, their identity was quickly known to everybody. If a cow calved or a sheep lambed, the news sent a tremor of excitement through the whole street, for such things were events of importance in the life of the community. If a boat was all but swamped at sea in a sudden storm, as was very often the case, the incident was on everybody's lips. Such were the topics of discussion at a *céilidh*.

But the coming of spring was eagerly awaited, for nowhere in the world does it perform such a miracle as in the Outer Isles. The ferment seemed to begin in the sea, for it cast out of its caves with a moaning like the noise of birth, fresh masses of brown seaweed that lay strewn along the beach. Shoals of haddock and saith appeared on the coast and the sea birds, noticing them, became wild and clamorous. They rose in white flocks from the sunless cliffs, passing in rhythmic flight over the bay, veering against the wind. The gannets dived and shouted, swooping and spinning down from great heights, splashing into the water with clasped wings.

A warmer wind blew in from the moors and produced a mysterious quickening in the dark soil of the crofts. Blood seemed to flow again in the veins of the earth, till it began to throb with the pulse of a new life. It cracked and burst, opening its pores to receive the germs of new crops. The villagers appeared in the fields, seized with the same strange quickening as if the beat of their blood were responding to the earth's pulse. On every hill the forms of workers appeared against the sky. On distant ridges a company of women, bent over their spades, looked like large, grotesque birds pecking at the soil. Their voices as they shouted over the fields were tremulous with eagerness and desire. Everywhere there was a lust for work. Spades were plunged into the moist soil; horses crawled along with their small ploughs, and in their wake a flock of ravenous sea birds snapped up worms and roots and grubs. Clouds of delicate grey mist rose from the moist earth, and in the fields everywhere was the acrid, satisfying smell of soil that had been newly delved. Seed was scattered on the furrows – mostly barley seed because in West Lewis they have great use for barley. They grind it in the village mills into meal for barley-bread, and if the harvest has been a successful one, they brew from the barley seed barrels of rich, creamy beer . . .

The village itself (called by the Norse *Siabost* or Steading by the Sea) sat on its warm ridges, all thoughts of its blotchy winter landscape forgotten. The green crops swayed lifelessly, waiting for the swish of summer rain. Down to the Butt, the villages of West Lewis were all visible, their windows reflecting the rays of the sun. Dimly the Butt lighthouse rose from its rocky perch, looking impotent and silly in the fierce light. Muirneag hill on the moors of Ness brooded over her widowhood. The four peaks of the Barvas hills threw their long shadows over the sheilings below them. Below Huitealam was Loch Raoinabhat, a straggling sheet of water from whose face the floating clouds in the sky were reflected like white flames. Beside the loch, in a circular hollow among the hills, was the lovely village of Dalbeg, with its few scattered houses. To the west lay the finest sea loch in the Hebrides, the mighty Loch Roag whose tides swirled round countless islands. The little island of Bernera lay in its mouth, a place that breeds the most dare-devil fishermen in the Hebrides. Outside Bernera the desolate rock of Bereasaidh appeared like the back of some huge whale. On this rock Neil MacLeod, the illustrious warrior of Lewis, spent three years during the clan warfare of the sixteenth century. Above Loch Roag rose the dark blue towers and pinnacles of the Uig mountains, the highest range in Lewis. Mealasbhal and Suainabhal loomed above their neighbours, Mealasbhal's frowning precipices and mountain chasms floodlit with strong light. The sands of Valtos Bay gleamed yellow in the distance. To the south the skyline was chequered with the vivid outlines of the Harris hills. And stretching towards them were the broad folds of Lewis moors, that seemed to burn and quiver and shake in the summer heat, like a landscape seen through the mad mind of Van Gogh. The purple and red blooms of heather lit up the moors, giving them the colour of *fion na Spaine*, the rich Spanish wine so often mentioned in waulking songs. Far across these purple fields was the hill of Roinabhal. It stood at the head of Loch Erisort, a serpentine sea loch that eats into the east of the island, shooting out long tongues among the quiet hills of Lochs. There is a whole parish called Lochs, and for good reason. The land is half covered with water. There are innumerable fresh-water lochs and so many arms of the sea that a man with a boat scarcely knows which one to use. The village of Maravig on Loch Erisort can be approached from the sea through five different channels. Loch Erisort has a company of splendid neighbours; in the same parish are Loch Sealg, Loch Claidh and Loch Seaforth, all of them associated with poaching adventures. For the Forest of Eisginn, into which they run, is the best deer forest in Scotland . . .

Uist has a reputation in the Outer Islands for yellow barley fields and noble horses. The island has been a famous mart for horses ever since the seventeenth century, when Allan of Clan Ranald brought home Spanish steeds to breed on his wide machairs. Allan's own stables were the wonder of many parishes. When he went on holiday to the Continent, it is said that his cavalcade clattered through the streets of Paris, each horse shod with shoes of gold stamped with the proud name of Clan Ranald. All this splendour is now dead, but the names of the Clan Ranald chieftains and the nobility of their deeds are rooted forever in the stories and legends of the islands. And in the Isle of Uist a child may still be rocked to sleep with the lullaby of Clan Ranald, which the bard MacCodrum composed while he walked with the infant chieftain in his arms twice round the garden of the child's home. Borve Castle, where for a time the chieftains lived, is now a toppling ruin on a machair in Benbecula. It is some hundreds of yards from the sea. Yet at one time, according to tradition, the waves of the Atlantic swilled round its rocky base, and a stately sailing ship with three white sails, moored herself below its walls. Since then the flood tides have thrown up banks of sand, the machair has surrounded the castle, and the gay waves have left off their flirting with its stones.

In all the Hebrides, Benbecula is the sea's dearest child. That is why the returning tide races so quickly over the sand, hurrying with pouted lips to kiss its shore. And when the night's embraces are over, the sea leaves Benbecula again, like a mother bird going to forage for its young. When the sea goes out, Benbecula is no longer an island. It is a patch of green earth in a desert of white sand: the North Ford and the South Ford are dry, and the crossings to the Uists are open to horses and carts. I saw the North Ford on an autumn evening from the village of Uachdar in Benbecula. It looked like a huge field of snow into which the thaw had set. For the dazzling whiteness was interrupted here and there with warmer colours. Wisps and strands of russet tangle were patterned upon it. Brown and red skerries rose up here and there, with little pools of foam floating about them. In the large sand furrows little green streams ran towards the sea, carrying along with them the slaver of brown spume that the tide had left behind it. Suddenly I heard the crack of whips, and from the headland on my right three gipsy gigs

133

rushed across the ford, like hurrying thieves. The horses ran at a merry gallop but their hooves made no murmur on the sands. Their dark manes flowed into the wind. The laughter of the gipsies rang out in the silence of the ford. In a moment their shapes became dim as they drew near the coast of Uist. Scarcely had they crossed when their tracks were covered up by the flowing tide. The sea was returning to Benbecula to protect its child . . .

Across the water from Eriskay is the Isle of Barra, known in Gaelic legend as *'Barraidh Ghorm NanLong'* – Blue Barra of the Ships. Its rounded breasts lie on the surface of a dim tide. Little boats with tawny sails steal out of its long creeks, manned by the cunning fishermen of Barra. The shadows of Kishmul's grey walls rise and fall in the Castle Bay, like the swaying blades of tangle below them. But Kishmul is no longer a centre for piracy. The MacNeills' sea-reiving is at an end. South of Barra, the lonely islands of Mingulay and Berneray mark the limits of the Hebrides . . .

The Blue Men of the Minch, according to Hebridean legend, sprang up from the sea in the Sound of Shiant and put to the skipper of every passing ship two lines of Gaelic poetry. Unless he could quote the next two lines of the text, they light-heartedly sank his ship. It meant that he was not of the blood. The Blue Men were artists who did not want the island culture to be contaminated, and perhaps it was their pranks that held off for such a long time the influence of the outside world . . .

Writers who in their dreams behold the Hebrides, have a misleading habit of suggesting that dreaming is as fashionable in the islands as it is among themselves. But the sweating labour of spring and autumn, and the continual fight with the sea does not leave much time for the weaving of dreams. Living is not an easy matter in the Hebrides. It is an exhausting struggle, but a struggle that is cheerfully accepted because it is familiar and has always been the way of life. There is neither pessimism nor melancholy anywhere, but a live spirit of gaiety that even the holy waters of the Church have not managed to quench. And strangely enough, the second menace to the culture of the Hebrides – a menace even greater than the economic one – is the Church, and the sterilizing religion which it preaches. As interpreted by the Presbyterian ministers of the Hebrides, life is identified with asceticism and repression. The crucifixion of the body is the monotonous theme of all their discourses. Drinking, dancing, music and recreation are officially condemned. But these gentlemen in their fanatical and destructive campaign forget that such taboos cannot be imposed on country people, whose nature it is to set more store on human values than on ascetic ones. And the more their human wants are denied them, the more they tend to excess. So that in the Isles the arts of drinking and dancing are still in a very healthy condition, for when they have to be pursued in secret, they become an exciting adventure.

HECTOR MacIVER, 'The Outer Isles',
in ed. G. Scott Moncrieff, *Scottish Country* (1935)

Old Woman

Your thorned back
heavily under the creel
you steadily stamped the rising daffodil.

Your set mouth
forgives no one, not even God's justice
perpetually drowning law with grace.

Your cold eyes
watched your drunken husband come
unsteadily from Sodom home.

Your grained hands
dandled full and sinful cradles.
You built for your children stone walls.

Your yellow hair
burned slowly in a scarf of grey
wildly falling like the mountain spray.

Finally, you're alone
among the unforgiving brass,
the slow silences, the sinful glass.

Who never learned,
not even aging, to forgive
our poor journey and our common grave,

while the free daffodils
wave in the valleys and on the hills
the deer look down with their instinctive skills,

and the huge seas
in which your brothers drowned sing slow
over the headland and the peevish crow.

IAIN CRICHTON SMITH, *Selected Poems* (1985)

Iona

We were now treading that illustrious Island, which was once
the luminary of the *Caledonian* regions, whence savage clans
and roving barbarians derived the benefits of knowledge, and
the blessings of religion. To abstract the mind from all local
emotion would be impossible, if it were endeavoured, and
would be foolish, if it were possible. Whatever withdraws us
from the power of our senses; whatever makes the past, the distant, or the future predominate over the present, advances us in
the dignity of thinking beings. Far from me and from my
friends, be such frigid philosophy as may conduct us indifferent and unmoved over any ground which has been dignified by
wisdom, bravery, or virtue. That man is little to be envied,
whose patriotism would not gain force upon the plain of *Mara-
thon*, or whose piety would not grow warmer among the ruins
of *Iona*!

SAMUEL JOHNSON,
A Journey to the Western Islands of Scotland (1775)

Clearances: An Eviction on Skye

One of the most vivid recollections which I retain of Kilbride is
that of the eviction or clearance of the crofts of Suishnish. The
corner of Strath between the two sea-inlets of Loch Slapin and

Loch Eishort had been for ages occupied by a community that cultivated the lower ground where their huts formed a kind of scattered village. The land belonged to the wide domain of Lord Macdonald, whose affairs were in such a state that he had to place himself in the hands of trustees. These men had little local knowledge of the estate, and though they doubtless administered it to the best of their ability, their main object was to make as much money as possible out of the rents, so as on the one hand, to satisfy the creditors, and on the other, to hasten the time when the proprietor might be able to resume possession. The interests of the crofters formed a very secondary consideration. With these aims, the trustees determined to clear out the whole population of Suishnish and convert the ground into one large sheep-farm, to be placed in the hands of a responsible grazier, if possible, from the south country.

I had heard some rumours of these intentions, but did not realize that they were in process of being carried into effect, until one afternoon, as I was returning from my ramble, a strange wailing sound reached my ears at intervals on the breeze from the west. On gaining the top of one of the hills on the south side of the valley, I could see a long and motley procession winding along the road that led north from Suishnish. It halted at the point of the road opposite Kilbride, and there the lamentation became loud and long. As I drew nearer, I could see that the minister with his wife and daughters had come out to meet the people and bid them all farewell. It was a miscellaneous gathering of at least three generations of crofters. There were old men and women, too feeble to walk, who were placed in carts; the younger members of the community on foot were carrying their bundles of clothes and household effects, while the children, with looks of alarm, walked alongside. There was a pause in the notes of woe as the last words were exchanged with the family of Kilbride. Everyone was in tears; each wished to clasp the hands that had so often befriended them, and it seemed as if they could not tear themselves away. When they set forth once more, a cry of grief went up to heaven, the long plaintive wail, like a funeral coronach, was resumed, and after the last of the emigrants had disappeared behind the hill, the sound seemed to re-echo through the whole wide valley of Strath in one prolonged note of desolation. The people were on their way to be shipped to Canada. I have often wandered since

137

then over the solitary ground of Suishnish. Not a soul is to be seen there now, but the greener patches of field and the crumbling walls mark where an active and happy community once lived.

SIR ARCHIBALD GEIKIE, *Scottish Reminiscences* (1904)

The Clearances

The thistles climb the thatch. Forever
this sharp scale in our poems,
as also the waste music of the sea.

The stars shine over Sutherland
in a cold ceilidh of their own,
as, in the morning, the silver cane

cropped among corn. We will remember this.
Though hate is evil we cannot
but hope your courtier's heels in hell

are burning: that to hear
the thatch sizzling in tanged smoke
your hot ears slowly learn.

IAIN CRICHTON SMITH, *Selected Poems 1955–1980* (1981)

Srath Nabhair

Anns an adhar dhubh-ghorm ud,
àirde na sìorraidheachd os ar cionn,
bha rionnag a' priobadh ruinn
's i freagairt mireadh an teine
ann an cabair taigh m' athar
a' bhlianna thugh sinn an taigh le bleideagan sneachda.

Agus siud a' bhlianna cuideachd
a shlaod iad a' chailleach don t-sitig,
a shealltainn cho eòlach 's a bha iad air an Fhirinn,
oir bha nid aig eunlaith an adhair
(agus cròthan aig na caoraich)
ged nach robh àit aice-se anns an cuireadh i a ceann fòidhpe.

A Shrath Nabhair 's a Shrath Chill Donnain,
is beag an t-iongnadh ged a chinneadh am fraoch àlainn
    oirbh,
a' falach nan lotan a dh' fhàg Pàdraig Sellar 's a sheòrsa,
mar a chunnaic mi uair is uair boireannach cràbhaidh
a dh' fhiosraich dòrainn an t-saoghail-sa
is sith Dhè 'na sùilean.

Strathnaver

In that blue-black sky,
as high above us as eternity,
a star was winking at us,
answering the leaping flames of fire
in the rafters of my father's house,
that year we thatched the house with snowflakes.

And that too was the year
they hauled the old woman out on to the dung-heap,
to demonstrate how knowledgeable they were in Scripture,
for the birds of the air had nests
(and the sheep had folds)
though she had no place in which to lay down her head.

O Strathnaver and Strath of Kildonan,
it is little wonder that the heather should bloom on your slopes,
hiding the wounds that Patrick Sellar, and such as he, made,
just as time and time again I have seen a pious woman
who has suffered the sorrow of this world,
with the peace of God shining from her eyes.

RUARAIDH MacTHÓMAIS (DERICK THOMSON)
in ed. Donald MacAuley, *Modern Scottish Gaelic Poems* (1976)

Terra Hyperborea

I am in the region known as Skye, in the Hebrides, on a large
queer island among islands, on an island consisting of fjords,
peat, rocks and summits; I collect coloured shells among bluish
or sallow pebbles, and by a special favour of heaven I find even
the excrement of the wild salmon which is the milch cow of

the Gaelic water-nymphs. The slopes ooze like a drenched sponge, the heather bruach catches in my feet, but then, readers, can be seen the islands of Raasay and Scalpay, Rum and Eigg, and then can be seen the mountains with strange and ancient names, such as Beinn na-Cailich and Sgurr na-Banachdich and Leacan Nighean an-i-Siosalaich, or Druim nan Cleochd, while those bald domes yonder are called merely Blaven, quite simply Blaven. And this rivulet here is simply Aan Reidhe Mhoire and that sandy inlet is merely Sran Ard-a-Mhullaich. These and all the other names demonstrate the beauty and strangeness of the Isle of Skye.

It is beautiful and poverty-stricken; and the native huts have such a prehistoric look, that they might have been built by the late Picts, concerning whom, as is known, there is nothing known. Then the Caledonian Gaels came here, and the Vikings from somewhere in Norway; King Hakon actually left behind him a stone stronghold, and the place is therefore called Kyle Akin. Apart from this, all these dwellers left the Isle of Skye in its original state, as it proceeded from God's hand: wild, forlorn and rugged, damp and sublime, terrible and winsome. Stone cottages are being overgrown with grass and moss, or are falling into decay, deserted by men.

Once a week the sun shines, and then the mountain peaks are revealed in all the inexpressible tints of blue; and there is blueness which is azure, mother-of-pearl, foggy or indigo, clouded like vapours, a hint or mere reminder of something beautifully blue. All these, and countless other shades of blueness I saw on the blue summits of Cuilin, but there, added to everything else, can be seen the blue sky and the blue bay, and this simply cannot be narrated; I tell you, unknown and divine virtues arose within me at the sight of this unbounded blueness.

But then the clouds creep forth from the valley and mountains, the sea turns grey, and a chill rain flows from the drenching slopes. In the home of some worthy folk the peat is burning on the hearth, a lady with a Greek profile sings Scottish ballads, and with the others I sing a strange and ancient song:

> 'tha tighin fodham, fodham, fodham,
> tha tighin fodham, fodham, fodham,
> tha tighin fodham, fodham, fodham,
> tha tighan fodham eirig.'

And then we all hold hands in a circle and sing something Scottish about parting or meeting again. Between the promontories of the island can be seen a narrow strip of open sea; thither, I am told, the whalers sail to Iceland or Greenland. Man, why do you feel sad when you look at that streak of open sea? Be greeted, O lands, which perchance I shall never see!

Ah, I have beheld blue and fiery seas and pliant beeches and palm-trees bending over azure waves; but these grey and cold lochs fairly bewitched me; look, yonder a crane is wading among the seaweed, and a gull or a sea-swallow is gliding over the waves with a wild and piercing cry; above the moorland a snipe is whistling and a flock of fieldfares are snorting, a shaggy little steer gazes at man, and on the bald hills the sheep are grazing, similar, from afar, to yellowish lice; and at evening myriads of tiny flies swarm forth and crawl into man's nose, while the northern day lasts till nearly midnight.

And the livid, plashing sea beneath one's feet, and the open road to the north . . .

KAREL ČAPEK, Letters from England (1925)

Virginia Woolf on Skye

To Vanessa Bell   Flodigarry Hotel, Portree,
                                     Isle of Skye
                                     25th June [1938]

Well, here we are in Skye, and it feels like the South Seas – completely remote, surrounded by sea, people speaking Gaelic, no railways, no London papers, hardly any inhabitants. Believe it or not, it is (in its way, as people say) so far as I can judge on a level with Italy, Greece or Florence. No one in Fitzroy Street will believe this, and descriptions are your abhorrence – further the room is pullulating and popping with Edinburgh tourists, one of whom owns spaniels, like Sally, but 'all mine are gun trained, the only thing they wont carry being hares' – so I cant run on, did you wish it. Only – well, in Duncan's highlands,[1] the colours in a perfectly still deep blue lake of green and purple trees reflected in the middle of the water which was enclosed with green reeds, and yellow flags, and the whole sky

[1] i.e. Duncan Grant, the artist

and a purple hill – well, enough. One should be a painter. As a writer, I feel the beauty, which is almost entirely colour, very subtle, very changeable, running over my pen, as if you poured a large jug of champagne over a hairpin. I must here tender my congratulations to Duncan upon being a Grant. We've driven round the island today, seen Dunvegan, encountered the children of the 27th Chieftain, nice red headed brats: the Castle door being open I walked in; they very politely told me the Castle was shut to visitors, but I could see the gardens. Here I found a gamekeepers larder with the tails of two wild cats. Eagles are said to abound and often carry off sheep: sheep and Skye Terriers are the only industries; the old women live in round huts exactly the shape of skye terriers; and you can count all the natives on 20 feet: but they are very rapacious in the towns, and its no use trying to buy anything, as the price, even of Sally's meat, is at least 6 times higher than in our honest land. All the same, the Scotch are great charmers, and sing through their noses like musical tea kettles.

VIRGINIA WOOLF, *Congenial Spirits:*
The Letters of Virginia Woolf (1989)

Crofter's kitchen, evening

A man's boots with a woman in them
Clatter across the floor. A hand
Long careless of the lives it kills
Comes down and thwacks on newspapers
A long black fish with bloody gills.

The kettle's at her singsong – minor
Prophetess in her sooty cave.
A kitten climbs the bundled net
On the bench and, curled up like a cowpat,
Purrs on the *Stornoway Gazette*.

The six hooks of a Mackerel Dandy
Climb their thin rope – an exclamation
By the curled question of a gaff.
Three rubber eels cling like a crayfish
On top of an old photograph.

Peats fur themselves in gray. The door
Bursts open, chairs creak, hands reach out
For spectacles, a lamp flares high . . .
The collie underneath the table
Slumps with a world-rejecting sigh.

NORMAN MacCAIG, *Collected Poems* (1990)

A Letter from D. H. Lawrence

Bailabhadan, Newtonmore, Inverness.
20 August 1926

Frieda sent me on your letter from Irschenhausen. I am glad
you like being there, but am surprised it is so cold. Here the
weather is mild, mixed rainy and sunny. The heather is out on
the moors: the day lasts till nine oclock: yet there is that dim,
twilight feeling of the north. We made an excursion to the
west, to Fort William and Mallaig, and sailed up from Mallaig
to the Isle of Skye. I liked it very much. It rains and rains, and
the white wet clouds blot over the mountains. But we had one
perfect day, blue and iridescent, with the bare northern hills
sloping green and sad and velvety to the silky blue sea. There is
still something of an Odyssey up there, in among the islands
and the silent lochs: like the twilight morning of the world, the
herons fishing undisturbed by the water, and the sea running
far in, for miles, between the wet, trickling hills, where the cottages are low and almost invisible, built into the earth. It is still
out of the world, and like the very beginning of Europe: though
of course, in August there are many tourists and motor-cars.
But the country is almost uninhabited.

The Letters of D. H. Lawrence 1924–1927, vol. 5,
ed. J. T. Boulton and L. Vasey (1987)

Rannoch, by Glencoe

Here the crow starves, here the patient stag
Breeds for the rifle. Between the soft moor
And the soft sky, scarcely room
To leap or soar. Substance crumbles, in the thin air

143

Moon cold or moon hot. The road winds in
Listlessness of ancient war,
Languor of broken steel,
Clamour of confused wrong, apt
In silence. Memory is strong
Beyond the bone. Pride snapped,
Shadow of pride is long, in the long pass
No concurrence of bone.

T. S. ELIOT, *Collected Poems* (1963)

Heavens Above!

And now to the mountains, to the interior of the country, to the region of the Gaelic language. Heavens above! never have I seen such a forlorn and sinister region; still the bare hills, but higher and direr; nothing but stunted birch-trees, and then not even those, but yellow gorse and heather, and then not even that, but oozing black peat, and on it only wisps of bog-cotton, which we call St Ivan's beard, and then not even that, but stones, stones, sheer stones with tough reed-stems.

Clouds drag their way across the grey baldness of the hills, there is a spatter of cold rain, mists rise above the black rocks, and a dark glen is revealed, mournful as the howling of a dog. For miles and miles neither dwelling nor man; and when a cottage does fly past it is as grey and stony as the rocks, and all by itself, nothing else for miles around. A lake without a fisherman, streams without a miller, pastures without a shepherd, road without a wayfarer. Only in the more fertile valleys graze the shaggy Scottish steers; they stand in the rain and lie down in the damp; perhaps that is why they are so overgrown with prickly tufts, as I have drawn them for you.

And the Scottish sheep have whole Havelocks of wool, and black masks on their faces; nobody tends them, only a small stone wall along the bare slopes indicates the presence of man; as far as this wall is my pasture.

And now the place is so deserted that there is neither flock nor property, only a ruined cottage and a tumbledown mound on the brown undulation of the mossy slope. The end of life, here nothing has changed for at least ten thousand years;

people have only made roads and built railways, but the earth has not changed; nowhere a tree or a shrub; only cold lakes, whins and ferns, unending brown gorse-land, endless black stones, ink-tinted mountain summits slit by silvery threads of torrents, black marshes of peat, cloudily smoking glens between the bald ridges of mountain-tops, and again a lake with dark reeds, its surface without birds, a region without people, disquiet without cause, a road without a goal, I do not know what I am seeking, but this anyhow is solitude; drink your fill of this unbounded sadness, before you return to the haunts of men, batten on solitude, unappeased soul; for you have seen nothing greater than this desolation.

And now I am driven along into the valley; by the roadside yellow sparks of gorse gush forth, dwarf pines crouch, stunted birch-trees have clutched at granite rubble; a black torrent leaps through the valley, here are now the pine-woods, the purple bloom of rhododendra and crimson digitalis; birch-trees, sumach, oaks and alders, Nordic wildness, ferns waist-high, and a dense forest of junipers; the sun pierces the clouds, and below glistens the deep strip of a new sea among the mountain peaks.

KAREL ČAPEK, *Letters from England* (1925)

Glencoe

Sigh, wind in the pine;
River, weep as you flow;
Terrible things were done
Long, long ago.

In daylight golden and mild
After the night of Glencoe
They found the hand of a child
Lying upon the snow.

Lopped by the sword to the ground
Or torn by wolf or fox,
That was the snowdrop they found
Among the granite rocks.

Oh, life is fierce and wild
And the heart of the earth is stone,
And the hand of a murdered child
Will not bear thinking on.

Sigh, wind in the pine,
Cover it over with snow;
But terrible things were done
Long, long ago.

DOUGLAS STEWART, *Glencoe* (1947)

Sun on the High Places

It was now high day, cloudless, and very hot. The valley was as clear as in a picture. About half a mile up the water was a camp of red-coats; a big fire blazed in their midst, at which some were cooking; and near by, on the top of a rock about as high as ours, there stood a sentry, with the sun sparkling on his arms. All the way down along the riverside were posted other sentries; here near together, there widelier scattered; some planted like the first, on places of command, some on the ground level and marching and countermarching, so as to meet half-way. Higher up the glen, where the ground was more open, the chain of posts was continued by horse-soldiers, whom we could see in the distance riding to and fro. Lower down, the infantry continued; but as the stream was suddenly swelled by the confluence of a considerable burn, they were more widely set, and only watched the fords and stepping-stones.

I took but one look at them, and ducked again into my place. It was strange indeed to see this valley, which had lain so solitary in the hour of dawn, bristling with arms and dotted with the red coats and breeches.

'Ye see,' said Alan, 'this was what I was afraid of, Davie: that they would watch the burn-side. They began to come in about two hours ago, and, man! but ye're a grand hand at the sleeping! We're in a narrow place. If they get up the sides of the hill, they could easy spy us with a glass; but if they'll only keep in the foot of the valley, we'll do yet. The posts are thinner down the water; and, come night, we'll try our hand at getting by them.'

'And what are we to do till night?' I asked.

'Lie here,' says he, 'and birstle.'[1]

That one good Scotch word, 'birstle', was indeed the most of the story of the day that we had now to pass. You are to remember that we lay on the bare top of a rock, like scones upon a girdle; the sun beat upon us cruelly; the rock grew so heated, a man could scarce endure the touch of it; and the little patch of earth and fern, which kept cooler, was only large enough for one at a time. We took turn about to lie on the naked rock, which was indeed like the position of that saint that was martyred on a gridiron; and it ran in my mind how strange it was, that in the same climate and at only a few days' distance, I should have suffered so cruelly, first from cold upon my island, and now from heat upon this rock.

All the while we had no water, only raw brandy for a drink, which was worse than nothing; but we kept the bottle as cool as we could, burying it in the earth, and got some relief by bathing our breasts and temples.

The soldiers kept stirring all day in the bottom of the valley, now changing guard, now in patrolling parties hunting among the rocks. These lay round in so great a number, that to look for men among them was like looking for a needle in a bottle of hay; and being so hopeless a task, it was gone about with the less care. Yet we could see the soldiers pike their bayonets among the heather, which sent a cold thrill into my vitals; and they would sometimes hang about our rock, so that we scarce dared to breathe.

It was in this way that I first heard the right English speech; one fellow as he went by actually clapping his hand upon the sunny face of the rock on which we lay, and plucking it off again with an oath.

'I tell you it's 'ot,' says he; and I was amazed at the clipping tones and the odd sing-song in which he spoke, and no less at that strange trick of dropping out the letter h. To be sure, I had heard Ransome; but he had taken his ways from all sorts of people, and spoke so imperfectly at the best, that I set down the most of it to childishness. My surprise was all the greater to hear that manner of speaking in the mouth of a grown man; and indeed I have never grown used to it; nor yet altogether with the English grammar, as perhaps a very critical eye might here and there spy out even in these memoirs.

[1] scorch

The tediousness and pain of these hours upon the rock grew only the greater as the day went on; the rock getting still hotter and the sun fiercer. There were giddiness, and sickness, and sharp pangs like rheumatism, to be supported. I minded then, and have often minded since, on the lines in our Scotch psalm:

> 'The moon by night thee small not smite,
> Nor yet the sun by day';

and indeed it was only by God's blessing that we were neither of us sun-smitten.

R. L. STEVENSON, *Kidnapped* (1886)

Loch Tay

If I were a poet like Karel Toman or Otakar Fischer, I would to-day write a short but beautiful poem. It would be about the Scottish lakes, the Scottish wind would be wafted through it, and the daily Scottish rain would bedew it; it would contain something about blue waves, gorse, bracken and wistful pathways; in it I should not mention that these wistful pathways are entirely begirt with a fence (perhaps to prevent enchantresses from going to dance there). I must say in crude prose how beautiful it is here; a blue and violet-coloured lake between bare hills – the lake is called Loch Tay and each valley is called Glen, each mountain Ben and each man Mac . . .

KAREL ČAPEK, *Letters from England* (1925)

East of Durness

I stopped the car, put up the hood, and lit a cigarette. Every living thing seemed to be waiting for that wave to sweep over it: the long grasses along the road were quite motionless; then I saw them trembling and waving beneath the soft gust of air that the wall of rain drove before it, and a moment afterwards a few drops pattered down: then a whole cataract descended on the roof of the car. The grasses, driven down flat, rebounded madly as if fighting for their life; shoots of light erratically pierced through the tumult of flying water from the sun still shining brightly somewhere behind the cloud; in a little while

148

it shone in full force, though the fringes of the shower were still trailing past the hills. Then in a few minutes the air was quite hot and still again, and as I put up the hood a grey cloud of horse-flies descended on me. I hastily started the car to get rid of them, but I was to see more of them later on. I now had a clear view of the wild rocky outline of the east coast of Loch Eriboll, a tossing confusion of black bluffs, which gave an impression of panic flight as they swept outwards towards the open sea. It was the wildest, though not the strangest scenery I had come to in the Highlands until now, and in that Sunday stillness, on the deserted road, it was a little frightening.

EDWIN MUIR, *Scottish Journey* (1935)

Contrasting Regions

One of the most exquisite pieces of inland scenery in the Highlands lies around the region of Achilty, Scatwell, and Lochluichart. It is a region of not very high mountains, intersecting wooded glens, and the upper waters of the Conon. It is a place where one can get lost in natural beauty, at once impressive and intimate. It is not a set piece, but is both before the eye and round the bend. There is one loch of birches and headlands, of islets and water lilies, which, when I came on it first, gave me the impression of never having been fished by mortal rod. (Actually, of course, it is highly 'preserved'.)

This is the very home of the birch, and on a sunny April day we rested on last year's dried bracken, through which the delicate wind-flowers or wood anemones were blooming, and looked on a birch caught in its own green fire. In a gorge where the sun's beams came slanting down on trees that hung high over the dark rushing torrent, the newly opened leaves held the light in a glory of translucence that the eye could hardly credit.

If the Scatwell-Achilty region of the Conon River provides one of the loveliest examples of a close gathering of hill and loch and wooded glen, perhaps its most perfect contrast is to be found on the road that runs from Latheron across the county of Caithness to Thurso. Here you have a prairie-like expanse of moor that can be come upon nowhere else in Scotland, not even on the Moor of Rannoch. Though it is not its extent that is the important matter, but its quality in light and texture. Rannoch is sterile and primeval. There are stretches of it that seem to contain the debris emptied out of God's barrows when in the beginning Scotland was made. There is a mood of the weary traveller in which this region can become horrific and overpowering. (I once tramped it all through a long night.)

But on the road to Thurso there is a low suavity of line, a smoothness of texture, a far light-filled perspective that holds the mind to wonder and a pleasant silence. Miles away the Scarabens and Morven rise from the moor in a long mountainous rampart against the sky. They hold the eyes steadily and without distraction. Their outlines are apprehended and dwelt upon. They are the natural 'backcloth' in blue or purple to the immense stage of the moor. And a magician attends to the lighting between the flying brightness of the morning and the wine-reds of still evening. Then, as the miles pass, beyond Morven, far into Sutherland, arise the peaks of the Griams and Ben Hope, and lastly, that enchanted mountain of the granite battlements, Ben Laoghal.

The Thurso River runs through bare flat country, and any guide book would pronounce it dull and uninteresting. There is one broken stretch around the ruins of Castle Dirlot, with potpool and gorge, but it is too short to affect the general character of this treeless river. And perhaps, to tell the truth, one would need to be a salmon-fisher before a liking for its character could be born, and remembered, and not unlovingly dwelt upon. There are days by the Thurso I would not willingly barter for days elsewhere. Many of its pools I know better than men whom I've met oftener. (We have camped on its upper reaches.) The wind blows there, and the sun races across leagues, and when the body is pleasantly tired of the heavy rod, and the wild duck even in the nesting season fly down (keeping to the line of their beloved river) and fly back, you may feel that the earth itself is with you and the world well lost.

NEIL GUNN, *Highland Pack* (1949)

Liberty Alone

At length it pleased God, who alone can heal after wounds, to restore us to liberty from these innumerable calamities, by our most serene prince, king and lord, Robert, who, for the delivering of his people and his own rightful inheritance from the enemies' hand, did, like another Joshua or Maccabeus, most cheerfully undergo all manner of toil, fatigue, hardship and hazard. The divine providence, the right of succession by the laws and customs of the kingdom (which we will defend till death), and the due and lawful consent and assent of all the people, made him our king and prince. To him we are obliged and resolved to adhere in all things, both upon account of his right and his own merit, as being the person who hath restored the people's safety in defence of their liberties. But, after all, if this prince shall leave these principles he hath so nobly pursued, and consent that we or our kingdom be subjected to the king or people of England, we will immediately endeavour to expel him as our enemy, and as the subverter both of his own and our rights, and will make another king who will defend our liberties. For so long as there shall but one hundred of us remain alive, we will never consent to subject ourselves to the dominion of the English. For it is not glory, it is not riches, neither is it honour, but it is liberty alone that we fight and contend for, which no honest man will lose but with his life.

The Declaration of Arbroath, 6 April 1320,
trans. in *Miscellanea Scotica* (1820)

Freedom

A! Fredome is a noble thing!
Fredome maiss man to haif liking:
Fredome all solace to man giffis:
He levis at ease that freely levis!
A noble heart may haif nane ease,
Na ellis nocht[1] that may him please,
Gif fredome failye; for free liking[2]
Is yearnit[3] owre all other thing.
Na he, that ay has levit free,
May nocht knaw weil the propertie,
The anger, na the wrechit dome,[4]
That is couplit to foul thyrldome.[5]
Bot gif he had assayit it,
Then all perquer[6] he suld it wit;[7]
And suld think fredome mar to prize
Than all the gold in warld that is.

JOHN BARBOUR (1316?–95)

[1] nor anything else; [2] pleasure in life; [3] longed for; [4] doom; [5] thralldom; [6] by heart; [7] know

Nane Mair Contrar

There is nocht tua nations vndir the firmament that ar mair contrar and different fra vthirs nor is Inglismen and Scottismen, quhoubeit that thai be within ane ile and nychtbours and of ane langage. For Inglismen ar subtil and Scottismen ar facile. Inglismen ar ambitius in prosperite and Scottismen ar humain in prosperite. Inglismen ar humil quhen thai ar subieckit be forse and violence, and Scottismen ar furius quhen thai ar violently subiekit. Inglismen ar cruel quhene thai get victorie, and Scottismen ar merciful quhen thai get victorie. And to conclude, it is onpossibil that Scottismen and Inglismen can remane in concord vndir ane monarche or ane prince, because there naturis and conditions ar as indefferent as is the nature of scheip and woluis.

The Complaynt of Scotland (1549)

152

My Lord Chancellor,

'When I consider this Affair of an UNION betwixt the Two Nations, as it is express'd in the several *Articles* thereof, and now the Subject of our Deliberation at this time; I find my Mind crowded with variety of very Melancholy Thoughts, and I think it my Duty to disburden my self of some of them, by laying them before, and exposing them to the serious Consideration of this Honourable House.

'I think I see *a Free and Independent Kingdom* delivering up That, which all the World hath been fighting for, since the days of *Nimrod*; yea, that for which most of all the Empires, Kingdoms, States, Principalities and Dukedoms of *Europe*, are at this very time engaged in the most Bloody and Cruel Wars that ever were, *to wit*, A Power to Manage their own Affairs by themselves, without the Assistance and Counsel of any other.

'I think I see *a National Church*, founded upon a Rock, secured by a *Claim of Right*, hedged and fenced about by the strictest and pointedest Legal Sanction that Sovereignty could contrive, voluntarily descending into a Plain, upon an equal level with *Jews, Papists, Socinians, Arminians, Anabaptists*, and other Sectaries, &c.

'I think I see *the Noble and Honourable Peerage of Scotland*, whose Valiant Predecessors led Armies against their Enemies upon their own proper Charges and Expenses, now divested of their Followers and Vassalages, and put upon such an Equal Foot with their Vassals, that I think I see a petty *English* Excise-man receive more Homage and Respect, than what was paid formerly to their *quondam Maccallanmores*.

'I think I see *the present Peers of Scotland*, whose Noble Ancestors conquered Provinces, over-run Countries, reduc'd and subjected Towns and fortify'd Places, exacted Tribute through the greatest part of *England*, now walking in the Court of Requests like so many *English* Attornies, laying aside their Walking Swords when in Company with the *English* Peers, lest their Self-defence should be found Murder.

'I think I see *the Honourable Estate of Barons*, the bold Asserters of the Nation's Rights and Liberties in the worst of Times, now setting a Watch upon their Lips and a Guard upon their Tongues, lest they be found guilty of *Scandalum Magnatum*.

'I think I see *the Royal State of Burrows* walking their desolate

Streets, hanging down their Heads under Disappointments; wormed out of all the Branches of their old Trade, uncertain what hand to turn to, necessitate to become Prentices to their unkind Neighbours; and yet after all finding their Trade so fortified by Companies, and secured by Prescriptions, that they despair of any success therein.

'I think I see *our Learned Judges* laying aside their Practices and Decisions, studying the Common Law of *England*, gravelled with Certiorares, *Nisi prius's*, Writs of Error, Verdicts indovar, *Ejectione firmæ*, Injunctions, Demurrs, &c. and frighted with Appeals and Avocations, because of the new Regulations and Rectifications they may meet with.

'I think I see *the Valiant and Gallant Soldiery* either sent to learn the Plantation Trade Abroad; or at Home Petitioning, for a small Subsistance as the Reward of their honourable Exploits, while their old Cores are broken, the common Soldiers left to Beg, and the youngest *English* Corps kept standing.

'I think I see *the Honest Industrious Tradesman* loaded with new Taxes, and Impositions, disappointed of the Equivalents, drinking Water in place of Ale, eating his fat-less Pottage, Petitioning for Encouragement to his Manufacturies, and Answered by counter Petitions.

'In short, I think I see *the Laborious Plew-man*, with his Corns spoiling upon his Hands, for want of Sale, Cursing the day of his Birth, dreading the Expense of his Burial, and uncertain whether to Marry or do worse.

'I think I see the Incureable Difficulties of the *Landedmen*, fettered under the Golden Chain of Equivalents, their pretty Daughters Petitioning for want of Husbands, and their Sons for want of Imployments.

'I think I see *our Mariners*, delivering up their Ships to their *Dutch* Partners; and what through Presses and Necessity, earning their Bread as Underlings in the Royal *English* Navy.

'But above all, *My Lord*, I think I see *our Ancient Mother* CALEDONIA, like *Cæsar* sitting in the midst of our Senate, Rufully looking round about her, Covering her self with her Royal Garment, attending the Fatal Blow, and breathing out her last with a *Et tu quoque mi fili.*'

LORD BELHAVEN in the last Scottish parliament, from Daniel Defoe, *History in the Union* (1709) from *The Treaty of Union of the Two Kingdoms of Scotland and England*

I. THAT the Two Kingdoms of Scotland and England, shall upon the first day of May next ensuing the date hereof, and forever after, be United into One Kingdom by the Name of GREAT BRITAIN: And that the Ensigns Armorial of the said United Kingdom be such as Her Majesty shall appoint and the Crosses of St Andrew and St George be conjoined in such manner as Her Majesty shall think fit, and used in all Flags, Banners, Standards and Ensigns both at Sea and Land.

II. THAT the Succession to the Monarchy of the United Kingdom of Great Britain and of the Dominions thereunto belonging after Her Most Sacred Majesty, and in default of Issue of Her Majesty be, remain and continue to the Most Excellent Princess Sophia Electoress and Dutchess Dowager of Hanover, and the Heirs of Her body, being Protestants, upon whom the Crown of England is settled by an Act of Parliament made in England in the twelfth year of the Reign of His late Majesty King William the Third entituled An Act for the further Limitation of the Crown and better securing the Rights and Liberties of the Subject: And that all Papists and persons marrying Papists, shall be excluded from and for ever incapable to inherit possess or enjoy the Imperial Crown of Great Britain, and the Dominions thereunto belonging or any part thereof; And in every such case the Crown and Government shall from time to time descend to, and be enjoyed by such person being a Protestant as should have inherited and enjoyed the same, in case such Papists or person marrying a Papist was naturally dead, according to the provision for the Descent of the Crown of England, made by another Act of Parliament in England in the first year of the Reign of their late Majesties King William and Queen Mary entituled An Act declaring the Rights and Liberties of the Subject, and settling the Succession of the Crown.

III. THAT the United Kingdom of Great Britain be Represented by one and the same Parliament to be stiled the Parliament of Great Britain.

as printed in G. S. PRYDE,
The Treaty of Union of Scotland and England (1950)

Verses Said to be Written on the Union

The Queen has lately lost a part
Of her entirely English heart,
For want of which by way of botch,
She pieced it up again with Scotch.
Blessed revolution, which creates
Divided hearts, united states.
See how the double nation lies;
Like a rich coat with skirts of frieze:
As if a man in making posies
Should bundle thistles up with roses.
Whoever yet a union saw
Of kingdoms, without faith or law.
Henceforward let no statesman dare,
A kingdom to a ship compare;
Lest he should call our commonweal,
A vessel with a double keel:
Which just like ours, new rigged and manned,
And got about a league from land,
By change of wind to leeward side
The pilot knew not how to guide.
So tossing faction will o'erwhelm
Our crazy double-bottomed realm.

JONATHAN SWIFT (1667–1745)

Two Views of the Union (1715)

When Andrew Fairservice (whom, by the way, the Bailie could not abide) chose to impute the accident of one of the horses casting his shoe to the deteriorating influence of the Union, he incurred a severe rebuke from Mr Jarvie.

'Whisht, sir! – whisht! it's ill-scraped tongues like yours, that make mischief atween neighbourhoods and nations. There's naething sae gude on this side o' time but it might hae been better, and that may be said o' the Union. Nane were keener against it than the Glasgow folk, wi' their rabblings and their risings, and their mobs, as they ca' them now-a-days. But it's an ill wind blaws naebody gude – Let ilka ane roose the ford as they find it – I say let Glasgow flourish! whilk is judiciously and elegantly putten round the town's arms, by way of by-word. – Now, since St Mungo catched herrings in the Clyde, what was ever like to gar us flourish like the sugar and tobacco trade? Will onybody tell me that, and grumble at the treaty that opened us a road west-awa' yonder?'

Andrew Fairservice was far from acquiescing in these arguments of expedience, and even ventured to enter a grumbling protest, 'That it was an unco change to hae Scotland's laws made in England; and that, for his share, he wadna for a' the herring-barrels in Glasgow, and a' the tobacco-casks to boot, hae gien up the riding o' the Scots Parliament, or sent awa' our crown, and our sword, and our sceptre, and Mons Meg, to be keepit by thae English pock-puddings in the Tower o' Lunnon. What wad Sir William Wallace, or auld Davie Lindsay, hae said to the Union, or them that made it?'

SIR WALTER SCOTT, *Rob Roy* (1818)

Such a parcel of rogues in a nation –

Fareweel to a' our Scotish fame,
   Fareweel our ancient glory;
Fareweel even to the Scotish name,
   Sae fam'd in martial story!
Now Sark rins o'er the Solway sands,
   And Tweed rins to the ocean,
To mark whare England's province stands,
   Such a parcel of rogues in a nation!

What force or guile could not subdue,
   Thro' many warlike ages,
Is wrought now by a coward few,
   For hireling traitors' wages.
The English steel we could disdain,
   Secure in valor's station;
But English gold has been our bane,
   Such a parcel of rogues in a nation!

157

O would, or I had seen the day
   That treason thus could sell us,
My auld grey head had lien in clay,
   Wi' BRUCE and loyal WALLACE!
But pith and power, till my last hour,
   I'll mak this declaration;
We're bought and sold for English gold,
   Such a parcel of rogues in a nation!

ROBERT BURNS (1759–96)

Scott on the Union

We ought not to be surprised that English statesmen, and Englishmen in general, are not altogether aware of the extent of the Scottish privileges, or that they do not remember, with the same accuracy as ourselves, that we have a system of laws peculiar to us, secured by treaties. These peculiarities have not, by any question lately agitated, been placed under their view and recollection. As one race grows up, and another dies away, remembrances which are cherished by the weaker party in a national treaty, are naturally forgotten by the stronger, and viewed, perhaps, as men look upon an old boundary stone, half-sunk in earth, half-overgrown with moss, and attracting no necessary attention, until it is appealed to as a proof of property. Such antiquated barriers are not calculated immediately to arrest the progress of statesmen intent upon some favourite object, any more than, when existing on the desolate mountain in their physical shape, such a bound-mark as I have described, always checks the eagerness of a stranger upon the moors, in keen and close pursuit of his game. But explain to the ardent young Southern sportsman that he trespasses upon the manor of another – convince the English statesman that he cannot advance his favourite object without infringing upon national right, – and, according to my ideas of English honour and good faith, the one will withdraw his foot within the boundary of private property, with as much haste as if he trod on burning marle; the other will curb his views of public good, and restrain even those within the limits which are prescribed by public faith. They will not, in either case, forget the precepts so often

158

reiterated in Scripture, fenced there with a solemn anathema, and received as matter of public jurisprudence by the law of every civilized country – 'Remove not the old land-mark, and enter not into the fields of the fatherless.' The high and manly sense of justice by which the English nation has been honourably distinguished through the world, will not, I am certain, debase itself by aggression towards a people, which is not indeed incapable of defending itself, but which, though fearless of inequality, and regardless of threats, is yet willing to submit even to wrong, rather than hazard the fatal consequences to be incurred by obstinate defence, *via facti*, of its just rights. We make the sense of English justice and honour our judge; and surely it would be hard to place us in a situation where our own sense of general mischief likely to ensue to the empire, may be the only check upon the sentiments which brave men feel, when called on to defend their national honour. There would be as little gallantry in such an aggression, as in striking a prisoner on parole . . .

A few general observations on England's late conduct to us, and I will release you.

A very considerable difference may be remarked, within these twenty-five years, in the conduct of the English towards such of the Scotch individuals, as either visit the metropolis as mere birds of passage, or settle there as residents. Times are much changed since the days of Wilkes and Liberty, when the bare suspicion of having come from North of the Tweed, was a cause of hatred, contempt, and obloquy. The good nature and liberality of the English seem now even to have occasioned a re-action in their sentiments towards their neighbours, as if to atone for the national prejudices of their fathers. It becomes every Scotsman to acknowledge explicitly and with gratitude, that whatever tenable claim of merit has been made by his countrymen for more than twenty years back, whether in politics, arts, arms, professional distinction, or the paths of literature, it has been admitted by the English, not only freely, but with partial favour. The requital of North Britain can be little more than good wishes and sincere kindness towards her southern Sister, and a hospitable welcome to such of her children as are led by curiosity to visit Scotland. To this ought to be added the most grateful acknowledgment.

But though this amicable footing exists between the public

of each nation, and such individuals of the other as may come into communication with them, and may God long continue it – yet, I must own, the conduct of England towards Scotland as a kingdom, whose crown was first united to theirs by our giving *them* a King, and whose dearest national rights were surrendered to them by an incorporating Union, has not been of late such as we were entitled to expect.

There has arisen gradually, on the part of England, a desire of engrossing the exclusive management of Scottish affairs, evinced by a number of circumstances, trifling in themselves, but forming a curious chain of proof when assembled together; many of which intimate a purpose to abate us, like old Lear, of our train, and to accustom us to submit to petty slights and mortifications, too petty perhaps individually to afford subject of serious complaint, but which, while they tend to lower us in our own eyes, seem to lay the foundation for fresh usurpations, of which this meditated measure may be an example.

This difference of treatment, and of estimation, exhibited towards *individuals* of the Scottish nation, and to the *nation itself* as an aggregate, seems at first sight an inconsistency. Does a Scotchman approach London with some pretension to character as a Preacher, a Philosopher, a Poet, an Economist, or an Orator, he finds a welcome and all-hail, which sometimes surprises those whom he has left on the northern side of the Tweed, – little aware, perhaps, of the paragon who had emigrated, till they heard the acclamations attending his reception – Does a gentleman of private fortune take the same route, he finds a ready and voluntary admission into the class of society for which he is fitted by rank and condition – Is the visitor one of the numerous class who wander for the chance of improving his fortunes, his national character as a Scotsman is supposed to imply the desirable qualities of information, prudence, steadiness, moral and religious feeling, and he obtains even a preference among the Southern employers, who want confidential clerks, land-stewards, head-gardeners, or fit persons to occupy any similar situation, in which the quality of trustworthiness is demanded.

But, on the other hand, if the English statesman has a point of great or lesser consequence to settle with Scotland *as a country*, we find him and his friends at once seized with a jealous, tenacious, wrangling, overbearing humour, and that they not only insist upon conducting the whole matter according to their own will, but are by no means so accessible to the pleas of reason, justice, and humanity, as might be expected from persons in other cases so wise and liberal. We cease at once to be the Northern Athenians, according to the slang of the day – the moral and virtuous people, who are practically and individually esteemed worthy of especial confidence. We have become the caterpillars of the island, instead of its pillars. We seem to be, in their opinion, once more transmuted into the Scots described by Churchill – a sharp sharking race, whose wisdom is cunning, and whose public spirit consists only in an illiberal nationality, inclining us, by every possible exertion of craft, to obtain advantage at the expense of England.

from SIR WALTER SCOTT, *A Letter to the Editor
of the* Edinburgh Weekly Journal, *from
Malachi Malagrowther, Esq. on the Proposed
Change of Currency* . . . (1826)

Some Parliamentarians

I
Keir Hardie

Hardie when I knew him had a white beard, a well polished bald head, with fringes of white bushy hair; he had deep set rather sombre eyes; was of short sturdy build; an old evangelical from the Ayrshire moors. David Lowe in describing the first meeting Hardie ever addressed – it was in 1879, and the occasion a presentation to Alexander Macdonald, the miners' leader – recalls how Hardie had prepared a long eulogium comparing Macdonald favourably with all the great men of history, beginning with Moses, but he never got farther down than Martin Luther because his description of Luther upset the predominantly Roman Catholic section of his audience, and the eulogist was actually threatened with physical violence.

Hardie was a collier, a journalist, an agitator who held fast to his faiths in all the storms and tempests of an agitator's life; an incorruptible if ever there was one. He had started out in adult life as a Good Templar, and there he remained to the end. He refused to speak for Labour Clubs which were licensed to retail alcohol, and was told: 'You'll drive out many good men from the Labour Party.' 'I know,' he replied, 'and if I speak there I'll drive out many good women.'

The snippet writers of the chit-chat columns called him Queer Hardie, and declared he had little sense of humour. That perhaps was true; he lived always on the edge of trouble and mass sorrow and hunger. But his face could light up with laughter, and he was filled to the brim with the old Scots ballads and with lore from the chap books. If you were interested in the politics of the left you were either a Hardie fan or you derided him as a sentimentalist. I was a Hardie fan.

II
David Kirkwood

One of David's best efforts was during a parliamentary speech upon the poverty of Clydebank. 'If the Prime Minister kent aboot it he widna tolerate it. If the King kent aboot it – ' (Cries of 'Order!' for you must not mention the King in debate!)

David tried again. 'If the Prime Minister kent aboot it he widna' tolerate it. If the King – ' (Louder shouts of 'Order!' during which a colleague whispers to David that the name of the King is barred!)

For a third time David essayed: 'If the Prime Minister kent aboot it, he widna' tolerate it. If' – (a pause during which the House was ready to shout the speaker down) – 'the Prince o' Wales's faither kent aboot it, he widna' tolerate it.'

Decorum disappeared and it is said that when King George heard the story, he slapped his knees with glee and added it to his ample repertoire.

III
Ramsay MacDonald

The classic instance of the man who lingered overlong in public affairs is Ramsay MacDonald. For the last six or seven years of his life he had lost his grip: become woolly, evasive, and liable to enmesh himself in a jumble of words. He could work off without a blush such drivelling rhodomontade as:

'We must go on and on, and on, and up and up and up.'

And:

'What we have to do is to pile up, and pile up and pile up the income of this industry in this way and that way and the other way . . .'

In Mr Churchill's vocabulary Ramsay MacDonald became 'a boneless wonder'. Mr Malcolm Muggeridge wrote of him that he had reached a state of 'doddering incoherency'.

IV
James Maxton

He had none of the heavy, forbidding economic and philosophical jargon about dialectical materialism and the like then the fashion, and considered the hallmark of the third degree Marxian. His was the merry jest and the quip, well mixed with the stuff for pathos and tears, and sauced with apt Biblical quotation and graphic description of social wrongs and injustices. His long black hair was bunched at the back *à la* Henry Irving. He not only preached the revolution; he looked it. Once – he told me the story himself – he had been induced to go to Inverness and act as best man at a friend's wedding; he had, he said, got for the first and last time a tall hat, and he was seated gloomily hunched up in a corner of the tearoom in Buchanan Street Station with his tall hat, and his long hair, awaiting the early morning train for the north. Enter an effusive, garishly dressed gentleman, and addressed Maxton:

'Hallo, chum, waitin' on the train?'

'Yes.'

'Where are you playing?'

'Playing?'

'Yes, old man. I see you're one of us. I'm on the halls myself!' . . .

THOMAS JOHNSTON, *Memories* (1952)

V
John Buchan as a Conservative Candidate, 1911–14

I came of a Liberal family, most of my friends were Liberals, I agreed with nine-tenths of the party's creed. Indeed, I think that my political faith was always liberalism – or rather 'liberality', as Gilbert Murray has interpreted the word. But when I stood for Parliament it had to be the other side.

Now that the once omnipotent Liberal party has so declined, it is hard to realize how formidable it was in 1911 – especially in Scotland. Its dogmas were so completely taken for granted that their presentation partook less of argument than of a tribal incantation. Mr Gladstone had given it an aura of earnest morality, so that its platforms were also pulpits and its harangues had the weight of sermons. Its members seemed to assume that their opponents must be lacking either in morals or mind. The Tories were the 'stupid' party; Liberals alone understood and sympathized with the poor; a working man who was not a Liberal was inaccessible to reason, or morally corrupt, or intimidated by laird or employer. I remember a lady summing up the attitude thus: Tories may think they are better born, but Liberals know that they are born better . . .

Old electioneering tactics can interest nobody, and they never greatly interested me. What made my work as a candidate a delight was the people I moved among. I did not want to be just any kind of Member of Parliament; I wanted to represent my own folk of the Border. . . . They had the qualities I most admired in human nature; realism coloured by poetry, a stalwart independence sweetened by courtesy, a shrewd kindly wisdom. To the first quality the ballads bear witness, to the second the history of Scotland. As examples of the third let me tell two stories.

Mr Gladstone once paid a visit to a Tweedside county, and in the afternoon went out for a walk and came to a gate which gave upon the glen. It was late in November, a snowstorm was threatening, and the sheep, as is their custom, were drawing out from the burn-side to the barer hill where drifts could not lie. An old shepherd was leaning on the gate, and to him Mr Gladstone spoke in his high manner. 'Are not sheep the most foolish of all animals? Here is a storm pending, and instead of remaining in shelter they are courting the fury of the blast. If I were a sheep I should remain in the hollows.' To which the shepherd replied: 'Sir, if ye were a sheep ye'd have mair sense.'

The second belongs to my own candidature. Heckling in the Borders is carried, I think, to a higher pitch of art than anywhere else in Britain. It is pursued for the pure love of the game, and I have known a candidate heckled to a standstill by his own supporters. Mr Lloyd George's Insurance Act had just been introduced, and at a meeting at remote Ettrickhead the speaker was defending it on the ground that it was a practical application of the Sermon on the Mount. A long-legged shepherd rose to question him, and the following dialogue ensued:

'Ye believe in the Bible, sir?'

'With all my heart.'

'And ye consider that this Insurance Act is in keepin' with the Bible?'

'I do.'

'Is it true that under the Act there's a maternity benefit, and that a woman gets the benefit whether she's married or no?'

'That is right.'

'D'ye approve of that?'

'With all my heart.'

'Well, sir, how d'ye explain this? The Bible says the wages of sin is death and the Act says thirty shillin's.'

JOHN BUCHAN, *Memory Hold-the-Door* (1940)

Devolution

... as to the future, we have to secure for Scotland a much more direct and convenient method of bringing her influence to bear upon her own purely domestic affairs. There is nothing which conflicts with the integrity of the United Kingdom in the setting up of a Scottish Parliament for the discharge of Scottish business. There is nothing which conflicts with the integrity of the United Kingdom in securing to Scotsmen in that or in some other way an effective means of shaping the special legislation which affects them and only them. Certainly I am of opinion that if such a scheme can be brought into existence it will mean a great enrichment not only of the national life of Scotland, but of the politics and public life of the United Kingdom.

SIR WINSTON CHURCHILL, from a speech given in Dundee,
3 October 1911

The case for small nationalism had first appeared to me in America, its original argument that it would make life more interesting. Small nations, as opposed to great, would produce diversity. Diversity is interesting, and so is responsibility. But political responsibility in a major state is so minified as to be invisible; it may exist in a satisfying degree only in a little country. At first it may seem frivolous to suggest that political change should be advocated to make the world more interesting; but the pursuit of wealth, which on all sides is most seriously regarded, has that as one of its three purposes: the others being, for a minority the achievement of power, and for the rest security. To seek a full life is laudable and sagacious. If life for the majority became more deeply interesting, majorities might lose the recurrent desire for death that lets them, once in a generation, be led to war . . .

Uniformity on the vast American scale, and a continuing passion for uniformity, appeared both wasteful and dangerous. Wasteful because uniformity nullified many natural differences that might usefully and gratefully be developed; and dangerous because life on a dead level sometimes produces the effect of a flat and open country in the light of noon: a tendency to panic. But if difference was cultivated, ramparts would be built that might stop the spread of hysterias and epidemic fear. Disaster is inseparable from the world, but it is the ever-increasing uniformity and interdependence of the world that carry infection of disaster . . .

And again I thought: Littleness – or reasonable littleness – for Efficiency. The megatherium, the sub-continent of India, and an army of five million soldiers were unmanageable things in comparison with a polo pony, the kingdom of Sweden, and Marlborough's men . . .

These general ideas being already in my mind, I heard with excitement the muttering noise in the North that Scottish Nationalists were making and the nurseling cry of what was hopefully described as a literary renaissance. There, it seemed, were people of my own conviction, a country well chosen for the experiment, and native sentiment to give it force. With my friend Francis Meiklejohn,[1] an ardent Nationalist, I dined in

[1] i.e. Moray McLaren

166

Soho and perceived my duty.

To begin with, we drank a little Pernod. It was after the second glass that I dedicated myself, and to mark the solemnity of the occasion we had some champagne. Not only our purpose, but our policy, grew enchantingly clear. Essential Scotland, we agreed, was represented by the court of King James IV and Edinburgh in the eighteenth century. Also of value were the Celtic ethos, the Norse propulsion, and such mastery of stock-breeding and agriculture as was displayed in Aberdeenshire and the Lothians. We must ignore, in our reconstruction of Scotland, the cultural blight of Presbyterianism and the industrial revolution.

'My dear fellow,' said Meiklejohn, 'let us admit two things: that in Scotland today there is much that will turn your stomach, but plenty to steal your heart. Let us be reasonable. We must extol our good qualities and admit our faults. There is nothing more horrible than Scotch meanness, but Scottish generosity is the most prodigal in the world. Our virtues are profound, our profligacy appalling. Quite appalling. We run to extremes. And that is going to be our salvation, because it means that we have unlimited enthusiasm. All we need, as a nation, is direction and a goal. To Scotland Renewed!'

Warmly I answered: 'How right you are! And let us remember that by nature and tradition we are less insular than the English, and so there should be little difficulty in rebuilding our diminished country. We shall look to the Continent. Our tariff policy shall be: Free Trade in Ideas. Our patriotism must not be narrow. We must borrow, not money but wisdom, from France and Scandinavia.'

'Our closest alliance,' said Meiklejohn, 'must be with France.'

'Of course,' I said, 'but Scandinavia can also teach. We shall attract, indeed, all those streams of European culture that now a foolish Government in London dams.'

'The great Wen,' said Meiklejohn.

'Not only culture,' I said, 'but claret.'

'From Bordeaux to Leith,' exclaimed Meiklejohn, 'there must be a continuous procession of ships loaded to the very gunwale with claret. It's our national drink.'

'A glass of champagne,' I suggested.

'When I die,' said Meiklejohn, 'and go to Heaven, I shall ask for an Austrian to provide my music, a Frenchman to cook my food, and a Scotsman of the eighteenth century to be my host.'

'Those are the lines,' I said, 'on which we must remake Scotland. We shall be national in order to be international. Consider the New Town of Edinburgh.'

'Charlotte Square!' shouted Meiklejohn. 'But it's enchanting!' . . .

Whatever its failings, our nationalism had not been born of a narrow provincial spirit. Its only defect, indeed, was a total disregard of the prevailing temper and the governing conditions of life in Scotland.

ERIC LINKLATER, The Man on My Back (1941)

Orwell's Prognosis, 1947

Up to date the Scottish Nationalist movement seems to have gone almost unnoticed in England. To take the nearest example to hand, I don't remember having seen it mentioned in *Tribune*, except occasionally in book reviews. It is true that it is a small movement, but it could grow, because there is a basis for it. In this country I don't think it is enough realized – I myself had no idea of it until a few years ago – that Scotland has a case against England. On economic grounds it may not be a very strong case. In the past, certainly, we have plundered Scotland shamefully, but whether it is *now* true that England as a whole exploits Scotland as a whole, and that Scotland would be better off if fully autonomous, is another question. The point is that many Scottish people, often quite moderate in outlook, are beginning to think about autonomy and to feel that they are pushed into an inferior position. They have a good deal of reason. In some areas, at any rate, Scotland is almost an occupied country. You have an English or anglicized upper class, and a Scottish working class which speaks with a markedly different accent, or even, part of the time, in a different language. This is a more dangerous kind of class division than any now existing in England. Given favourable circumstances it might develop in an ugly way, and the fact that there was a progressive Labour Government in London might not make much difference.

No doubt Scotland's major ills will have to be cured along with those of England. But meanwhile there are things that could be done to ease the cultural situation. One small but not negligible point is the language. In the Gaelic-speaking areas, Gaelic is not taught in the schools. I am speaking from limited experience, but I should say that this is beginning to cause resentment. Also, the BBC only broadcasts two or three half-hour Gaelic programmes a week, and they give the impression of being rather amateurish programmes. Even so they are eagerly listened to. How easy it would be to buy a little goodwill by putting on a Gaelic programme at least once daily.

At one time I would have said that it is absurd to keep alive an archaic language like Gaelic, spoken by only a few hundred thousand people. Now I am not so sure. To begin with, if people feel that they have a special culture which ought to be preserved, and that the language is part of it, difficulties should not be put in their way when they want their children to learn it properly. Secondly, it is probable that the effort of being bi-lingual is a valuable education in itself. The Scottish Gaelic-speaking peasants speak beautiful English, partly, I think, because English is an almost foreign language which they sometimes do not use for days together. Probably they benefit intellectually by having to be aware of dictionaries and grammatical rules, as their English opposite numbers would not be.

At any rate, I think we should pay more attention to the small but violent separatist movements which exist within our own island. They may look very unimportant now, but, after all, the Communist Manifesto was once a very obscure document, and the Nazi Party only had six members when Hitler joined it.

GEORGE ORWELL, *Collected Essays*, vol. 4 (1970)

The Past: Essential Facts of Scottish History

2.1 Much ink is wasted on the question whether the Scots are a nation. Of course they are. They were both a nation and a state until 1707. The state was wound up by a Treaty which clearly recognized the nation and its right to distinctive government in a fundamental range of home affairs. The fact that institutional forms, however empty, reflecting these distinctions have been preserved to the present day demonstrates that no one in British government has dared to suggest openly that the nation no longer exists or that the case for distinctiveness has now disappeared.

2.2 Scottish nationhood does not rest on constitutional history alone. It is supported by a culture reaching back over centuries and bearing European comparison in depth and quality, nourished from a relatively early stage by an education system once remarkable by European standards. Since the Union, the strength of that culture has fluctuated but there is no ground for any claim that, overall or even at any particular time, it has benefited from the Union. On the contrary the Union has always been, and remains, a threat to the survival of a distinctive culture in Scotland.

2.3 The international zenith reached by that culture in the late eighteenth century is sometimes facilely attributed to the Union, but that leaves for explanation the subsequent decline of the culture as the Union became more established. No doubt some benefit was derived from the relatively settled state of Scotland at the time. More, probably, stemmed from the minimal interference of London in Scottish affairs in those days. But the roots of that philosophical, literary and scientific flowering lay in the social soil of Scotland itself and its long-established cross-fertilization with mainland Europe.

2.4 That cross-fertilization diminished as the pull of London increased and the effects of the removal of important stimuli to Scottish confidence and self respect were felt. In the mid-nineteenth century Scottish culture eroded and became inward-looking in consequence. It has struggled with mixed success to revive as Scots realized what they were in danger of losing. The twentieth century, up to and including the present day, has been a period of extraordinary fertility in all fields of the Scottish arts; literature, visual and dramatic arts, music, traditional crafts, philosophic and historical studies. In particular the indigenous languages of Scotland, Gaelic and Scots, are being revived in education, the arts and social life. We think it no accident that this trend has accompanied an increasingly vigorous demand for a Scottish say in Scotland's government.

2.5 The nation was not conquered but it did not freely agree to the Union of the Parliaments in 1707. We need not go into the details of the negotiations about the Union. What is beyond dispute is that the main impetus for Union came from the English and it was brought about for English reasons of state. Likewise, the form of Union was not what the Scots would have chosen but what the English were prepared to concede. However, the considerable guarantees which Scots won in the Treaty of Union reflected the fact that, until the Treaty was implemented, they had a Parliament of their own to speak for them.

2.6 The matters on which the Treaty guaranteed the Scots their own institutions and policies represented the bulk of civil life and government at the time; the Church, the Law and Education. However, there was never any mechanism for enforcing respect for the terms of the Treaty of Union. Many of its major provisions have been violated, and its spirit has never affected the huge areas of government which have evolved since. The say of Scotland in its own government has diminished, is diminishing and ought to be increased.

2.7 The forms of Scottish autonomy which, until recently, had multiplied for almost a century are misleading. The Scottish Office can be distinguished from a Whitehall Department only in the sense that it is not physically located in Whitehall (and much of its most important work is done in Whitehall). The Secretary of State may be either Scotland's man in the Cabinet or the Cabinet's man in Scotland, but in the last resort he is invariably the latter. Today, he can be little else, since he must impose on Scotland policies against which an overwhelming majority of Scots have voted.

from Report of the Constitutional Steering Committee
Presented to the Campaign for a Scottish Assembly,
Edinburgh July 1988, as printed in ed. O. D. EDWARDS,
A Claim of Right for Scotland (1989)

Hill of Benarty

Happy the man who belongs to no party,
But sits in his ain house, and looks at Benarty.

SIR MICHAEL MALCOLM OF LOCHORE (C. 1795)

Religion

from *St Columba's Rule*

A mind prepared for red martyrdom. A mind fortified and steadfast for white martyrdom. Forgiveness from the heart to everyone. Constant prayers for those who trouble thee. Follow almsgiving before all things. Take not of food until you art hungry. The love of God with all thy heart and all thy strength. The love of thy neighbour as thyself. Abide in God's testaments throughout all times. Thy measure of prayer shall be until thy tears come; or thy measure of work of labour until thy tears come.

St Andrew

St Andrew was of course the first disciple called by our Lord, and the first thing he had done was to bring his brother Peter to Jesus. If his missionary work was done anywhere it was done in Greece and in the regions around the Black Sea, a fact which gave him an important place in the Russian Church, which shared with Scotland the badge representing the saltire-shaped cross on which he was martyred at Patras, on the Gulf of Corinth. His remains were subsequently taken to Constantinople and, much later, in the thirteenth century, to Amalfi. This was all remote enough from the historical inhabitants of Scotland. But the Scots were later to believe that they were descended from a prince of Greece, and Bede had said that the Picts came from Scythia, the region north of the Black Sea. Besides, the Scots claimed to possess relics of the apostle, including an arm bone which signified his readiness to protect them, and this was explained by a fable relating that St Regulus had removed relics of Andrew from Constantinople and brought them to St

Andrews. A companion tale related to a King Angus. Angus, king of the Picts from about 730 to 761, was a great warrior, battling against the Scots of Dalriada, the Angles of Northumbria and the Britons of Strathclyde, and legend relates that in one of his campaigns he had a vision of the cross of St Andrew – a white diagonal cross – against the blue sky. King Angus may very well have been the founder of the monastery dedicated to St Andrew which was established at the place in Fife since known by the saint's name. The saltire became the Scottish national emblem and when, much later, it was adopted as the foundation for the Union Jack, the background continued to represent the blue sky against which King Angus saw the white cross twelve hundred years ago.

GORDON DONALDSON, *Scotland: Church and Nation through Sixteen Centuries* (1972)

The Scottish Talent

They can admire John Knox and Mary Queen of Scots . . . a feat impossible to other nations.

W. ROBERTSON NICOLL, *People and Books* (1926)

Knox

I

[Knox] has told us what passage in the Scriptures led him to embrace the new faith; it was the seventeenth chapter of the Gospel of St John.

This chapter contains the last prayer of Jesus with His disciples before His betrayal . . .

EDWIN MUIR, *John Knox* (1929)

John's Gospel, 17

Sae Jesus spak tae them. Syne he luikit up til heiven an said, 'Faither, the hour hes come. Glorifíe thy son, at the Son may glorifíe thee, an bi the pouer thou hes gíen him owre aa lívin may gíe eternal life til aa at thou hes gíen him. This is eternal life – kennin thee, the ae true God, an him thou hes sent, Jesus Christ. I hae glorifíed thee on the yird bi cairriein throu til its end the wark thou gíed me tae dae. An nou glorifíe thou me, Faither, at thy side, wi the glorie I bruikit aside thee afore the warld begoud.

'I hae made kent thy name til the men at thou hes gíen me out o the warld. They war thine, an thou hes gíen them tae me, an they hae hauden leal tae thy Wurd. Nou ken they at aa thou hes gíen me comes frae thee; for I hae taucht them what thou taucht me, an they hae walcomed it, an weill ken they nou at I cam frae thee, an belíeve at thou sent me. I pray for them: I prayna for the warld, but for them at thou hes gíen me, because they ar thine – aa at is mine is thine, an what is thine is mine – an I hae been glorifíed in them. No lang am I nou for this warld, but they bide ey i the warld, as I gang my waas tae thee. Halie Faither, keep them sauf bi the pouer o thy name, at they may be ane, een as we ar ane.

'Whan I wis wi them, I keepit them sauf bi the pouer o thy name at thou hes gíen me; I gairdit them weill, an no ane o them aa hes gane the Black Gate, binna him at wis weirdit tae gang that gate, at the wurd o Scriptur micht come true. Nou I am comin tae thee, but afore I quat the warld, I speak thir wurds, sae at they may hae i their hairts the joy at I hae in mine. I hae gíen them thy Wurd; an the warld hates them, because they belangna the warld, een as I belangna the warld. I pray-ye-na tae tak them out o the warld, but tae keep them sauf frae the Ill Ane. They belangna the warld, een as I belangna the warld. Consecrate them bi the trowth; thy Wurd is the trowth. As thou hes sent me intil the warld, een sae hae I sent them intil the warld. It is for their sakes I consecrate mysel, at they, tae, may be consecrate bi the trowth. But I prayna for them alane: I pray for them as weill at belíeves in me throu the wurd at they speak. May they aa be ane; may they be in us, een as thou, Faither, is in me, an I in thee, sae at the warld may belíeve at thou hes sent me. I hae gíen them the glorie at thou hes gíen me, at they aa may be ane, een as we ar ane, I in them, an thou in me, sae at the warld may ken at thou hes sent me an luved them, een as thou hes luved me.

'Faither, it is my will at they, thy gift tae me, may be wi me

whaur I am, sae at they may behaud my glorie at thou hes gíen
me for the luve thou buir me afore the founds o the warld wis
laid. O richteous Faither, the warld kens-thee-na, but I ken
thee, an thir o mine kens nou at thou hes sent me. I hae made
thy name kent tae them, an will mak it ey the mair kent, at the
luve thou hes borne me may be i their hairts, an I in them!'

> John's Gospel, 17, *The New Testament in Scots,*
> trans W. L. LORIMER (1985)[1]

This chapter is of crucial importance for the understanding of
Knox. It led logically to Calvinism. In the most absolute terms
it stated the doctrines of election, of special grace, and of
assured salvation. It welded the invisible Church into a firm
and everlasting body; it welded that Church to Christ and
through Christ to God; and it welded Knox . . .

> EDWIN MUIR, *op. cit.*

II

Adversity, in fact, improved him. In prosperity he hardened, in
success he became intolerable, in the changing gamble for
success he became monstrous.

> *ibid.*

III

Knox had served as a slave on the French galleys for eighteen
months after the assassination of Cardinal Beaton in 1546, he
had definite and clear beliefs on the part the Reformation must
play in Scotland, and in the years of his exile he had wandered
from haunt to haunt of the European revolutionaries (much as
Lenin did in the first decade of the twentieth century) testing
out his own creed in converse and debate with Calvin and the
like innovators. Once again a Scotsman had arisen capable of
apprehending the direction of the historic forces, and determined to enchannel those for the benefit of a Commons' Scotland. The nauseous character of his political allies in Scotland

---

[1] In this context, the translation is anachronistic. Knox preached from the Bible in English
and as a Reformer was concerned with it in Greek.

did not deter him from the conflict. In the triumphant Parliament summoned in 1560 the Protestants under his direction established the Reformed Church, forbade the mass, and practically legalized the wholesale seizure of Church property. Knox's intentions with regard to the disposal of that property were definite and unshakable: it would be used for the relief of the poor, for the establishment of free schools, for the sustentation of a free people's priesthood. But, though he had foreseen the direction of the historic forces thus far, history proved on the side of his robbing allies, not on his. The Covenant left the Commons poorer than ever and Knox an embittered and sterile leader, turning from his battle in the cause of the people to sardonic denunciations of the minor moral lapses of the young Queen.

He was a leader defeated: and history was to ascribe to him and his immediate followers, and with justice, blame for some of the most terrible aberrations of the Scots spirit in succeeding centuries. Yet Knox himself was of truly heroic mould; had his followers, far less his allies, been of like mettle, the history of Scotland might have been strangely and splendidly different. To pose him against the screen of antique time as an inhibition-ridden neurotic (as is the modern fashion) who murdered the spirit and hope of an heroic young queen, is malicious distortion of the true picture. The 'heroic young queen' in question had the face, mind, manners and morals of a well-intentioned but hysterical poodle.

LEWIS GRASSIC GIBBON, 'The Antique Scene',
Scottish Scene (1934)

IV

Withal he had considerable confidence in himself, and in the uprightness of his own disciplined emotions, underlying much sincere aspiration after spiritual humility. And it is this confidence that makes his intercourse with women so interesting to a modern. It would be easy, of course, to make fun of the whole affair, to picture him strutting vaingloriously among these inferior creatures, or compare a religious friendship in the sixteenth century with what was called, I think, a literary friendship in the eighteenth. But it is more just and profitable to recognize what there is sterling and human underneath all

177

his theoretical affectations of superiority. Women, he has said in his 'First Blast,' are 'weak, frail, impatient, feeble, and foolish'; and yet it does not appear that he was himself any less dependent than other men upon the sympathy and affection of these weak, frail, impatient, feeble, and foolish creatures; it seems even as if he had been rather more dependent than most.

R. L. STEVENSON,
'John Knox and his Relations to Women' (1874)

Mary Queen of Scots

I
Alas! Poor Queen

She was skilled in music and the dance
And the old arts of love
At the court of the poisoned rose
And the perfumed glove,
And gave her beautiful hand
To the pale Dauphin
A triple crown to win –
And she loved little dogs
    And parrots
  And red-legged partridges
And the golden fishes of the Duc de Guise
And a pigeon with a blue ruff
She had from Monsieur d'Elbœuf.

Master John Knox was no friend to her;
She spoke him soft and kind,
Her honeyed words were Satan's lure
The unwary soul to bind
'Good sir, doth a lissome shape
And a comely face
Offend your God His Grace
Whose Wisdom maketh these
Golden fishes of the Duc de Guise?'

She rode through Liddesdale with a song;
'Ye streams sae wondrous strang,
Oh, mak' me a wrack as I come back
But spare me as I gang,'
While a hill-bird cried and cried
Like a spirit lost
By the grey storm-wind tost.

Consider the way she had to go.
Think of the hungry snare,
The net she herself had woven,
Aware or unaware,
Of the dancing feet grown still,
The blinded eyes –
Queens should be cold and wise,
And she loved little things,
      Parrots
   And red-legged partridges
And the golden fishes of the Duc de Guise
And the pigeon with the blue ruff
She had from Monsieur d'Elbœuf.

MARION ANGUS, *Selected Poems* (1950)

II

. . . a legend, to be a good enduring legend, should have some
congruity with the land of its birth. And to this postulate Mary
conforms, having been brave, energetic, and unfortunate. She
conforms to the idea of Scotland in that, despite her many virtues, she lacked the co-ordinating factor, the mating principle,

to bring them success or fruition. That incompleteness has always been Scotland's destiny. There is, moreover, something Scottish and uncomely in the fact that her son went to London, where he became wealthy, famous, and something of a joke: falling heir to that which his mother had ruled and lost, and that which she had worked for and never won, he was yet disinherited of her courage and her beauty and her grace. And the beauty that she failed to transmit is also part of her title to be Scotland's Queen: to be, not merely to have been. – A romantic assertion? But

> 'Vivre sans rêve, qu'est-ce?
> Et j'aime la Princesse Lointaine!'

Sir Francis Knollys, meeting Mary in Carlisle, wrote of her to Cecil: 'This lady and princess is a notable woman. She seemeth to regard no ceremonious honour besides the acknowledging of her estate regal. She showeth a disposition to speak much, to be bold, to be pleasant, and to be very familiar. She showeth a great desire to be avenged of her enemies; she showeth a readiness to expose herself to all perils in hope of victory; she delighteth much to hear of hardiness and valiancy, commending by name all approved hardy men of her country, although they be her enemies; and she commendeth no cowardness even in her friends. The thing that most she thirsteth after is victory, and it seemeth to be indifferent to her to have her enemies diminish, either by the sword of her friends, or by the liberal promises and rewards of her purse, or by division and quarrels raised among themselves; so that for victory's sake pain and perils seemeth pleasant unto her, and in respect of victory, wealth and all things seemeth to her contemptuous and vile.'

There indeed is a proper queen for the high hills, snow-covered, with the sunlight a blinding gleam in the corries, and blue shadows on the dappled snow; for Scotland in the gipsy colours of autumn, of silver birch and discoloured leaf and the solid black-hearted green of the pines; Scotland of swift amber streams and silver firths that take the knees of the mountains in their arms; of the islands that float on the western sea under sails of indigo and pearl and the vapour of gold; Scotland of pibrochs and the silenced music of the harp, of *Christ's Kirk on the Green*, of Urquhart, and rough bothy-singers; of the makars and the ballads, of the chivalry that rode to Flodden, of broken clans and banished men, of battlefields from Lucknow to the Somme; of beauty that brings no profit but to the heart, and of disaster that wrings the heart . . . True, there is another Scotland, somewhat provincial in spirit and circumscribed in its imagination; a lion couchant, with the unaspiring steeple of a depressing church and a factory chimney for supporters; a country whose native violence and traditionally dogged temper have violently asserted and now most doggedly maintain a standard of unflinching mediocrity. The sentiments and the smoke of this other Scotland somewhat obscure the old romantic kingdom – but what of it?

> Tecum Scotia nostra conparatur?
> O saeclum insapiens et infacetum!

ERIC LINKLATER, *Mary, Queen of Scots* (1933)

The Creed

We trow[1] in God allanerlie,
Full of all micht and majestie,
Maker of hevin and eird sa braid,
Quhilk hes himself our Father maid:
And we his sonnis ar in deid,
He will us keip in all our neid,
Baith saull and body to defend
That na mischance sall us offend:
He takis cure baith day and nicht
To save us throw his godly micht
Fra Sathanis subteltie and slicht.

We trow in Jesus Christ his Sone,
God, lyke in gloir, our Lord alone;
Quhilk, for his mercy and his grace,
Wald man be borne to mak our peace,
Of Mary mother, Virgin chaist,
Consavit be the Haly Gaist,

181

And for our saik on croce did die
Fra sin and hell to make us fre,
And rais from deith, throw his Godheid,
Our Mediatour and our remeid
Sall cum to judge baith quick and deid.

We trow in God the Haly Spreit,
In all distres our comfort sweit,
We trow the Kirk Catholick be
And faithfull Christin companie
Throw all the warld with ane accord,
Remissioun of our sin we trow;
And this same flesche that levis now
Sall stand up at the latter day
And bruik[2] eternal lyfe for ay.

WEDDERBURN BROTHERS,
The Gude and Godlie Ballatis (c. 1542)

[1] believe; [2] enjoy

A Post-Reformation Catholic Prayer

Iniquitie on eirth is so increst,
All flesh bot few with falset[1] is defyld,
Givin ou'r of God, with gredynes beguyld
So that the puir, but pitie, ar opprest.
God in his justice dou na mair digest
Sik sinfull swyn with symonie defyld
But must revenge, thair vyces ar so vyld,
And pour doun plagues of famin, sword and pest.
Aryse O Lord, delyver from the lave[2]
Thy faithfull flock befor that it infect!
Thou sees how Satan sharps[3] for to dissave,
If it were able, even thyn awin elect.
Sen conscience, love and cheritie all laiks,[4]
Lord, short the season for the chosens saiks.

ALEXANDER MONTGOMERIE (c. 1545–98)

[1] falsehood; [2] rest; [3] plays-tricks; [4] is lacking

Father James Macbreck to Father General [of the Society of Jesus]
(Stonyhurst MSS)

Very Rev. Father in Christ,   From Scotland, 13th June,
Pax Christi.   the holy Feast of Pentecost, 1641

I do not know whether your Paternity ever received a letter I
wrote last December, with full particulars of the state of this
distracted Church. Since then things have become more and
more confused and imperilled every day. The enemy are mad
with fury, in full strength, and able to do just what they please.
They are resolved to stamp out the last sparks of true religion,
and leave neither name nor trace of Catholic in any part of this
accursed land. Their devilish Covenant, renewed three years
ago, is offered to all without exception, and those who refuse it
are set down as enemies of their country, and of the godless
heresy which they call the Reformed religion, and prosecuted
with the utmost rigour. They are put in prison and their goods
escheated; unless they fly the country, leaving home, family,
and children behind them. But there are too many – alas! – who
have not before their eyes the words of Christ, 'Whoever shall
deny me before men, him will I also deny before my Father,'
and 'What doth it profit?'

In all the years I have been working in this barren and
troubled vineyard of the Lord, I have scarcely had two or three
of tolerable quiet. From one side or another, persecution was
sure to come; but neither I nor any other Catholic has, since the
first overthrow of the Catholic faith in this country, ever before
experienced a trial so universal and terrible as this. I am now
the only one of us left in the south of Scotland; God only knows
how long I shall be able to remain. I am determined to stay as
long as I can find a corner wherein to lay my head; though I
may have to live in extreme misery, in perpetual danger, and
continual fear. God grant I may be the means of saving one
single soul from the shipwreck! may the good Jesus deign to
show me what I have to suffer for His Name, and would that
for Him I might be allowed to die. Your Paternity will excuse
my not writing oftener in these troubled times. We can neither
write nor send letters safely; hardly any one will take them, for
fear of discovery. While I write, I have to escape this very night,
and am in such straits that I scarcely know where to go. I fear

we shall all have occasion to say with Jeremias li. 9: 'We would have cured Babylon, but she is not healed; let us forsake her, because her judgment hath reached even to the heavens, and is lifted up to the clouds.' I am obliged to send this through Germany, to a friend of our Society at Olmütz [i.e. Olomouc, in Czechoslovakia]. I write by stealth, surrounded by dangers. I commend myself and all this afflicted Mission to your most Holy Sacrifices and prayers.

Your most unworthy son and servant in Christ,

JAMES MacBRECK
as printed in W. F. LEITH S.J.,
Memoirs of Scottish Catholics, vol. 1. (1909)

Covenanters

I

They preached a creed which, in most of its details, is now forgotten, and the language of which is fantastic or ridiculous to our ears. They laid down as the necessary and universal progress towards salvation a rigid curriculum of experiences – 'exercise', 'law-work', 'discovery of interest', 'damps', 'challenge', 'outgate', 'assurance'. Well might a later seventeenth-century Scotsman exclaim: 'I doubt it hath occasioned much unnecessary disquiet to some holy persons that they have not found such a regular and orderly transaction in their souls as they have seen described in the books. . . . God hath several ways of dealing with the souls of men, and it sufficeth if the work be accomplished whatever the methods have been.' But behind their narrowness and their legal jargon we can see in many the true exaltation of the saint. Among the crudities and absurdities of their sermons and biographies there are passages of apostolic power, visions such as George Fox records in his journal, which led them to an ecstasy of praise, moments of deep tenderness towards the souls of their flocks. They must be judged by their work, and beyond doubt they gave to the Scottish people a moral seriousness, a conception of the deeper issues of life, and an intellectual *ascesis*, gifts which may well atone for their many infirmities.

Yet there is much to be atoned for, and the immediate result of their predominance was not less disastrous than beneficent. 'Deliver me, O Lord,' was the cry of Archbishop Leighton, 'from the errors of wise men, yea, and of good men.' They perverted the Gospel into a thing of subtle legal conundrums; they made morality difficult by destroying its rational basis; they took the colour out of life for their people by condemning the innocencies of the world with a more than monastic austerity; they inflamed the superstitions of the country by peopling it with a fanciful pandemonium. If any one has the patience to labour through a dozen volumes of their sermons, he will be aghast at the childishness and irreverence of much of their teaching. Like an African witch-doctor, they 'smelled out' offenders, and they were the principal upstay of witch-burning. Miracles and portents adorned their path, and natural laws were suspended to point their lessons. They magnified their office till they hedged themselves round with a false divinity. The clouds of their dogmatic terrors darkened the world for their hearers, and condemned weak spirits to religious mania. Their neurotic supernaturalism, which saw judgments and signs in the common incidents of life, weakened in the people the power of rational thought. If they gave manhood and liberty to Scotland, they did much to sap the first and shackle the second. Condemning natural pleasures and affections, they drew a dark pall over the old merry Scottish world, the world of the ballads and the songs, of frolics and mummings and 'blithesome bridals', and, since human nature will not be denied, drove men and women to sinister and perverted outlets. In a word, they established over the whole of human life, alike in its public duties and in its most intimate private affairs, a harsh and senseless tyranny, and against them, as the delegates of heaven, there was no appeal. Tougher spirits might emerge unscathed and even fortified, but the frail were warped and demented. Yet it was the strongest thing in Scotland, and presently in all the Lowlands it had made good its sway over every class of the people; *ruere in servitium consules, patres, eques.*

JOHN BUCHAN, *Montrose* (1928)

II

'Stay, passenger, take notice what thou reads,
At Edinburgh lie our bodies, here our heads:
Our right hands stood at Lanark, these we want,
Because with them we signed the Covenant.'

Epitaph on a tombstone at Hamilton

III

Macbriar was then moved forward to the post of examination.

'Were you at the battle of Bothwell Bridge?' was, in like manner, demanded of him.

'I was,' answered the prisoner, in a bold and resolute tone.

'Were you armed?'

'I was not – I went in my calling as a preacher of God's word, to encourage them that drew the sword in His cause.'

'In other words, to aid and abet the rebels?' said the Duke.

'Thou hast spoken it,' replied the prisoner.

'Well, then,' continued the interrogator, 'let us know if you saw John Balfour of Burley among the party? – I presume you know him?'

'I bless God that I do know him,' replied Macbriar; 'he is a zealous and a sincere Christian.'

'And when and where did you last see this pious personage?' was the query which immediately followed.

'I am here to answer for myself,' said Macbriar, in the same dauntless manner, 'and not to endanger others.'

'We shall know,' said Dalzell, 'how to make you find your tongue.'

'If you can make him fancy himself in a conventicle,' answered Lauderdale, 'he will find it without you. – Come, laddie, speak while the play is good – you're too young to bear the burden will be laid on you else.'

'I defy you,' retorted Macbriar. 'This has not been the first of my imprisonments or of my sufferings; and, young as I may be, I have lived long enough to know how to die when I am called upon.'

'Ay, but there are some things which must go before an easy death, if you continue obstinate,' said Lauderdale, and rung a small silver bell which was placed before him on the table.

A dark crimson curtain, which covered a sort of niche, or Gothic recess in the wall, rose at the signal, and displayed the public executioner, a tall, grim, and hideous man, having an oaken table before him, on which lay thumb-screws, and an iron case, called the Scottish boot, used in those tyrannical days to torture accused persons. Morton, who was unprepared for this ghastly apparition, started when the curtain arose, but Macbriar's nerves were more firm. He gazed upon the horrible apparatus with much composure; and if a touch of nature called the blood from his cheek for a second, resolution sent it back to his brow with greater energy.

'Do you know who that man is?' said Lauderdale, in a low, stern voice, almost sinking into a whisper.

'He is, I suppose,' replied Macbriar, 'the infamous executioner of your bloodthirsty commands upon the persons of God's people. He and you are equally beneath my regard; and, I bless God, I no more fear what he can inflict than what you can command. Flesh and blood may shrink under the sufferings you can doom me to, and poor frail nature may shed tears, or send forth cries; but I trust my soul is anchored firmly on the rock of ages.'

'Do your duty,' said the Duke to the executioner.

The fellow advanced, and asked, with a harsh and discordant voice, upon which of the prisoner's limbs he should first employ his engine.

'Let him choose for himself,' said the Duke; 'I should like to oblige him in anything that is reasonable.'

'Since you leave it to me,' said the prisoner, stretching forth his right leg, 'take the best – I willingly bestow it in the cause for which I suffer.'

The executioner, with the help of his assistants, enclosed the leg and knee within the tight iron boot, or case, and then placing a wedge of the same metal between the knee and the edge of the machine, took a mallet in his hand, and stood waiting for further orders. A well-dressed man, by profession a surgeon, placed himself by the other side of the prisoner's chair, bared the prisoner's arm, and applied his thumb to the pulse, in order to regulate the torture according to the strength of the patient. When these preparations were made, the President of the Council repeated with the same stern voice the question 'When and where did you last see John Balfour of Burley?'

The prisoner, instead of replying to him, turned his eyes to heaven as if imploring Divine strength, and muttered a few words, of which the last were distinctly audible, 'Thou hast said thy people shall be willing in the day of thy power!'

The Duke of Lauderdale glanced his eye around the Council as if to collect their suffrages, and, judging from their mute signs, gave on his part a nod to the executioner, whose mallet instantly descended on the wedge, and, forcing it between the knee and the iron boot, occasioned the most exquisite pain, as was evident from the flush which instantly took place on the brow and on the cheeks of the sufferer. The fellow then again raised his weapon, and stood prepared to give a second blow.

'Will you yet say,' repeated the Duke of Lauderdale, 'where and when you last parted from Balfour of Burley?'

'You have my answer,' said the sufferer resolutely, – and the second blow fell. The third and fourth succeeded; but at the fifth, when a larger wedge had been introduced, the prisoner set up a scream of agony.

Morton, whose blood boiled within him at witnessing such cruelty, could bear no longer, and, although unarmed and himself in great danger, was springing forward, when Claverhouse, who observed his emotion, withheld him by force, laying one hand on his arm and the other on his mouth, while he whispered, 'For God's sake, think where you are!'

This movement, fortunately for him, was observed by no other of the councillors, whose attention was engaged with the dreadful scene before them.

'He is gone,' said the surgeon – 'he has fainted, my Lords, and human nature can endure no more.'

'Release him,' said the Duke; and added, turning to Dalzell, 'He will make an old proverb good, for he'll scarce ride today, though he has had his boots on. I suppose we must finish with him?'

'Ay, despatch his sentence, and have done with him; we have plenty of drudgery behind.'

SIR WALTER SCOTT, *Old Mortality* (1816)

Samuel Rutherford

To his Reverend and Dear Brother, Mr David Dickson,
on the Death of his Son
(GOD'S SOVEREIGNTY, AND DISCIPLINE BY AFFLICTION)

Reverend and Dear Brother, – Ye look like the house whereof ye are a branch: the cross is a part of the liferent that lieth to all the sons of the house. I desire to suffer with you, if I could take a lift of your house-trial off you; but ye have preached it ere I knew anything of God. Your Lord may gather His roses, and shake His apples, at what season of the year He pleaseth. Each husbandman cannot make harvest when he pleaseth, as He can do. Ye are taught to know and adore His sovereignty, which He exerciseth over you, which yet is lustred with mercy. The child hath but changed a bed in the garden, and is planted up higher, nearer the sun, where he shall thrive better than in this outfield muir-ground. Ye must think your Lord would not want him one hour longer; and since the date of your loan of him was expired (as it is, if ye read the lease), let Him have His own with gain, as good reason were. I read on it an exaltation and a richer measure of grace, as the sweet fruit of your cross; and I am bold to say, that that college where your Master hath set you now shall find it.

I am content that Christ is so homely with my dear brother David Dickson, as to borrow and lend, and take and give with him. And ye know what are called the visitations of such a friend: it is, Come to the house, and be homely with what is yours. I persuade myself, upon His credit, that He hath left drink-money, and that He hath made the house the better of Him. I envy not His waking love, who saw that this water was to be passed through, and that now the number of crosses lying in your way to glory are fewer by one than when I saw you. They must decrease. It is better than any ancient or modern commentary on your text, that ye preach upon in Glasgow. Read and spell right, for He knoweth what He doeth. He is only lopping and snedding a fruitful tree, that it may be more fruitful. I congratulate heartily with you His new welcome to your new charge.

Dearest brother, go on, and faint not. Something of yours is in heaven, beside the flesh of your exalted Saviour; and ye go on after your own. Time's thread is shorter by one inch than it was. An oath is sworn and past the seals, whether afflictions will or not, ye must grow, and swell out of your shell, and live, and triumph, and reign, and be more than a conqueror. For your Captain, who leadeth you on, is more than conqueror, and He maketh you partaker of His conquest and victory. Did not love to you compel me, I would not fetch water to the well, and speak to one who knoweth better than I can do what God is doing with him.

Remember my love to your wife, to Mr John, and all friends there. Let us be helped by your prayers, for I cease not to make mention of you to the Lord, as I can.

Grace be with you.

Yours in his sweet Lord Jesus,   S.R.

St Andrews, May 28, 1640

Letters of Samuel Rutherford (1600–61), ed. A. A. Bonar (1899)

Religion and the Rise of Capitalism

I

By the 1690s the number of cases [of witchcraft] coming up were so few that the local outbreak in Renfrewshire in 1697 when a laird's eleven-year-old [Christian Shaw, daughter of the laird of Bargarran] accused a number of her father's servants and tenants and tenants' children of bewitching her caused widespread reverberations, comment, and disquiet, and made this case one of the best documented of all Scottish cases. Seven out of twenty accused were executed in 1697 but other cases arising out of it were still pending in 1699.

CHRISTINA LARNER, Enemies of God:
The Witch-hunt in Scotland (1981)

II

Christian continued to swoon every quarter of an hour and to produce strange objects from her mouth. For the first three days after her arrival in Glasgow, bundles of hair as before. For four days following, coal cinders about the size of chestnuts, some of them so hot that they could scarcely be handled. Then came two days when she brought up great quantities of straw, one piece at a time. Each piece was tightly folded and when stretched out to its full length was both long and broad; in one of them a small pin was found. After the straw came bones of fowls and small bones from the heads of cows, and then small sticks of fir, one of them about four inches long, of a sort used for candles in country districts.

If anyone saw a bone or stick in her mouth and tried to pull it out, her teeth were immediately clenched on it, or it was drawn back into her throat. When Archibald Bannatyne of Kellie, younger (a McGilchrist relation), came to call, he caught sight of the shin-bone of a duck in her mouth, gripped it and had to pull very hard before he got it out. He said afterwards that he could feel something drawing it back into her throat. She could never explain how these things came to be in her mouth, and when she got rid of them she immediately recovered from her fit for the time being.

On this second visit to Glasgow Christian quickly became a celebrity. The McGilchrists were well known there, and her Uncle John, still only twenty-four years old, was already on his way to becoming Town Clerk. Everyone lived within walking distance of one another. It would have been impossible to suppress the news of Christian's miraculous behaviour if the family had wanted to. As it was, they needed all the credible witnesses they could get. John McGilchrist's journal of the illness was growing, and he was not writing it as an aspiring author but because he wanted to prove something beyond a shadow of doubt. He believed, as her mother did, that the child was bewitched.

Christian's behaviour grew more and more startling. She disgorged 'unclean hay mixed with dung, as if it had been taken out of a dung-hill'. The taste and smell were so vile that each time she put some of this out she had to rinse her mouth with water. For about twenty-four hours she put out wild-fowl feathers of various sorts. After that came a gravel-stone, which, observers thought, must have been passed by some person in a gravel fit; some small white stones; a whole nut gall (used to make ink); lumps of candle grease and eggshells. Sometimes after she had brought up these things she became very violent, crying out piteously at the pain which wracked her body. In her distress she would try to climb the walls of the chamber, and it took four people to hold her down.

During her lucid times she explained that in her fits a number of people were tormenting her. She could describe them in detail, but did not always know their names. Some of those she named were recognized by the spectators as 'persons of ill fame'. They belonged to the class of vagabond beggars, the nightmare fringe of Scottish society, creatures who knocked at every kitchen door, pestered travellers on the roads and appeared like grinning death's-heads at baptisms, weddings and funerals, demanding largesse. One of them came begging at her uncle's door, and Christian saw him. He was among the crew who tormented her, she said, but she could not name him. His name was Alexander Anderson, and he came from Inchinnan, a parish bordering her own.

ISABEL ADAM, *Witch Hunt* (1978)

III

In 1721 a young woman called Christian Miller [i.e. Christian Shaw] was left a widow. Living in Johnstone, close to Paisley, she supported herself by spinning linen yarn for thread. She was able to bleach it 'to perfection', and her white linen thread was so much admired that it was bought by lace makers in the southwest of England. Quick to build on this success Christian Miller acquired a thread-mill from Holland, and soon, with her mother and sister, had established a profitable thread-making business.

By 1744 thread-making was flourishing in Paisley, with 93 mills operating. By 1789 nearly five thousand people were employed in thread-making and Paisley was well known for a variety of high quality threads. The next chapter in the story of Paisley thread-making features two names which became virtually synonymous with sewing thread: Clark and Coats. They both set up in the Paisley area in the 1820s, and to both has been attributed the invention of cotton sewing thread. Whoever was the first, by the end of the century there were two Paisley firms pre-eminent in the production of sewing thread, Messrs J & P Coats and Messrs Clark and Co. Their success was partly the result of keenness and enterprise, helped considerably by the increasingly widespread use of the sewing machine and the growing needs of both factory and home dressmaking.

In 1889 the two firms co-operated to form a distributing centre called The Cotton Agency, later the Central Agency. Seven years later the firms amalgamated, by which time a large part of the world's thread industry was controlled from Paisley. They expanded into Europe, and as early as the 1860s had established works in the USA. It was a striking achievement.

For more than two centuries Paisley was associated with high quality products and with industrial and commercial initiative. The town's achievements were hard won. There were reversals and depressions, high emigration in the nineteenth century fuelled by frustration as well as lack of work, and often considerable suffering amongst those on whose labour the town's success depended. But the spirit of Paisley was remarkable, and it seems wholly appropriate that the town's enterprise should be remembered in the shawls that are now collector's items, in the pattern that has become a household name, and Coats thread which is used throughout the world. Visit Paisley itself, and the street names of the Earl of Abercorn's new town, Gauze, Silk, Inkle, Thread, provide forthright evidence of a productive past.

JENNI CALDER, 'Paisley: a Textile Town'
in ed. Jenni Calder, *The Enterprising Scot* (1986)

On the Presbyterians

The Anglican religion only extends to England and Ireland. Presbyterianism is the dominant religion in Scotland. This Presbyterianism is nothing more than pure Calvinism as it was established in France and survives in Geneva. As the priests in this sect receive very small stipends from their churches, and so cannot live in the same luxury as bishops, they have taken the natural course of decrying honours they cannot attain. Picture the proud Diogenes trampling underfoot the pride of Plato: the Scottish Presbyterians are not unlike that proud and tattered reasoner. They treated Charles II with much less respect than Diogenes had treated Alexander. For when they took up arms on his behalf against Cromwell who had deceived them, they made the poor King put up with four sermons per day, they forbade him to play cards, they sat him on the stool of repentance, with the result that Charles soon grew tired of being King of these pedants and escaped from their clutches like a schoolboy playing truant.

VOLTAIRE, *Letters on England* (1733), trans. L. Tancock (1980)

The Fate of an Episcopalian Chaplain to the Jacobite Army

The first period after the end of the civil war was characterized by the inhuman cruelties of the victor, His Royal Highness the Duke of Cumberland. The present Lord Roseberry (1914) describes him as 'the slave of violent passions' and adds:

'Success in battle was destined to develop the worst phase of his character, *i.e.* a brutal disregard of all the dictates of justice and common humanity, when dealing with a brave but vanquished enemy. No blacker, no bloodier page will be found in the history of any country than that, which records the atrocities perpetrated at Culloden at the command and under the eye of a British Monarch's son.'

And, since that is the deliberate opinion of so eminent a modern Statesman and Historian on the 'Liberal' side of politics, it enables us to accept the following general account of matters given by one of Bishop Alexander's Clergy, *i.e.* the Rev. Robert Lyon of Perth, as not unduly exaggerated:

'The Church of Scotland is now, alas! devoted in the intention of her adversaries to utter destruction, which I fervently pray God to prevent. Her oratories have been profaned and burnt, her holy altars desecrated, her priests outrageously plundered, deprived and some of them imprisoned and treated with uncommon cruelty, her faithful members almost deprived of the means of Salvation, and this mostly done without a form of law by a hostile force especially appointed by him, who calls himself the Duke of Cumberland, and who (God grant him a timely repentance and forgive him!) has occasioned the painful and untimely death of many innocent and inoffensive persons, and by wilful fire and sword and by every means of torment, distress and barbarity, exceeding Glencoe's massacre itself, has brought a dreadful desolation on my dear country.'

194

The writer of the above words himself became one of the royal 'Butcher's' victims, and we proceed to narrate his story.

In the Spring of 1745 his movements became mysterious even to his trusted friends. Thus on March 30th, the Rev. W. Erskine of Muthill wrote as follows to the Bishop concerning him:

'R.L.'s enclosed Letter came to my Hands this day in one to myself, by which he tells me that he hopes to satisfy me at meeting how he came to be two nights at Drummond Castle last week without seeing me. I shall not pass a hasty Sentence against him, but I should think his excuse would need to be pretty relevant.'

The fact evidently was that the Prince had resolved that his army should behave with restraint and humanity and one obvious means of obtaining this end was to enlist the services of loyal Chaplains of good character. Now Mr Lyon assuredly came under that head, and it seems pretty clear that Lord Ogilvy's purpose in bringing him to Drummond Castle on the errand which puzzled Mr Erskine so much was to induce him to follow the Jacobite army, when the time should come, in the capacity of a Chaplain.

In this, that Officer was successful. Mr Lyon himself tells us that it was in response to the prayers of many that he entered upon the risky undertaking. Perhaps it was represented to him that it was safe for him to do so, inasmuch as, 'thinking it inconsistent with his sacred Character,' he neither intended to, nor did he, bear arms, but only lent his aid in maintaining those principles of order and humanity which marked the conduct of the Prince's troops.

The date at which he actually joined the forces has not been ascertained, but it is certain that Charles entered Perth on Sept. 3rd, 1745, and in doing so received an enthusiastic public welcome, and that he attended 'Episcopal' worship, conducted by the Rev. Mr Armstrong, in the Middle Kirk on Sunday, Sept. 8th. This is certainly the likely time for our eager Presbyter to have taken the plunge. It is recorded indeed that, after the Prince had marched south and gained the victory of Prestonpans, near Edinburgh, there were great rejoicings in the Fair City and 'the windows of Mr Lyon's house were illuminated, and the letters C.P.R. (Charles Prince Regent) in large

Characters, with lights shining through them', but that may imply no more than that he waited behind for a little, or that though he was at Prestonpans with the Army, he had left directions with his sister Cicely as to what to do in case of victory. The following extract from a letter addressed on Jan. 6th, 1746, to the Bishop, shews us that he did leave Perth about this time:

'I know not, R.R. Sir, if Mr Lyon acquainted you, ere he left us, but he never so much as signified to one of his Congregation and we are now but Indifferently off. I think we deserved better treatment from him.'

No account of his actual arrest after the great catastrophe survives, but somewhere he fell into the hands of the victorious Hanoverian forces. When the trial came on at Carlisle, he 'was forced,' he said, 'by surprise and the advice of his counsel' to confess the part he had taken in the campaign. 'Upon which,' he continues, 'my pretended Judges declared, and the Jury found me guilty of high treason and levying war' and he was accordingly sentenced to be executed at Penrith on Oct. 28th. Before that date he composed two long documents, the one a letter of farewell to his friends, and the other a speech to be delivered on the scaffold. The Primus and Bishop Alexander, with commendable courage, ran the risk involved in writing him a sympathetic letter of consolation and, after celebrating the Holy Communion for 50 out of his 77 condemned fellow-prisoners, he was led with them to the scaffold, where they were each hanged for three minutes and then disembowelled.

Some of the sawdust was collected by sorrowing friends and preserved as a relic.

G. T. S. FARQUHAR, *Three Bishops of Dunkeld 1743–1808* (1915)

196

Holy Willie's Prayer

And send the Godly in a pet to pray
POPE

Argument

Holy Willie was a rather oldish batchelor Elder in the parish of Mauchline, and much and justly famed for that polemical chattering which ends in tippling Orthodoxy, and for that Spiritualized Bawdry which refines to Liquorish Devotion. – In a Sessional process with a gentleman in Mauchline, a M.ʳ Gavin Hamilton, Holy Willie, and his priest, father Auld, after full hearing in the Presbytry of Ayr, came off but second best; owing partly to the oratorical powers of M.ʳ Rob.ᵗ Aiken, M.ʳ Hamilton's Counsel; but chiefly to M.ʳ Hamilton's being one of the most irreproachable and truly respectable characters in the country. – On losing his Process, the Muse overheard him at his devotions as follows –

O thou that in the heavens does dwell!
Wha, as it pleases best thysel,
Sends ane to heaven and ten to h–ll,
  A' for thy glory!
And no for ony gude or ill
  They've done before thee. –

I bless and praise thy matchless might,
When thousands thou has left in night,
That I am here before thy sight,
  For gifts and grace,
A burning and a shining light
  To a' this place. –

What was I, or my generation,
That I should get such exaltation?
I, wha deserv'd most just damnation,
  For broken laws
Sax thousand years ere my creation,
  Thro' Adam's cause!

When from my mother's womb I fell,
Thou might hae plunged me deep in hell,
To gnash my gooms, and weep, and wail,
             In burning lakes,
Where damned devils roar and yell
                Chain'd to their stakes. –

Yet I am here, a chosen sample,
To shew thy grace is great and ample:
I'm here, a pillar o' thy temple
             Strong as a rock,
A guide, a ruler and example
                To a' thy flock. –

[O L—d thou kens what zeal I bear,
When drinkers drink, and swearers swear,
And singin' there, and dancin' here,
             Wi' great an' sma';
For I am keepet by thy fear,
                Free frae them a'. –]

But yet – O L—d – confess I must –
At times I'm fash'd wi' fleshly lust;
And sometimes too, in warldly trust
             Vile Self gets in;
But thou remembers we are dust,
                Defil'd wi' sin. –

O L—d – yestreen – thou kens – wi' Meg –
Thy pardon I sincerely beg!
O may 't ne'er be a living plague,
             To my dishonor!
And I'll ne'er lift a lawless leg
                Again upon her. –

Besides, I farther maun avow,
Wi' Leezie's lass, three times – I trow –
But L—d, that friday I was fou
             When I cam near her;
Or else, thou kens, thy servant true
                Wad never steer her. –

Maybe thou lets this fleshy thorn
Buffet thy servant e'en and morn,
Lest he o'er proud and high should turn,
        That he's sae gifted;
If sae, thy hand maun e'en be borne
        Untill thou lift it. –

L—d bless thy Chosen in this place,
For here thou has a chosen race:
But G–d, confound their stubborn face,
        And blast their name,
Wha bring thy rulers to disgrace
        And open shame. –

L—d mind Gaun Hamilton's deserts!
He drinks, and swears, and plays at cartes,
Yet has sae mony taking arts
        Wi' Great and Sma',
Frae G–d's ain priest the people's hearts
        He steals awa. –

And when we chasten'd him therefore,
Thou kens how he bred sic a splore,
And set the warld in a roar
        O' laughin at us:
Curse thou his basket and his store,
        Kail and potatoes. –

L—d hear my earnest cry and prayer
Against that Presbytry of Ayr!
Thy strong right hand, L—d, make it bare
        Upon their heads!
L—d visit them, and dinna spare,
        For their misdeeds!

O L—d my G–d, that glib-tongu'd Aiken!
My very heart and flesh are quaking
To think how I sat, sweating, shaking,
        And p–ss'd wi' dread,
While Auld wi' hingin lip gaed sneaking
        And hid his head!

L—d, in thy day o' vengeance try him!
L—d visit him that did employ him!
And pass not in thy mercy by them,
        Nor hear their prayer;
But for thy people's sake destroy them,
        And dinna spare!

But L—d, remember me and mine
Wi' mercies temporal and divine!
That I for grace and gear may shine,
        Excell'd by nane!
And a' the glory shall be thine!
        Amen! Amen!

ROBERT BURNS (1759–96)

The Twenty-third Psalm O King Dauvit

Composed on St Andrew's Day, 1942, in Edinburgh Prison

The late Moray MacLaren in *The Scots* (1951) tells how 'a Scottish writer who was speaking in support of a Scottish Nationalist political candidate at a rural district in the East Lowlands found himself at an informal meeting of farmers and small town business men. They asked him whether all this revival of the Scottish language was not "so much nonsense", and whether anything that he had written in this kind could really be understood by them – plain ordinary Scots folk. For an answer this rather peculiar-looking literary man, black-bearded and immensely elongated, drew himself up to his full six and a half feet and recited to them his own translation of the Twenty-third Psalm in Scots. When he had finished there was a long silence; and the present writer can vouch for it that one or two of these practical East Coast Lowland farmers were near to tears.'

The Lord's my herd, I sall nocht want.[1]
  Whaur green the gresses grow
sall be my fauld. He caas[2] me aye
  whaur fresh sweet burnies rowe.[3]

200

He gars[4] my saul be blyth aince mair
    that wandert was frae hame,
and leads me on the straucht smaa gait[5]
    for sake o His ain name.

Tho I suld gang the glen o mirk[6]
    I'ld grue[7] for nae mischance,
Thou bydes[8] wi me, Thy kent[9] and cruik[10]
    maks aye my sustenance.

Thou spreids ane brod[11] and gies me meat[12]
    whaur aa my faes[13] may view,
Thou sains[14] my heid wi ulyie[15] owre
    and pours my cogie[16] fou.

Nou seil[17] and kindliness sall gae
    throu aa my days wi me,
and I sall wone[18] in God's ain hous
    at hame eternallie.

DOUGLAS YOUNG, *A Clear Voice:*
Douglas Young, Poet and Polymath (1976)

[1] lack; [2] drives; [3] roll; [4] makes; [5] straight narrow track; [6] darkness; [7] feel a chill of horror; [8] dost remain; [9] shepherd's long pole for leaping hedges, etc.; [10] crook; [11] board, table; [12] food; [13] enemies; [14] dost bless; [15] oil; [16] bowl; [17] blessing; [18] dwell

'Geegs'

'Did you never have any religious background?' he asked, his voice pitched deliberately casual. He always felt embarrassed about these questions, Moseby thought.

'Church. Nothing very intensive. Why?'

'Why?' And he turned on Moseby, pausing a moment then coming to his desk. 'Why, because that's the other basic component of the Lowlands, West Coast male. Along with sex. What people don't realize about us' – it gave Moseby a strange feeling to hear the pronoun – 'is that we are existentialists, classically so, and that the twin pillars of our existentialism are religion and sexuality.'

'That makes our basic emotion guilt then.'

'My wife calls it "geegs". I think that's better, it's a more existentially expressive phrase I think. Do you know it?'

'"Geegs". Dirty things, spittles in the dust, that class of item.'

'Yes, Nancy is very sensitive to the geegs, in other people too. She says it's the hallmark of a metaphysical revulsion against our fleshly existence.'

'Does she?'

'You don't agree.' Moseby shrugged elaborately.

'I don't know. Really I don't. I think we are all a bit sex-obsessed because we've all got the feeling it's dirty, we're all a bit pervy.'

'But that's simply the eschatological emphasis of Calvinism being denied by a positive life force. It is a metaphysical assertion.' He smiled, jerkily and got up from his seat, going back to stand at the window. 'I've decided to give up this thing with Jennie,' he said.

'Where does that put your metaphysical assertions then?' Moseby said, annoyed at this having come up again.

'Within religion there is room for the mortification of the flesh.'

ALAN SHARP, *A Green Tree in Gedde* (1965)

Slow Train, Edinburgh to Dundee, around 1920

The morning slow train from Edinburgh to Dundee used to stop (as I suppose it still does) at many of the Fife coast towns on the way. This is why the train used to be, in the 1920, the favourite mode of transport of those Edinburgh Jews who made a precarious living as itinerant salesmen, peddling anything from sewing needles to ready-made dresses among the good housewives and fisherfolk of Fife. They were the 'trebblers', in their own Scots-Yiddish idiom; they had come as young men from Lithuania or Poland seeking freedom and opportunity but somehow had never got on as they had planned. Those with more push and enterprise had moved westward to Glasgow and often on from there to America; a few had managed to build up flourishing businesses in Edinburgh; but the trebblers were the failures, who spent their days carrying their battered suitcases from door to door in the little grey towns of Fife, to return home in the evening with a pound or so gained to a shabby but comfortable flat in one of the more run-down districts of Edinburgh. There, in old stone buildings where the gentry and nobility of Scotland had lived in the eighteenth and early nineteenth centuries, within a stone's throw of the 'Royal Mile' with its violent and picturesque historical associations, they re-created the atmosphere of the Ghetto and lived a life of self-contained Jewish orthodoxy. Edinburgh, one of the few European capitals with no anti-semitism in its history, accepted them with characteristic cool interest. In its semi-slums they learned such English as they knew, which meant in fact that they grafted the debased Scots of the Edinburgh streets on to their native Yiddish to produce one of the most remarkable dialects ever spoken by man . . . Their sons and daughters, making full use of the city's admirable educational facilities, grew up to be doctors and scientists and professors, changing their names from Pinkinsky to Penn, from Finkelstein to Fenton, for Turiansky to Torrence. But they themselves, the Scottish-Jewish pioneers who never quite got where they wanted to go, changed nothing. On Fridays in the winter, when the sun set early, they would be home by the middle of the afternoon, to welcome the Sabbath. On Saturday, of course, as well as on all Jewish festivals, there was no 'trebbling'. And on weekdays in the Dundee train they would chant their morning prayers, strapping their phylacteries on to arm and forehead . . .

Recently I received a letter from the son of the man who was stationmaster at one of the small railway stations where the earliest trebblers would alight; he told me how, at the very beginning of this century, these Jewish immigrants, not yet knowing any English, would converse with his father, they talking in Yiddish and he in broad Scots, with perfectly adequate mutual intelligibility. Scots-Yiddish as a working language must have been developing rapidly in the years immediately preceding the First World War. It must have been one of the most short-lived languages in the world. I should guess that 1912 to 1940 was the period of its flourishing. The younger generation, who grew up in the 1920s and 1930s, of course did not speak it, though they knew Yiddish; and while there is an occasional old man in Edinburgh who speaks it today, one has to seek it out in order to find it, and in another decade it will be gone for ever. 'Aye man, ich hob' getrebbelt mit de five o'clock train,' one trebbler would say to another. 'Vot time's yer barmitzvie, laddie?' I was once asked. 'Ye'll hae a drap o' bramfen (whisky). It's Dzon Beck. Ye ken: "Nem a schmeck fun Dzon Beck."' ('Take a peg of John Begg', the advertising slogan of John Begg whisky.) There was one word in the Scots-Yiddish vocabulary that has always puzzled me: this was 'bleggage', applied to an ill-behaved youngster. My father used to maintain that it was a corruption of 'blackguard', and perhaps it was a mixture of 'blackguard' and 'baggage'. Whatever its origin, it was a fine, expressive word, and it was never more effectively used than one Sabbath morning in 1919 when a number of enterprising youngsters had climbed on to the roof of the Graham Street synagogue and were making a noise on the skylight. The *chazan* (cantor) stopped his singing, banged his large prayer book with the flat of his hand, and cried out: 'Shah! Mak a quietness! *Bleggages*!' This was just after my father had accepted his appointment as Edinburgh rabbi, and the incident was symbolic of the kind of chaos he was determined to put a stop to.

DAVID DAICHES, *Two Worlds* (1956)

'And Yet'

What do we mean by Calvinism when we speak of Scotland? Not merely the beastliness of Predestination and Holy Willie's

Prayer. The image is the Kirk in the moorlands, man face to face with God; *reductio ad simplicitatem.* It is God felt as a pure Wind of Reason and also as something beyond reason. Kipling caught how it made sense of this world – 'predestination in the stride o'yon connecting-rod'; but, being rooted in the Psalms, it also recognizes the vastness of the desert's desolation. It makes an intellectual appreciation of the existential position and adds 'and yet . . .'

ALLAN MASSIE, 'Retrospective'
in ed. Trevor Royle, *Jock Tamson's Bairns* (1977)

The Rowan Tree

Vanishing Village

Some years ago, when many of the roads in the east of Fife were still used but by few, a visitor to the district chanced to ride from the south coast to St Andrews by that across the uplands. He had heard of Dunino Church, and knew something of its associations. He therefore resolved to make a detour to visit it. A somewhat rough track leads down to a bridge across the Pitmilly Burn, not yet united to her sister streams. Thence there diverges a broad and well-made path, cut in the hillside, and climbing among the trees to the kirk and the manse. Leaving this for the moment he continued on the level track round the flank of the hill, and saw before him on the farther side of the stream a picturesque hamlet. Some of the cottages were thatched, some tiled; but all were covered with roses and creepers. In front a strip of garden, stretching to the burn, was trimly kept, and full of old-world flowers; behind, it took on more the nature of a kail-yard. At the east end, on slightly higher ground, a smithy closed the prospect, save for the trees that shut out the farther windings of the Den.

No sound broke the stillness of the summer noon but the flow of the burn. At one or two of the doors there stood an old man in knee-breeches and broad bonnet, or a woman in a white mutch and a stuff gown, while in the entrance to the forge the smith leant motionless on his hammer . . .

Peace brooded like a benediction over the hollow. Half in a dream, he turned and climbed to the church, nor, as time pressed when he had seen it, did he return that way.

No sense of the abnormal had occurred to the intruder. He encountered no living thing till he had passed back to the high road. All was solitude.

A year or little more elapsed ere the wanderer came thither again. It was autumn, and tints of russet and gold were stealing into the colour of the woodlands. This time he was accompanied by a companion to whom he had told the story of his glimpse of 'the most old-world hamlet in Fife'. Where he had left the highway they diverged from it and, crossing the bridge, prepared to sketch the Arcady to be revealed.

The cottages were gone.

The burn flowed through the Den as when last he saw it, but its farther bank was bare. The smith, like the cottages and those whose simple lives were passed in them, had returned to the world of dreams, and where it had stood appeared a croft, the house on which itself seemed old. The wanderer could but assure his questioning companion of the truth of his vision, and leave the riddle to be solved by other minds than his.

Both the *Statistical Accounts* state that there has been no village in the parish 'within living memory'; but the population in Sir John Sinclair's day was only one-half of what it had been, and there were then thirty-one fewer inhabited houses than at an earlier date.

The author is informed on excellent authority that there were at one time at least three or four cottages and a black-smith's shop at the place described. It is said these were taken down 'some time last century'.

J. WILKIE, *Bygone Fife North of the Lomonds* (1938)

The Cross-roads

'Wha bides in yon hoose we hae tae pass
    Yont – div ye see it?'
There's nae hoose there. It's a theek o' grass
    And auld stanes wi' it.'
'But oh! yon thing by the wa' that lurks!
    Is it soond or sicht?'
'It's just the breith o' the grazin' stirks
    Or the white haar[1] crawlin' amang the birks wi' the fa' o' nicht.'

'There's a windy keekin' amang the thorn
    And the branches thrawin – '
*''Twill be tae seek when the morn's morn
    Comes tae the dawin'!'*
'But man, foo² that? For it's there the noo,
    And I see it plain – '
*'Gin ye be sober, I doot I'm fou,
    For I see nane.'*

'There's an auld wife's lee that I fain wad loss,
    Sair sair I fear it,
O' an ill man's hoose whaur the twa roads cross
    And his lair³ that's near it;
Yet gin ye'll meet him by birk or broom
    Ye canna tell – '
*'It's nocht but havers. The road is toom,
    And there's nane ye'll meet sic a nicht o'gloom, but just mysel'.*

'But bide a wee till we kneel and pray,
    For I'd fain be prayin'.'
*'Stand up, stand up – for I daurna say
    The words ye're sayin'!
But rise and gang tae the kirkyaird heid
    And plead yer best
Whaur they wadna bury the ootcast deid
    For a sad saul spent wi' the weird it's dree'd, and I'll maybe rest!"*

VIOLET JACOB, *The Scottish Poems of Violet Jacob* (1944)
¹ sea-mist; ² how; ³ grave

Thomas Rymer

True Thomas lay o'er yond grassy bank,
    And he beheld a lady gay,
A lady that was brisk and bold,
    Come riding o'er the fernie brae.¹

Her skirt was of the grass-green silk,
    Her mantel of the velvet fine,
At ilka² tate³ o' her horse's mane
    Hung fifty siller bells and nine.

True Thomas he took off his hat,
    And bowed him low down till his knee:
'All hail, thou mighty Queen of Heaven!
    For your like on earth I never did see.'

'O no, O no, True Thomas,' she says,
    'That name does not belong to me;
I am but the queen of fair Elfland,
    And I am come here for to visit thee.

'But ye maun go wi' me now, Thomas,
    True Thomas, ye maun go wi' me,
For ye maun serve me seven years,
    Thro weel or wae, as may chance to be.'

She turned about her milk-white steed,
    And took True Thomas up behind,
And aye whene'er her bridle rang,
    The steed flew swifter than the wind.

For forty days and forty nights
    He wade thro red blude to the knee,
And he saw neither sun nor moon,
    But heard the roaring of the sea.

O they rade on, and farther on,
    Until they came to a garden green:
'Light down, light down, ye ladie free,
    Some of that fruit let me pull to thee.'

'O no, O no, True Thomas,' she says,
    'That fruit maun not be touched by thee,
For a' the plagues that are in hell
    Light on the fruit of this countrie.

'But I have a loaf here in my lap,
    Likewise a bottle of claret wine,
And now ere we go farther on,
    We'll rest a while, and ye may dine.'

When he had eaten and drunk his fill,
   'Lay down your head upon my knee,'
The lady sayd, 'ere we climb yon hill,
   And I will show you ferlies[4] three.

'O see not ye yon narrow road,
   So thick beset wi' thorns and briers?
That is the path of righteousness,
   Tho after it but few enquires.

'And see not ye yon braid braid road,
   That lies across yon lilly leven?[5]
That is the path of wickedness,
   Tho some call it the road to heaven.

'And see not ye that bonny road,
   Which winds about the fernie brae?
That is the road to fair Elfland,
   Where you and I this night maun gae.

'But Thomas, ye maun hold your tongue,
   Whatever you may hear or see,
For gin[6] ae word you should chance to speak,
   You will neer get back to your ain countrie.'

He has gotten a coat of the even cloth,
   And a pair of shoes of velvet green,
And till seven years were past and gone
   True Thomas on earth was never seen.

[1] fern-covered slope; [2] each; [3] lock; [4] wonders, strange sights; [5] glade; [6] if

The Stown Bairn

O dinna ye spy yon castel braw
   Ayont the gress-green riggs o' sea,
There's a tower intil't and a bower intil't
   And a louping lyon has power intil't
Rampin' amang the win's that thraw
   Yon banner bousteouslie.

O whaten a castel is yon, ma minnie,
    That harles the hert's bluid oot o' me
And beckons me owre a warld o' watters
    To seek its weird or dee?

You castel braw, ma bonny bit hinny,
    It is the Scottis Glamourie;
There's a spell intil't and a well intil't
    And the sang o' a siller bell intil't,
But the braes abune it are dowf and whinny,
    And the bracken buries the lea.
It's noo a ship wi' the haar for sail,
    And syne a strength, as ye may see,
Forbye it's a hill wi' a hollow ha',
    Whaur the fludes sough eerilie.

O minnie, see yon mune-white steed
    That sowms sae soople owre the sea;
Wi' a horn on his heid, he mak's sic speid
    As alanerlie the clan o' the deid,
And I ken he's fain o' me.
    O whaur are ye, ma gentle bairn
This moment was upon ma knee?
    I cuddled ye i' the cruik o' ma airm,
And noo ye're awa frae me!

LEWIS SPENCE, *Collected Poems* (1953)

The Horseman's Word

This was a kind of cross between a farm servant freemasonry, a working-class Hellfire Club, and a 'primitive rebel' trade union. The sessions of The Horseman's Word – particularly the initiation ceremonies, when youthful recruits to the industry were given the works – could boast their own orally trans-mitted freemason-type ritual, scarifying oaths and all, but they rapidly turned into uproarious drinking bouts in which the bluest of bawdy toasts were exchanged, and 'The Ball of Kirriemuir' was the order of the day . . .

*

It was in the North-East – Aberdeenshire, Banffshire and the Mearns – that one could still find in the 1950s the remnants of the clandestine organization of the Damned – and in quite a good state of preservation, at that. Aberdeenshire has always been a noted place for balladry, and it was no surprise for researchers from the School of Scottish Studies to find that the county still contained many fine ballad singers, some of them quite young. What *did* come as a definite surprise was that the organization of the non- (or anti-) Elect – which looked as if it had some sort of link with the witch cult of the seventeenth century – was a going concern all over the Scottish North-East until roughly the period of World War I, and that its fantastic ritual was still fresh in the minds of a good number of the older people.

The name of the cult – as stated earlier – was the Horseman's Word, and it embraced virtually the entire farm labourer population of the North-East. Its principal ceremony, which was most often celebrated around Martinmas, was an elaborate initiation rite in the course of which the young lads of the neighbourhood were made 'Horsemen'.

> Between the manager and the greep
> 'Tis there that I do hang my whip.
> Between the stable and the cartshed
> 'Twas there a Horseman I was made.

The number of initiates taking part in the capers had to be an odd number, preferably 13; the place chosen was always a barn a good bit off the beaten track. To avoid detection, the locale of meeting was changed frequently. When the seniors of the cult had collected the names of sufficient novices, they passed round the word to attend; this was sometimes done by sending a single horse-hair in an envelope to the brother invited.

Each novice was told of the summons to attend by a 'made Horseman'. He was also told that he had to bring with him a bottle of whisky, a jar of berries (or jam), and a loaf of bread. There is a verse of *Nicky Tams*, often sung and seldom understood, which puts the matter succinctly:

> It's first I gaed on for baillie loon,
> An' syne I gaed on for third:
> An' syne of course I had to get
> The Horseman's grip an' Word. . . .

212

On the appointed night, when the rest of the farm world were safely bedded, the novices were roused and convoyed across country to the barn selected for the ceremony. On the way they were blindfolded. When the horsemen got to the door of the barn, they gave the 'Horseman's knock' (three measured raps), pawed three times on the door with hands or feet, and whinnied like horses. Inside the door stood the 'minister', and the following interrogation took place:

'Who cometh? In the name of the Word speak your name.'
'A brother.'
'A brother of what?'
'Of horsemanry.'
'Who bade ye come here?'
'The Devil.'
'What way did ye come? The crooked way, or the straight way of the path?'
'By the hooks and crooks of the road.'
'In what light did ye come?'
'The stars and the light of the moon.'
'What's the tender of the oath?'
'Hele, conceal, never reveal: neither write, nor dite, nor recite; nor cut, nor carve, nor write in sand.'

Towards midnight the ceremony began. The novices, still blindfolded, knelt in a circle around the 'minister', each with his left foot bare and his left hand raised. The 'minister' rehearsed the mysteries of the Word: he told the lads the name of the first Horseman, which was Cain (Tubal Cain?), and gave them the Word itself, which was another word written backwards. He also revealed the two verses of the Bible which were to be read backwards when a Horseman wished to invoke the aid of the Devil.

As the novices received the Word they swore 'neither to write, nor dite, nor recite' it. Immediately afterwards the 'minister' tried to trick them into breaking their oath. The blindfold would be raised slightly to allow each boy to see paper in front of him, and the command would be given – 'Now you have the Word: write it'.

Occasionally a sharp lad would be fly enough to refuse, but the average greenhorn fell for the trick. He would take the proffered pen or pencil to write the Word, but before he could write the first letter, he would be given a 'lick' over the fingers with

213

the backchain of a cart or the stock of a horsewhip. Several old men to whom I have talked in Buchan and Stra'bogie still bear the marks of this 'lick' on their fingers.

After this – the ritual infliction of pain – the novices were pushed one by one into the cauf-hoose of the barn for 'a shak o' Auld Hornie'. No horseman was a right 'made Horseman' if he had not shaken hands with the Devil, so everyone had to go through it. Sometimes the 'Deil' was a man dressed in a calf-skin rubbed with phosphorus; sometimes he was a live calf or goat. In either case, the novice felt a hoof pressed into his hand, and he was ordered to shake it.

This completed the initiation. After it the bottles of whisky were uncorked, and the meeting became less formal. The newly initiated horsemen were given 'information' by their seniors, in which practical hints on the managing of horses were mixed up with the wildest of supernatural folklore. Stories were related of the prowess of some famous Horseman, who with the Devil's assistance could make stallions dance around the corn-yard, and follow at his heels wherever he went.

If a horseman who had signed himself over to the Deil had trouble with some coarse, ill-natured mare, all he had to do was this: take her collar and bridle to the crossroads, 'say over his lessons' (i.e. recite two verses of the Bible backwards), and a horse would appear. He would have good cause for fear, because the horse would be the Devil – but if he took courage, slipped the collar over the uncanny cratur's head and mounted it, he would never afterwards have trouble from his pair of horse.

('The Deil is a gey handy man' – as one old chap put it to me – 'a gey handy man.')

As the drinking got going, the horsemen would challenge each other on points of horsemanry and rehearse a number of esoteric shibboleths. One question often put was – 'Where were ye made a Horseman?' To this the correct answer went as follows:

> In a Horseman's hall
>   where the sun never shone
>   where the wind never blew
>   where a cock never crew
>   and the feet of a maiden never trod.

A question put to the greenhorns, and which they were now supposed to be able to tackle, was 'Fat d'ye need maist?' (What do you need most?) The correct statutory answer here was 'More light' but other more ribald answers were suggested by senior horsemen . . .

Sooner or later during the proceedings the ceremonial Horseman's toast was given:

> Here's to the horse wi' the four white feet,
>   The chestnut tail and mane –
> A star on his face and a spot on his breast,
>   And his master's name was Cain.

Drinking and revelry went on until dawn, when the horsemen staggered off to their own farms – to Auchnamoon, say, or Satyrhills or Cairnadellie – to cope with horses in the cold light of day.

HAMISH HENDERSON, 'The Ballad, the Folk and the Oral Tradition' in ed. Edward J. Cowan, *The People's Past* (1980)

The Rowan Tree

So late as 1860 I have seen the rowan tree trained in the form of an arch over the byre door, and in another case over the gate of the farmyard, as a protection to the cows. It was also believed that a rowan tree growing in a field protected the cattle against being struck by lightning.

> 'Lest witches should obtain the power
> Of Hawkie's milk in evil hour,
> She winds a red thread round her horn,
> And milks thro' row'n tree night and morn;
> Against the blink of evil eye
> She knows each antidote to ply.'

JAMES NAPIER, *Folk Lore* (1879)

The Witch Cake

I saw yestreen, I saw yestreen,
Little wis ye what I saw yestreen,
The black cat pyked out the gray ane's een,
At the hip o' the hemlock knowe yestreen.

Wi' her tail i' her teeth she whomel'd roun',
Wi' her tail i' her teeth she whomel'd roun',
'Til a braw star drapt frae the lift aboon,
An' she keppit it e'er it wan to the grun'.

She hynt them a' in her mow' an' chowed,
She hynt them a' in her mow' an' chowed,
She drabbled them owre wi' a black tade's blude,
An' baked a bannock, – an' ca'd it gude!

She haurned it weel wi' ae blink o' the moon,
She haurned it weel wi' ae blink o' the moon,
An withre-shines thrice she whorled it roun',
'There's some sall skirl ere ye be done.'

'Some lass maun gae wi' a kilted sark,
Some priest maun preach in a thackless kirk;
Thread maun be spun for a dead man's sark,
A' maun be done e'er the sang o' the lark.'

Tell nae what ye saw yestreen,
Tell nae what ye saw yestreen,
There's ane may gaur thee sich an' graen,
For telling what ye saw yestreen!

ANON

216

Tam o' Shanter. A Tale

Of Brownyis and of Bogillis full is this buke.

GAWIN DOUGLAS

When chapman billies leave the street,
And drouthy neebors, neebors meet,
As market-days are wearing late,
An' folk begin to tak the gate;
While we sit bousing at the nappy,
And getting fou and unco happy,
We think na on the lang Scots miles,
The mosses, waters, slaps, and styles,
That lie between us and our hame,
Whare sits our sulky sullen dame,
Gathering her brows like gathering storm,
Nursing her wrath to keep it warm.

This truth fand honest *Tam o' Shanter*,
As he frae Ayr ae night did canter,
(Auld Ayr, wham ne'er a town surpasses,
For honest men and bonny lasses.)

O *Tam*! hadst thou but been sae wise,
As ta'en thy ain wife *Kate*'s advice!
She tauld thee weel thou was a skellum,
A blethering, blustering, drunken blellum;
That frae November till October,
Ae market-day thou was nae sober;
That ilka melder, wi' the miller,
Thou sat as lang as thou had siller;
That every naig was ca'd a shoe on,
The smith and thee gat roaring fou on;
That at the L—d's house, even on Sunday,
Thou drank wi' Kirkton Jean till Monday.
She prophesied that late or soon,
Thou would be found deep drown'd in Doon;
Or catch'd wi' warlocks in the mirk,
By *Alloway*'s auld haunted kirk.

Ah, gentle dames! it gars me greet,
To think how mony counsels sweet,
How mony lengthen'd sage advices,
The husband frae the wife despises!

But to our tale: Ae market-night,
Tam had got planted unco right;
Fast by an ingle, bleezing finely,
Wi' reaming swats, that drank divinely;
And at his elbow, Souter *Johnny*,
His ancient, trusty, drouthy crony;
Tam lo'ed him like a vera brither;
They had been fou for weeks thegither.
The night drave on wi' sangs and clatter;
And ay the ale was growing better:
The landlady and *Tam* grew gracious,
Wi' favours, secret, sweet, and precious:
The Souter tauld his queerest stories;
The landlord's laugh was ready chorus:
The storm without might rair and rustle,
Tam did na mind the storm a whistle.

Care, mad to see a man sae happy,
E'en drown'd himsel amang the nappy:
As bees flee hame wi' lades o' treasure,
The minutes wing'd their way wi' pleasure:
Kings may be blest, but *Tam* was glorious,
O'er a' the ills o' life victorious!

But pleasures are like poppies spread,
You seize the flower, its bloom is shed;
Or like the snow falls in the river,
A moment white – then melts for ever;
Or like the borealis race,
That flit ere you can point their place;
Or like the rainbow's lovely form
Evanishing amid the storm. –
Nae man can tether time or tide;
The hour approaches *Tam* maun ride;
That hour, o' night's black arch the key-stane,
That dreary hour he mounts his beast in;

And sic a night he taks the road in,
As ne'er poor sinner was abroad in.

The wind blew as 'twad blawn its last;
The rattling showers rose on the blast;
The speedy gleams the darkness swallow'd;
Loud, deep, and lang, the thunder bellow'd:
That night, a child might understand,
The Deil had business on his hand.

Weel mounted on his gray mare, *Meg*,
A better never lifted leg,
Tam skelpit on thro' dub and mire,
Despising wind, and rain, and fire;
Whiles holding fast his gude blue bonnet;
Whiles crooning o'er some auld Scots sonnet;
Whiles glowring round wi' prudent cares,
Lest bogles catch him unawares:
Kirk-Alloway was drawing nigh,
Whare ghaists and houlets nightly cry. –

By this time he was cross the ford,
Whare, in the snaw, the chapman smoor'd;
And past the birks and meikle stane,
Whare drunken *Charlie* brak's neck-bane;
And thro' the whins, and by the cairn,
Whare hunters fand the murder'd bairn;
And near the thorn, aboon the well,
Whare *Mungo*'s mither hang'd hersel. –
Before him *Doon* pours all his floods;
The doubling storm roars thro' the woods;
The lightnings flash from pole to pole;
Near and more near the thunders roll:
When, glimmering thro' the groaning trees,
Kirk-Alloway seem'd in a bleeze;
Thro' ilka bore the beams were glancing;
And loud resounded mirth and dancing. –

Inspiring bold *John Barleycorn*!
What dangers thou canst make us scorn!
Wi' tippeny, we fear nae evil;
Wi' usquabae, we'll face the devil! –
The swats sae ream'd in *Tammie*'s noddle,
Fair play, he car'd na deils a boddle.
But *Maggie* stood right sair astonish'd,
Till, by the heel and hand admonish'd,
She ventured forward on the light;
And, vow! *Tam* saw an unco sight!
Warlocks and witches in a dance;
Nae cotillion brent new frae *France*,
But hornpipes, jigs, strathspeys, and reels,
Put life and mettle in their heels.
A winnock-bunker in the east,
There sat auld Nick, in shape o' beast;
A towzie tyke, black, grim, and large,
To gie them music was his charge:
He screw'd the pipes and gart them skirl,
Till roof and rafters a' did dirl. –
Coffins stood round, like open presses,
That shaw'd the dead in their last dresses;
And by some devilish cantraip slight
Each in its cauld hand held a light. –

By which heroic *Tam* was able
To note upon the haly table,
A murderer's banes in gibbet airns;
Twa span-lang, wee, unchristen'd bairns;
A thief, new-cutted frae a rape,
Wi' his last gasp his gab did gape;
Five tomahawks, wi' blude red-rusted;
Five scymitars, wi' murder crusted;
A garter, which a babe had strangled;
A knife, a father's throat had mangled,
Whom his ain son o' life bereft,
The grey hairs yet stack to the heft;
Wi' mair o' horrible and awefu',
Which even to name wad be unlawfu'.
And how *Tam* stood, like ane bewitch'd,
And thought his very een enrich'd;
Even Satan glowr'd, and fidg'd fu' fain,
And hotch'd and blew wi' might and main:
Till first ae caper, syne anither,
Tam tint his reason a' thegither,
And roars out, 'Weel done, Cutty-sark!'
And in an instant all was dark:
And scarcely had he Maggie rallied,
When out the hellish legion sallied.

As bees bizz out wi' angry fyke,
When plundering herds assail their byke;
As open pussie's mortal foes,
When, pop! she starts before their nose;
As eager runs the market-crowd,
When 'Catch the thief!' resounds aloud;
So Maggie runs, the witches follow,
Wi' mony an eldritch skreech and hollow.

Ah, *Tam*! Ah, *Tam*! thou'll get thy fairin!
In hell they'll roast thee like a herrin!
In vain thy *Kate* awaits thy comin!
Kate soon will be a woefu' woman!
Now, do thy speedy utmost, Meg,
And win the key-stane* of the brig;
There at them thou thy tail may toss,

A running stream they dare na cross.
But ere the key-stane she could make,
The fient a tail she had to shake!
For Nannie, far before the rest,
Hard upon noble Maggie prest,
And flew at *Tam* wi' furious ettle;
But little wist she Maggie's mettle –
Ae spring brought off her master hale,
But left behind her ain gray tail:
The carlin claught her by the rump,
And left poor Maggie scarce a stump.

Now, wha this tale o' truth shall read,
Ilk man and mother's son, take heed:
Whene'er to drink you are inclin'd,
Or cutty-sarks run in your mind,
Think, ye may buy the joys o'er dear,
Remember Tam o' Shanter's mare.

ROBERT BURNS (1759–96)

*It is a well known fact that witches, or any evil spirits, have no power to follow a poor wight any farther than the middle of the next running stream. – It may be proper likewise to mention to the benighted traveller, that when he falls in with *bogles*, whatever danger may be in his going forward, there is much more hazard in turning back.

Languages and Literature

Romance and Gossip

In many countries Scotland is known as a land of romance; Scott was chiefly responsible for spreading this idea of Scotland over the world. There is a genuine romantic strain in the Scottish character, and especially among the peasantry. Scotland is a country in which history turns very easily into legend. Scottish children first hear of Wallace and Bruce, Mary Stuart and Bonnie Prince Charlie, as figures in legend or folksong. And this gift for poeticizing history is so strong that it often runs counter to the religious convictions and prejudices of the people. Scotland has been a Protestant nation for four hundred years; yet the four main figures which it has turned into legend – Wallace and Bruce, Mary Stuart and Prince Charlie – are all Catholics. These legendary figures were created by the peasantry, not by the aristocracy or the poets; they were shaped by the communal poetic genius, and handed on from generation to generation by word of mouth, very often by people who could not either read or write. The Scottish ballads, some of them about kings and princes, some about local characters, long forgotten, some about supernatural happenings, murders, tragic love affairs, were handed on in the same way. There are hundreds of them, and they contain the greatest poetry that Scotland has produced. We do not know now who made them, or how they were made, for it took generations to cast them into the shape in which we know them. They bring us back again to the Scottish people and its part in the making of Scotland; for it was the people who created these magnificent poems. The greatest poetry of most countries has been written by the educated middle and upper classes; the greatest poetry of Scotland has come from the people.

It is curious that this people, with its theology, its passion for liberty, its insatiable interest in human life, its critical temper, should have influenced the literature of other countries purely through its romantic genius, as if that were the rarest gift it had to give. James MacPherson, the author of 'Ossian', Lord Byron, and Walter Scott, have had a more profound effect on the literatures of Europe from Russia to Spain than any other three writers born in Great Britain during the last two hundred years. Scott was very close to the Border ballads, and MacPherson to the legends of the Scottish Highlands, and Byron had the explosive genius which had appeared already in Burns; that is to say, the gifts they exercised so magnificently were gifts which had been bred among the Scottish peasantry. By the accident of genius these gifts were suddenly displayed before Europe and greeted as rare and strange; and if we try to view them through the eyes of Europe we seem to catch a fleeting glimpse of the Scottish genius at its best, as it can be at moments when it has forgotten its gravity and its canny commonsense . . .

For its size, Scottish literature has created a greater number of characters (drawn from life) than any other literature in the world; and it has produced the two greatest biographies in the English language: Boswell's 'Life of Dr Johnson', and Lockhart's 'Life of Scott'. So much, then, for the Scots' boundless, insatiable interest in their fellow men and women; they are tireless gossips and anecdotists.

EDWIN MUIR,
The Scots and their Country (1946)

Border Ballads

Like the Homeric Greeks, they were cruel, coarse savages, slaying each other as the beasts of the forest; and yet they were also poets who could express in the grand style the inexorable fate of the individual man and woman, the infinite pity for all the cruel things which they none the less perpetually inflicted upon one another. It was not one ballad-maker alone but the whole cut-throat population who felt this magnanimous sorrow, and the consoling charm of the highest poetry.

... If the people had not loved the songs, many of the best would have perished. The Border Ballads, for good and for evil, express this society and its quality of mind.

G. M. TREVELYAN,
Clio. A Muse (1913)

The Wife of Usher's Well

There lived a wife at Usher's Well,
   And a wealthy wife was she;
She had three stout and stalwart sons,
   And sent them oer the sea.

They hadna been a week from her,
   A week but barely ane,
Whan word came to the carline[1] wife
   That her three sons were gane.

They hadna been a week from her,
   A week but barely three,
Whan word came to the carlin wife
   That her sons she'd never see.

I wish the wind may never cease,
   Nor fishes in the flood,
Till my three sons come hame to me,
   In earthly flesh and blood.

It fell about the Martinmass,
   When nights are lang and mirk,
The carlin wife's three sons came hame,
   And their hats were o the birk.[2]

It neither grew in syke[3] nor ditch,
   Nor yet in ony sheugh;[4]
But at the gates o Paradise,
   That birk grew fair eneugh.

Blow up the fire, my maidens!
  Bring water from the well!
For a' my house shall feast this night,
  Since my three sons are well.

And she has made to them a bed,
  She's made it large and wide,
And she's taen her mantle her about,
  Sat down at the bed-side.

Up then crew the red, red cock,
  And up and crew the grey;
The eldest to the youngest said,
  'Tis time we were away.

The cock he hadna crawd but once,
  And clappd his wings at a',
When the youngest to the eldest said,
  Brother, we must awa.

The cock doth craw, the day doth daw,
  The channerin[5] worm doth chide;
Gin we be mist out o our place,
  A sair pain we maun bide.

Fare ye weel, my mother dear!
  Fareweel to barn and byre!
And fare ye weel, the bonny lass
  That kindles my mother's fire!

ANON

[1] old woman; [2] birch; [3] marshy hollow, small rill; [4] a hollow; [5] scolding, fretful

Folk

At camp fires in the berryfields of Blairgowrie, in council houses at Perth, and in the heart of secret-looking woodlands in the Mearns (an ancestral hideout) members of the travelling fraternity, young and old, sang rare Child ballads, lyric love-songs, execution broadside ballads, kid's rhymes, contemporary pop songs, you name it, they sang it. The only trouble (if you can call it trouble) was that everyone sang, or wanted to sing, right down to the smallest children: at an encampment near Laurencekirk, in 1953, a teenage girl who was tone deaf sang a long version of a classic ballad into the microphone for the Kentucky singer Jean Ritchie; the other travellers were far too well-mannered to pass any comment while the song was being recorded – or indeed afterwards – although I intercepted some embarrassed glances.

What one encountered, in that drystick wood, in Jeannie Robertson's house in Causewayend, and at the Standing Stones berry field on the road to Essendy, was this wonderful fluid thing representing the actual world of the ballad singers, a shared sensibility still artistically vital and fertile. Singers who *are* singers remake their own versions, which may gel for themselves and others, or may dissipate again … The greatest thrill is to hear one's own songs sung in new variants by singers who feel themselves totally free to remake them in any old way – or in any new way – that seems good to them.

HAMISH HENDERSON,
'The Ballad, the Folk and the Oral Tradition'
in ed. Edward J. Cowan, *The People's Past* (1980)

On Visiting the Tomb of Burns

The town, the churchyard, and the setting sun,
  The clouds, the trees, the rounded hills all seem,
  Though beautiful, cold – strange – as in a dream,
I dreamed long ago, now new begun.
The short-liv'd, paly Summer is but won
  From Winter's ague, for one hour's gleam;
  Though sapphire-warm, their stars do never beam:
All is cold Beauty; pain is never done:

For who has mind to relish, Minor-wise,
　　The Real of Beauty, free from that dead hue
　　　Sickly imagination and sick pride
Case wan upon it! Burns! with honour due
　　I oft have honour'd thee. Great shadow, hide
Thy face; I sin against thy native skies.

(1818)
JOHN KEATS

Burns and Popular Poetry

For a Scotsman to see Burns simply as a poet is almost impossible. Burns is so deeply imbedded in Scottish life that he cannot be detached from it, from what is best and what is worst in it, and regarded as we regard Dunbar or James Hogg or Walter Scott. He is more a personage to us than a poet, more a figurehead than a personage, and more a myth than a figurehead. To those who have heard of Dunbar he is a figure, of course, comparable to Dunbar; but he is also a figure comparable to Prince Charlie, about whom everyone has heard. He is a myth evolved by the popular imagination, a communal poetic creation, a Protean figure; we can all shape him to our own likeness, for a myth is endlessly adaptable; so that to the respectable this secondary Burns is a decent man; to the Rabelaisian, bawdy; to the sentimentalist, sentimental; to the Socialist, a revolutionary; to the Nationalist, a patriot; to the religious, pious; to the self-made man, self-made; to the drinker, a drinker. He has the power of making any Scotsman, whether generous or canny, sentimental or prosaic, religious or profane, more wholeheartedly himself than he could have been without assistance; and in that way perhaps more human. He greases our wheels; we could not roll on our way so comfortably but for him; and it is impossible to judge impartially a convenient appliance to which we have grown accustomed . . .

But the national poet of Scotland is too conventional a term for him; the poet of the Scottish people is better, for all claim him. And by the people I do not mean merely the ploughman and the factory worker and the grocer's assistant, but the lawyer, the business man, the minister, the bailie – all that large class of Scotsmen who are not very interested in literature, not very cultivated, and know little poetry outside the poetry of Burns. It is these who have fashioned the popular image of Burns; and this is what really happens when a poet is taken into the life of a people. He moulds their thoughts and feelings; but they mould his too, sometimes long after he is dead. They make current a vulgarized image of him, and a vulgarized reading of his poetry; they take him into their life, but they also enter into his; and what emerges as the popular picture is a cross between the two. What is good in this bargain is self-evident – that the words and thoughts and feelings of a great poet become the common property of his people. The disadvantages I have tried to describe; they are natural and inevitable; compared to the single great advantage they do not matter very much, unless to those who cannot endure a normal dose of vulgarity. But they exist, and those who are advocating a more popular note in poetry at present should take them into account. For Burns is an object-lesson in what poetic popularity really means – the prime object-lesson in the poetry of the world, perhaps the unique instance.

EDWIN MUIR, 'Burns and Popular Poetry',
in *Essays on Literature and Society* (1965)

Song – For a' that and a' that –

Is there, for honest Poverty
 That hings his head, and a' that;
The coward-slave, we pass him by,
 We dare be poor for a' that!
 For a' that, and a' that,
  Our toils obscure, and a' that,
 The rank is but the guinea's stamp,
  The Man's the gowd for a' that. –

What though on hamely fare we dine,
 Wear hoddin grey, and a' that.
Gie fools their silks, and knaves their wine,
 A Man's a Man for a' that.
 For a' that, and a' that,
  Their tinsel show, and a' that;
 The honest man, though e'er sae poor,
  Is king o' men for a' that. –

Ye see yon birkie ca'd, a lord,
 Wha struts, and stares, and a' that,
Though hundreds worship at his word,
 He's but a coof for a' that.
 For a' that, and a' that,
  His ribband, star and a' that,
 The man of independant mind,
  He looks and laughs at a' that. –

A prince can mak a belted knight,
 A marquis, duke, and a' that;
But an honest man's aboon his might,
 Gude faith he mauna fa' that!
 For a' that, and a' that,
  Their dignities, and a' that,
 The pith o' Sense, and pride o' Worth,
  Are higher rank than a' that. –

230

Then let us pray that come it may,
    As come it will for a' that,
That Sense and Worth, o'er a' the earth
    Shall bear the gree, and a' that.
  For a' that, and a' that,
    Its comin yet for a' that,
  That Man to Man the warld o'er,
    Shall brothers be for a' that. –

ROBERT BURNS (1759–96)

Gentlemanly Speech

I

Sir A. 'I have been correcting several Scotch accents in my friend Boswell. I doubt, Sir, if any Scotchman ever attains to a perfect English pronunciation.' *Johnson.* 'Why, Sir, few of them do, because they do not persevere after acquiring a certain degree of it. But, Sir, there can be no doubt that they may attain to a perfect English pronunciation, if they will. We find how near they come to it; and certainly, a man who conquers nineteen parts of the Scottish accent, may conquer the twentieth. But, Sir, when a man has got the better of nine tenths, he grows weary, he relaxes his diligence, he finds he has corrected his accent so far as not to be disagreeable, and he no longer desires his friends to tell him when he is wrong; nor does he choose to be told. Sir, when people watch me narrowly, and I do not watch myself, they will find me out to be of a particular county. In the same manner, Dunning may be found out to be a Devonshire man. So most Scotchmen may be found out. But, Sir, little aberrations are of no disadvantage. I never catched Mallet in a Scotch accent; and yet Mallet, I suppose, was past five-and-twenty before he came to London.'

Upon another occasion I talked to him on this subject, having myself taken some pains to improve my pronunciation, by the aid of the late Mr Love, of Drury-lane theatre, when he was a player at Edinburgh, and also of old Mr Sheridan. Johnson said to me, 'Sir, your pronunciation is not offensive.' With this concession I was pretty well satisfied; and let me give my countrymen of North-Britain an advice not to aim at absolute

231

perfection in this respect; not to speak *High English*, as we are apt to call what is far removed from the *Scotch*, but which is by no means *good English*, and makes, 'the fools who use it', truly ridiculous. Good English is plain, easy and smooth in the mouth of an unaffected English Gentleman. A studied and factitious pronunciation, which requires perpetual attention and imposes perpetual constraint, is exceedingly disgusting. A small intermixture of provincial peculiarities may, perhaps, have an agreeable effect, as the notes of different birds concur in the harmony of the grove, and please more than if they were all exactly alike.

JAMES BOSWELL, *Life of Johnson* (1791)

II

Lord Elibank was a great Scotsman when in England, and a great Englishman when in Scotland. A neighbour of his in East Lothian was holding forth on the superior qualities of the Scots. 'I don't dispute that,' said Elibank, 'but I think they do one thing better.' – 'You mean, my lord, they make better cheese, but I deny that.' 'No, laird, I only think they speak better English.'

HENRY MacKENZIE (1745–1831),
ed. H. W. Thompson, *The Anecdotes and Egotisms* (1927)

III

Really it is admirable how many Men of Genius this Country produces at present. Is it not strange that, at a time when we have lost our Princes, our Parliaments, our independent Government, even the Presence of our chief Nobility, are unhappy, in our Accent & Pronunciation, speak a very corrupt Dialect of the Tongue which we make use of; is it not strange, I say, that, in these Circumstances we shou'd really be the People most distinguish'd for Literature in Europe?

DAVID HUME (1711–76) in 1757

The Maker to Posterity

Far 'yont amang the years to be
When a' we think, an' a' we see,
An' a' we luve, 's been dung ajee
    By time's rouch shouther,
An' what was richt and wrang for me
    Lies mangled throu'ther,

It's possible – it's hardly mair –
That some ane, ripin' after lear –
Some auld professor or young heir,
    If still there's either –
May find an' read me, an' be sair
    Perplexed, puir brither!

'What tongue does your auld bookie speak?'
He'll spier; an' I, his mou to steik:
'No bein' fit to write in Greek,
    I wrote in Lallan,
Dear to my heart as the peat reek,
    Auld as Tantallon.

'Few spak it than, an' noo there's nane.
My puir auld sangs lie a' their lane,
Their sense, that aince was braw an' plain,
    Tint a'thegether,
Like runes upon a standin' stane
    Amang the heather.

'But think not you the brae to speel;
You, tae, maun chow the bitter peel;
For a' your lear, for a' your skeel,
    Ye're nane sae lucky;
An' things are mebbe waur than weel
    For you, my buckie.

'The hale concern (baith hens an' eggs,
Baith books an' writers, stars an' clegs)
Noo stachers upon lowsent legs
    An' wears awa';
The tack o' mankind, near the dregs,
    Rins unco' law.

'Your book, that in some braw new tongue,
Ye wrote or prentit, preached or sung,
Will still be just a bairn, an' young
In fame an' years,
Whan the hale planet's guts are dung
About your ears;

'An' you, sair gruppin' to a spar
Or whammled wi' some bleezin' star,
Cryin' to ken whaur deil ye are,
Hame, France, or Flanders –
Whang sindry like a railway car
An' flie in danders.'

R. L. STEVENSON

Entreaties

In his well-known letter to the *Bombay Courier*, he [Col.-Gen. Sir J. Malcolm] says: 'When he arrived at Calcutta in 1806, I was most solicitous regarding his reception in the society of the Indian Capital. I entreat you, Leyden (I said to him the day he landed), to be careful of the impression you make on your entering this community. For God's sake learn a little English, and be silent upon literary subjects, except among literary men.

'"Learn English!" he exclaimed, "no, never; it was my trying to learn that language that spoilt my Scots; and as to being silent, I will promise to hold my tongue if you will make fools hold theirs."'

JOHN REITH, *Life of Dr John Leyden* (1909)

Sir James Murray,
Editor of the Oxford English Dictionary,
in Edinburgh, 1870

How thoroughly Scotch even literary men speak here. I could hardly believe it. I never noticed it as much before. I find per contra that I am taken for out-and-out English by every one. How funny, since all Londoners could tell me to be Scotch at

once – and even hear you as Scotch from your contact with me
– and yet here nobody suspects me to be anything but English
who does not know!

quoted in K. M. ELISABETH MURRAY,
Caught in the Web of Words (1979)

Speech and Death

On their return to Peckham she became desperately ill. James
nursed her, noting with interest, in spite of his distress, that
when in delirium she dropped the refined speech he had so
much admired and reverted to the broad Scotch of her childhood.

K. M. ELISABETH MURRAY,
Caught in the Web of Words (1979)

Wee

I

Hundreds of mothers throughout Aberdeenshire and
Banffshire every night put their 'little wee bit loonikies' and
'little wee bit lassickies' to their 'bedies', while the infant of the
household, described as the 'little wee eenickie', that is a 'teeny
weeny eenie' – lies in its 'cradlie'. A thousand and one
examples will leap to your minds: – 'The boatie rows': 'sic
mannie, sic horsie'; 'the ewie wi' the crookit horn' – as against
Burns's 'Ca' the ewes tae to the knowes'; a 'sheltie': a 'sheepie', a
'lammie', a 'burnie', a 'quinie' and so on through a whole catalogue of diminutives, sometimes five and six thick. Indeed, 'a
little wee bit loonikie' represents five diminutives. These
diminutives are, I say, just as frequently used as ever they have
been. They are even employed by people who have sloughed
nearly every other vestige of the vernacular, for the very simple
reason that they cannot slough the mentality which the diminutive represents and which it can evaluate as nothing else can
do . . .

For nursery rhymes the diminutive is unsurpassable for its

sense of tender perception of the fascinating helplessness of the object addressed. Take for instance:

> Dance to your daddie,
> My bonnie laddie.
> Dance to your daddie, my bonnie lamb!
> And ye'll get a fishie
> In a little dishie –
> Ye'll get a fishie when the boat comes hame.
>
> Dance to your daddie,
> My bonnie laddie,
> Dance to your daddie, my bonnie lamb!
> And ye'll get a coatie,
> And a pair o' breekies –
> You'll get a whippie and a soople tam.

J. M. BULLOCH, 'The Delight of the Doric in the Diminutive' in W. A. Craigie *et al.*, *The Scottish Tongue* (1924)

II

Diminutives are our only emotional outlets. We have practically no endearments. The southerner spreads himself out on 'dears', 'darlings', 'beloveds' and such-like saccharinities. The tidal wave of passion swamps the Scot. Even the mildest of ordinary, everyday loves remain unexpressed either directly or indirectly because there is no vocabulary for them. It is somebody of Barrie's, I think, who says: 'Love ye? Weesht! Fat kin' o' a word's that to be makin' eese o' – an' fowk a' weel eneuch.' In a vague unformulated fashion we consider tenderness a weakness, very nearly an indecency. At any rate we fight shy of it. We *are* shy of it. 'Love, but dinna lat on' about sums up all the erotic philosophy of the hill plaid and the sleeved weskit. So in our soft moments – no dithyrambics, no little urbanities, or amiabilities. We just drop into diminutives.

MARY SYMON (1863–1938), *op. cit.*

III
The Voyeur

what's your favourite word dearie
is it wee
I hope it's wee
wee's such a nice wee word
like a wee hairy dog
with two wee eyes
such a nice wee word to play with dearie
you can say it quickly
with a wee smile
and a wee glance to the side
or you can say it slowly dearie
with your mouth a wee bit open
and a wee sigh dearie
a wee sigh
put your wee head on my shoulder dearie
oh my
a great wee word
and Scottish
it makes you proud

TOM LEONARD, *Intimate Voices* (1984)

English Words

Words? I don't know about that. You see, the Southerners haven't got the monopoly of written English. The American dramatist, Maxwell Anderson, once said that the first qualification of a writer of plays was that he should be an Irishman because the Irish write the best English. The second qualification was to be a Scotsman, because the Scots write better English than the Irish.

JAMES BRIDIE to Moray McLaren, *A Small Stir* (1949)

this is thi
six a clock
news thi
man said n
thi reason
a talk wia
BBC accent
iz coz yi
widny wahnt
mi ti talk
aboot thi
trooth wia
voice lik
wanna yoo
scruff. if
a toktaboot
thi trooth
lik wanna yoo
scruff yi
widny thingk
it wuz troo.
jist wanna yoo
scruff tokn.
thirza right
way ti spell
ana right way
ti tok it. this
is me tokn yir
right way a
spellin. this
is ma trooth.
yooz doant no
thi trooth
yirsellz cawz
yi canny talk
right. this is
the six a clock
nyooz. belt up.

TOM LEONARD, from 'Unrelated Incidents',
Intimate Voices (1984)

Saints and Gargoyles

This mixing of contraries – 'intermingledoms', to recall Burns's word – helps to explain the presence of certain qualities which have come to be considered as characteristic of Scottish literature. In the first place, it throws some light on that talent for the picturesque so generally allowed to northern writers. And what is the picturesque, in spite of the cheapening of the term in the marketplace, but the quality which, as Hazlitt tells us, 'depends chiefly on the principle of discrimination and contrast' and 'runs imperceptibly into the fantastical and grotesque'? In other words, in its exercise and effect it does not show mere sensitiveness to fact, with or without the art of intensifying and completing the impression by the heaping-up of details. Scottish literature is not so placid. If we neglect its more striking or astonishing extravagances, we have to account for that prevailing sense of movement, that energy and variety, call it what we like, that stirs even its most narrative mood. If a formula is to be found it must explain this strange combination of things unlike, of things seen in an everyday world and things which, like the elf-queen herself, neither earth nor heaven will claim. This mingling, even of the most eccentric kind, is an indication to us that the Scot, in that medieval fashion which takes all things as granted, is at his ease in both 'rooms of life', and turns to fun, and even profanity, with no misgivings. For Scottish literature is more medieval in habit than criticism has suspected, and owes some part of its picturesque strength to this freedom in passing from one mood to another. It takes some people more time than they can spare to see the absolute propriety of a gargoyle's grinning at the elbow of a kneeling saint.

G. GREGORY SMITH, *Scottish Literature* (1919)

Scottish Vernacular

We have been enormously struck by the resemblance – the moral resemblance – between Jamieson's Etymological Dictionary of the Scottish language and James Joyce's *Ulysses*. A *vis comica* that has not yet been liberated lies bound by desuetude and misappreciation in the recesses of the Doric: and its potential uprising would be no less prodigious, uncontrollable, and

239

utterly at variance with conventional morality than was Joyce's tremendous outpouring. The Scottish instinct is irrevocably, continuously, opposed to all who 'are at ease in Zion'. It lacks entirely the English sense of 'the majesty of true corpulence'. Sandy is our national figure – a shy, subtle, disgruntled, idiosyncratic individual – very different from John Bull. And while the Irish may envisage their national destiny as 'the dark Rosaleen' and the thought of England may conjure up pictures of roast beef and stately homes, Scotland is always 'puir auld Scotland'. Dr Walter Walsh recently referred to the affinity between the Scots and the Spartans and voiced a deep national feeling when he deprecated material well-being and comfort of mind or body. It is of first-rate significance, revealing that what really does most profoundly appeal to us is not pleasure but pain, to remember what happened at the concert given by Serge Koussevitzki in Edinburgh recently. (It has a bearing on what we are subsequently to say of the mystical relation of Scotland and Russia.) A newspaper critic described it thus: 'He (Koussevitzki) rose to his greatest heights when he came to the modern Russians. There were the introduction to Moussorgski's opera "Khovanschchina", Rimsky Korsakov's "The Flight of the Bumble Bee", Rachmaninoff's "Vocalise" and Tchaikovski's "Fifth Symphony" . . . Two of them had to be repeated, but the symphony marked the climax of the concert. Koussevitzki extracted from it *the last ounce of agony and gloom* with which it is charged. It was all very exciting, and at the close there were scenes unparalleled at these concerts. An Edinburgh audience, reputed to be reserved, rose to its feet, cheered and shouted bravos.' – That's us all over! Joy and gladness are all very well in their way – but gloom is what really gets us and we do enjoy agony! . . .

Burns himself had no wish for the increase of mere human self-satisfaction. It is deeply significant that he wrote

> O wad some power the giftie gie's
> To see oorsels as ithers see's

– not, 'O gie the gift to ither folk to see us as we see oorsels.'

And one of the most distinctive characteristics of the Vernacular, part of its very essence, is its insistent recognition of the body, the senses. The Vernacular is almost startlingly at one with Rabbi Ben Ezra,

> Let us not always say
> *Spite of this flesh to-day*
> I strove, made head . . .

In other words, in Meredith's phrase, the Vernacular can never consent to 'forfeit the beast wherewith we are cross'. This explains the unique blend of the lyrical and the ludicrous in primitive Scots sentiment. It enables us to realize very clearly just what Matthew Arnold meant when he called Burns 'a beast with splendid gleams' – and the essence of the genius of our race, is, in our opinion, the reconciliation it effects between the base and the beautiful, recognizing that they are complementary and indispensable to each other.

The Scottish Vernacular is the only language in Western Europe instinct with those uncanny spiritual and pathological perceptions alike which constitute the uniqueness of Dostoevski's work, and word after word of Doric establishes a blood-bond in a fashion at once infinitely more thrilling and vital and less explicable than those deliberately sought after by writers such as D. H. Lawrence in the medium of English which is inferior for such purposes because it has entirely different natural bias which has been so confirmed down the centuries as to be insusceptible of correction. The Scots Vernacular is a vast storehouse of just the very peculiar and subtle effects which modern European literature in general is assiduously seeking and, if the next century is to see an advance in mental science equal to that which the last century has marked in material science, then the resumption of the Scots Vernacular into the mainstream of European letters, in a fashion which the most enthusiastic Vernacularist may well hesitate to hope for, is inevitable. The Vernacular is a vast unutilized mass of lapsed observation made by minds whose attitudes to experience and whose speculative and imaginative tendencies were quite different from any possible to Englishmen and Anglicized Scots to-day. It is an inchoate Marcel Proust – a Dostoevskian debris of ideas – an inexhaustible quarry of subtle and significant sound.

HUGH MacDIARMID, 'A Theory of Scots Letters' (1923)
in ed. Alan Bold, *The Thistle Rises* (1984)

The Watergaw

Ae weet forenicht[1] i' the yow-trummle[2]
I saw yon antrin[3] thing,
A watergaw[4] wi' its chitterin'[5] licht
Ayont[6] the on-ding;[7]
An' I thocht o' the last wild look ye gied
Afore ye deed!

There was nae reek[8] i' the laverock's[9] hoose
That nicht – an' nane i' mine;
But I hae thocht o' that foolish licht
Ever sin' syne;
An' I think that mebbe at last I ken
What your look meant then.

HUGH MacDIARMID,
The Complete Poems (1978)

[1] early evening; [2] ewe-tremble (i.e. cold spell in summer after sheep-shearing); [3] strange; [4] faint or broken rainbow; [5] shivering; [6] beyond; [7] downpour; [8] smoke; [9] lark (line evokes wind and darkness).

Literary Problems

The riddle which confronted me in approaching Scott himself, by far the greatest creative force in Scottish literature as well as one of the greatest in English, was to account for a very curious emptiness which I felt behind the wealth of his imagination. Many critics have acknowledged this blemish in Scott's work, but have either made no attempt to account for it, or else have put it down to a defect in Scott's mind and character. Yet men of Scott's enormous genius have rarely Scott's faults; they may have others but not these particular ones; and so I was forced to account for the hiatus in Scott's endowment by considering the environment in which he lived, by invoking the fact – if the reader will agree it is one – that he spent most of his days in a hiatus, in a country, that is to say, which was neither a nation nor a province, and had, instead of a centre, a blank, an Edinburgh, in the middle of it. But this Nothing in which Scott wrote was not merely a spatial one; it was a temporal Nothing as well, dotted with a few disconnected figures arranged at abrupt intervals: Henryson, Dunbar, Allan Ramsay, Burns, with a rude buttress of ballads and folk songs to shore them up and keep them from falling. Scott, in other words, lived in a community which was not a community, and set himself to carry on a tradition which was not a tradition; and the result was that his work was an exact reflection of his predicament. His picture of life had no centre, because the environment in which he lived had no centre. What traditional virtue his work possessed was at second hand, and derived mainly from English literature, which he knew intimately but which was a semi-foreign literature to him. Scotland did not have enough life of its own to nourish a writer of his scope; it had neither a real community to foster him nor a tradition to direct him; for the anonymous ballad tradition was not sufficient for his genius . . .

So that my inquiry into what Scotland did for Scott came down finally to what it did not do for Scott. What it did not do, or what it could not do. Considered historically these alternatives are difficult to separate.

Having traced Scott's greatest fault to his geographical and historical position as a writer, I began to wonder what he might have been, given his genius, if he had been born into a genuine organic society such as England, or even into a small self-subsistent state like Weimar. Could he possibly have left his picture of life in such a tentative state, half flesh and blood and half pasteboard, unreal where he dealt with highly civilized people, and real where he dealt with peasants, adventurers and beggars? Would he not have been forced to give it unity? or rather, would not a sociological unity at least have been there without his having to make a specific effort to achieve it? . . .

But behind this problem of the Scottish writer there is another which, if not for the individual author, for Scotland itself is of crucial importance. This is the problem of Scottish literature, and it is clearly a question for the Scottish people as a whole, not for the individual Scottish writer; for only a people can create a literature. The practical present-day problem may be put somewhat as follows: that a Scottish writer who wishes to achieve some approximation to completeness has no choice except to absorb the English tradition, and that if he thoroughly does so his work belongs not merely to Scottish literature but to

243

English literature as well. On the other hand, if he wishes to add to an indigenous Scottish literature, and roots himself deliberately in Scotland, he will find there, no matter how long he may search, neither an organic community to round off his conceptions, nor a major literary tradition to support him, nor even a faith among the people themselves that a Scottish literature is possible or desirable, nor any opportunity, finally, of making a livelihood by his work. All these things are part of a single problem which can only be understood by considering Scottish literature historically, and the qualities in the Scottish people which have made them what they are; it cannot be solved by writing poems in Scots, or by looking forward to some hypothetical Scotland in the future . . .

Every genuine literature, in other words, requires as its condition a means of expression capable of dealing with everything the mind can think or the imagination conceive. It must be a language for criticism as well as poetry, for abstract speculation as well as fact, and since we live in a scientific age, it must be a language for science as well. A language which can serve for one or two of those purposes but not for the others is, considered as a vehicle for literature, merely an anachronism. Scots has survived to our time as a language for simple poetry and the simpler kind of short story, such as *Thrawn Janet*; all its other uses have lapsed, and it expresses therefore only a fragment of the Scottish mind. One can go further than this, however, and assert that its very use is a proof that the Scottish consciousness is divided. For, reduced to its simplest terms, this linguistic division means that Scotsmen feel in one language and think in another; that their emotions turn to the Scottish tongue, with all its associations of local sentiment, and their minds to a standard English which for them is almost bare of associations other than those of the classroom. If Henryson and Dunbar had written prose they would have written in the same language as they used for poetry, for their minds were still whole; but Burns never thought of doing so, nor did Scott, nor did Stevenson, nor has any Scottish writer since. In an organic literature poetry is always influencing prose, and prose poetry; and their interaction energizes them both. Scottish poetry exists in a vacuum; it neither acts on the rest of literature nor reacts to it; and consequently it has shrunk to the level of anonymous folk-song.

Hugh MacDiarmid has recently tried to revive it by impregnating it with all the contemporary influences of Europe one after another, and thus galvanize it into life by a series of violent shocks. In carrying out this experiment he has written some remarkable poetry; but he has left Scottish verse very much where it was before. For the major forms of poetry rise from a collision between emotion and intellect on a plane where both meet on equal terms; and it can never come into existence where the poet feels in one language and thinks in another, even though he should subsequently translate his thoughts into the language of his feelings. Scots poetry can only be revived, that is to say, when Scotsmen begin to think *naturally* in Scots. The curse of Scottish literature is the lack of a whole language, which finally means the lack of a whole mind.

EDWIN MUIR, *Scott and Scotland* (1936)

Celtic Twilight

It is a very different type of romanticism that has been predicated of the Gael and his poetry. The special brand of romanticism attributed to the Gael and his poetry is a romanticism of the escapist, other-worldly type, a cloudy mysticism, the type suggested by the famous phrase, 'Celtic Twilight'. This Celtic Twilight never bore any earthly relation to anything in Gaelic life or literature. It was merely one of the latest births of the English literary bourgeoisie, and its births are to Gaelic eyes exceedingly strange, whether they be Mr John Duncan's St Bride or the late Mrs Kennedy-Fraser's 'Mairead òg with her sea-blue eyes of witchery' . . .

I suppose that many with Celtic pretensions will be shocked at a declaration that Gaelic poetry has not less but more than common realism. They invoke the names of 'Ossian' MacPherson, 'Fiona MacLeod', Kenneth MacLeod and Marjorie Kennedy-Fraser, and hosts of lesser Twilightists, but they will have no competent native critic on their side. Of course, with the kind of people who call Mrs Kennedy-Fraser's travesties of Gaelic songs 'faithful reproductions of the spirit of the original', I have no dispute. They are harmless as long as ignorance and crassness are considered failings in criticism of poetry. They have had their hour in the drawing-rooms of Edinburgh and London; they have soothed the ears of old ladies of the Anglo-Saxon bourgeoisie: they have spoken after dinner, hiding with a halo the bracken that grew with the Clearances; they have cherished the Iubhrach Bhallach and forgotten the 'Annie Jane' that went down in the Kyle of Vatersay, and some of them have had their earthly reward.

SORLEY MacLEAN,
Ris a' Bhruthaich. Criticism and Prose Writings (1985)

Manners

John Clerk (afterwards a judge by the title of Lord Eldin) was arguing a Scotch appeal case before the House of Lords. His client claimed the use of a mill stream by a prescriptive right. Mr Clerk spoke broad Scotch, and argued that 'the *watter* had rin that way for forty years. Indeed naebody kenn'd how long, and why should his client now be deprived of the watter?' etc. The chancellor, much amused at the pronunciation of the Scottish advocate, in a rather bantering tone asked him, 'Mr Clerk, do you spell water in Scotland with two t's?' Clerk, a little nettled at this hit at his national tongue, answered, 'Na, my Lord, we dinna spell watter (making the word as short as he could) wi' twa t's, but we spell mainners (making the word as long as he could) wi' twa n's.'

E. B. RAMSAY, *Reminiscences of Scottish Life and Character*, 22nd ed. (1879)

Canedolia

An Off-Concrete Scotch Fantasia

ao! hoy! awe! ba! mey!

who saw?
rhu saw rum. garve saw smoo. nigg saw tain. lairg saw lagg. rigg saw eigg. largs saw haggs. tongue saw luss. mull saw yell. stoer saw strone. drem saw muck. gask saw noss. unst saw cults. echt saw banff. weem saw wick. trool saw twatt.

how far?
from largo to lunga from joppa to skibo from ratho to shona from
ulva to minto from tinto to tolsta from soutra to marsco from
braco to barra from alva to stobo from fogo to fada from gigha to
gogo from kelso to stroma from hirta to spango.

what is it like there?
och it's freuchie, it's faifley, it's wamphray, it's frandy, it's
sliddery.

what do you do?
we foindle and fungle, we bonkle and meigle and maxpoffle. we
scotstarvit, armit, wormit, and even whifflet. we play at crosstobs,
leuchars, gorbals, and finfan. we scavaig, and there's aye a bit of
tilquhilly. if it's wet, treshnish and mishnish.

what is the best of the country?
blinkbonny! airgold! thundergay!

and the worst?
scrishven, shiskine, scrabster, and snizort.

listen! what's that?
catacol and wauchope, never heed them.

tell us about last night
well, we had a wee ferintosh and we lay on the quiraing. it was
pure strontian!

but who was there?
petermoidart and craigenkenneth and cambusputtock and
ecclemuchty and corriehulish and balladolly and altnacanny and
clauchanvrechan and stronachlochan and auchenlachar and
tighnacrankie and tilliebruaich and killieharra and invervannach
and achnatudlem and machrishellach and inchtamurchan and
auchterfechan and kinlochculter and ardnawhallie and
invershuggle.

and what was the toast?
schiehallion! schiehallion! schiehallion!

EDWIN MORGAN, *Poems of Thirty Years* (1982)

Hallaig

'Tha tìm, am fiadh, an coille Hallaig'

Tha bùird is tàirnean air an uinneig
troimh 'm faca mi an Aird an Iar
's tha mo ghaol aig Allt Hallaig
'na craoibh bheithe, 's bha i riamh

eadar an t-Inbhir 's Poll a' Bhainne,
thall 's a bhos mu Bhaile-Chùirn:
tha i 'na beithe, 'na calltuinn,
'na caorunn dhìreach sheang ùir.

Ann an Screapadal mo chinnidh,
far robh Tarmad 's Eachunn Mór,
tha 'n nigheanan 's am mic 'nan coille
ag gabhail suas ri taobh an lóin.

Uaibhreach a nochd na coilich ghiuthais
ag gairm air mullach Cnoc an Rà,
dìreach an druim ris a' ghealaich –
chan iadsan coille mo ghràidh.

Fuirichidh mi ris a' bheithe
gus an tig i mach an Càrn,
gus am bi am bearradh uile
o Bheinn na Lice f' a sgàil.

Mura tig 's ann theàrnas mi a Hallaig
a dh' ionnsaigh sàbaid nam marbh,
far a bheil an sluagh a' tathaich,
gach aon ghinealach a dh' fhalbh.

Tha iad fhathast ann a Hallaig,
Clann Ghill-Eain's Clann MhicLeòid,
na bh' ann ri linn Mhic Ghille-Chaluim:
Chunnacas na mairbh beò.

Na fir 'nan laighe air an lianaig
aig ceann gach taighe a bh' ann,
na h-ighean an 'nan coille bheithe,
dìreach an druim, crom an ceann.

Hallaig

'Time, the deer, is in the wood of Hallaig'

The window is nailed and boarded
through which I saw the West
and my love is at the Burn of Hallaig,
a birch tree, and she has always been

between Inver and Milk Hollow,
here and there about Baile-chuirn:
she is a birch, a hazel,
a straight, slender young rowan.

In Screapadal of my people
where Norman and Big Hector were,
their daughters and their sons are a wood
going up beside the stream.

Proud tonight the pine cocks
crowing on the top of Cnoc an Ra,
straight their backs in the moonlight –
they are not the wood I love.

I will wait for the birch wood
until it comes up by the cairn,
until the whole ridge from Beinn na Lice
will be under its shade.

If it does not, I will go down to Hallaig,
to the Sabbath of the dead,
where the people are frequenting,
every single generation gone.

They are still in Hallaig,
MacLeans and MacLeods,
all who were there in the time of Mac Gille Chaluim:
the dead have been seen alive.

The men lying on the green
at the end of every house that was,
the girls a wood of birches,
straight their backs, bent their heads.

Eadar an Leac is na Feàrnaibh
tha 'n rathad mór fo chóinnich chiùin,
's na h-igheanan 'nam badan sàmhach
a' dol a Chlachan mar o thùs.

Agus a' tilleadh as a' Chlachan,
á Suidhisnis 's á tir nam beò;
a chuile té òg uallach
gun bhristeadh cridhe an sgeòil.

O Allt na Feàrnaibh gus an fhaoilinn
tha soilleir an dìomhaireachd nam beann
chan eil ach coimhthional nan nighean
ag cumail na coiseachd gun cheann.

A' tilleadh a Hallaig anns an fheasgar,
anns a' chamhanaich bhalbh bheò,
a' lìonadh nan leathadan casa,
an gàireachdaich 'nam chluais 'na ceò,

's am bòidhche 'na sgleò air mo chridhe
mun tig an ciaradh air na caoil,
's nuair theàrnas grian air cùl Dhùn Cana
thig peileir dian á gunna Ghaoil;

's buailear am fiadh a tha 'na thuaineal
a' snòtach nan làraichean feòir;
thig reothadh air a shùil 'sa' choille:
chan fhaighear lorg air fhuil ri m' bheò.

Between the Leac and Fearns
the road is under mild moss
and the girls in silent bands
go to Clachan as in the beginning,

and return from Clachan
from Suisnish and the land of the living;
each one young and light-stepping,
without the heartbreak of the tale.

From the Burn of Fearns to the raised beach
that is clear in the mystery of the hills,
there is only the congregation of the girls
keeping up the endless walk,

coming back to Hallaig in the evening,
in the dumb living twilight,
filling the steep slopes,
their laughter a mist in my ears,

and their beauty a film on my heart
before the dimness comes on the kyles,
and when the sun goes down behind Dun Cana
a vehement bullet will come from the gun of Love;

and will strike the deer that goes dizzily,
sniffing at the grass-grown ruined homes;
his eye will freeze in the wood,
his blood will not be traced while I live.

SORLEY MacLEAN,
From Wood to Ridge – Collected Poems (1989)

252

Hospitality
(and Other Potations)

'And, my lords and lieges, let us all to dinner, for the cockie-leekie is a-cooling.'

SIR WALTER SCOTT, *The Fortunes of Nigel* (1822)

Dinner is the English meal, breakfast the Scotch. An Englishman's certainty of getting a good dinner seems to make him indifferent about his breakfast, while the substantiality of a Scotchman's breakfast impairs, or at least might be said to impair, his interest in his dinner.

LORD COCKBURN, *Circuit Journeys* (1888)

Haggis

The Recipe

Clean a sheep's pluck thoroughly. Make incisions in the heart and liver to allow the blood to flow out, and parboil the whole, letting the windpipe lie over the side of the pot to permit the discharge of impurities; the water may be changed after a few minutes' boiling for fresh water. A half-hour's boiling will be sufficient; but throw back half of the liver to boil till it will grate easily; take the heart, the half of the liver, and part of the lights, trimming away all skins and black-looking parts, and mince them together. Mince also a pound of good beef suet and four or more onions. Grate the other half of the liver. Have a dozen of small onions peeled and scalded in two waters to mix with this mince. Have some finely-ground oatmeal, toasted slowly before the fire for hours, till it is of a light brown colour and perfectly dry. Less than two teacupfuls of meal will do for this quantity of meat. Spread the mince on a board and strew the meal lightly over it, with a high seasoning of pepper, salt and a little cayenne, first well mixed. Have a haggis bag (i.e. a sheep's paunch) perfectly clean, and see that there be no thin part in it, else your whole labour will be lost by its bursting. Some cooks use two bags, one as an outer case. Put in the meat with a half-pint of good beef gravy, or as much strong broth as will make it a very thick stew. Be careful not to fill the bag too full, but allow the meat room to swell; add the juice of a lemon or a little good vinegar; press out the air and sew up the bag, prick it with a large needle when it first swells in the pot to prevent bursting; let it boil slowly for three hours if large.

'MISTRESS MARGARET DODDS',
The Cook and Housewife's Manual (1826)

Porridge

'The halesome parritch, chief o' Scotia's food.' – Burns.

(The One and Only Method)
Oatmeal, salt, water.

It is advisable to keep a goblet exclusively for porridge.

Allow for each person one breakfastcupful of water, a handful of oatmeal (about an ounce and a quarter), and a small saltspoonful of salt. Use fresh spring water and be particular about the quality of the oatmeal. Midlothian oats are unsurpassed the world over.

Bring the water to the boil and as soon as it reaches boiling-point add the oatmeal, letting it fall in a steady rain from the left hand and stirring it briskly the while with the right, sunwise, or the right-hand turn for luck – and convenience. A porridge-stick, called a spurtle, and in some parts a theevil, or, as in Shetland, a gruel-tree, is used for this purpose. Be careful to avoid lumps, unless the children clamour for them. When the porridge is boiling steadily, draw the mixture to the side and put on the lid. Let it cook for from twenty to thirty minutes according to the quality of the oatmeal, and do not add the salt, which has a tendency to harden the meal and prevent its swelling, until it has cooked for at least ten minutes. On the other hand, never cook porridge without salt. Ladle straight into porringers or soup plates and serve with small individual bowls of cream, or milk, or buttermilk. Each spoonful of porridge, which should be very hot, is dipped in the cream or milk, which should be quite cold, before it is conveyed to the mouth.

F. MARIAN McNEILL, The Scots Kitchen (1929)

Potage à la Meg Merrilies de Derncleugh

Meg, in the meanwhile, went to a great black cauldron that was boiling on a fire on the floor, and lifting the lid, an odour was diffused through the vault which, if the vapours of a witch's cauldron could in aught be trusted, promised better things than the hell-broth which such vessels are usually supposed to contain. It was in fact the savour of a goodly stew, composed of fowls, hares, partridges, and moorgame, boiled in a large mess with potatoes, onions, and leeks, and from the size of the cauldron, appeared to be prepared for half-a-dozen of people at least.

'So ye hae eat naething a' day?' said Meg, heaving a large portion of this mess into a brown dish, and strewing it savourily with salt and pepper.

'Nothing,' answered the Dominie – *'scelestissima!* – that is – gudewife.'

'Hae, then,' said she, placing the dish before him, 'there's what will warm your heart.'

'I do not hunger – *malefica* – that is to say – Mrs Merrilies!' for he said unto himself, 'the savour is sweet, but it hath been cooked by a Canidia or an Ericthoe.'

'If ye dinna eat instantly, and put some saul in ye, by the bread and the salt, I'll put it down your throat wi' the cutty spoon, scaulding as it is, and whether ye will or no. Gape, sinner, and swallow!'

Sampson, afraid of eye of newt, and toe of frog, tigers' chaudrons, and so forth, had determined not to venture; but the smell of the stew was fast melting his obstinacy, which flowed from his chops, as it were, in streams of water, and the witch's threats decided him to feed. Hunger and fear are excellent casuists.

'Saul,' said Hunger, 'feasted with the witch of Endor.' – 'And,' quoth Fear, 'the salt which she sprinkled upon the food showeth plainly it is not a necromantic banquet, in which that seasoning never occurs.' – 'And besides,' says Hunger, after the first spoonful, 'it is savoury and refreshing viands.'

'So ye like the meat?' said the hostess.

'Yea,' answered the Dominie, 'and I give thee thanks – *sceleratissima!* – which means – Mrs Margaret.'

'Aweel, eat your fill; but an ye kenn'd how it was gotten, ye maybe wadna like it sae weel.' Sampson's spoon dropped in the act of conveying its load to his mouth. 'There's been mony a moonlight watch to bring a' that trade thegither,' continued Meg – 'the folk that are to eat that dinner thought little o' your game-laws.'

SIR WALTER SCOTT, *Guy Mannering* (1815)

Salmon

Scotch salmon has a texture and flavour superior to most. At one time it was so plentiful that it is said that servants complained when given it too often for meals.

Certainly, Defoe commented on its abundance and cheapness, particularly in the north. But disease and over-fishing took their toll, and by the early 1900s it was already food for the rich. It is a very versatile fish, equally good hot or cold, poached, grilled or baked.

Poaching should be very gently done, the fish put into cold water which is slowly brought to boil, the heat then immediately reduced so that the water merely simmers for about one minute. The heat is then turned off and the fish left in the water, covered, until quite cold.

Herring

When Dorothy Wordsworth and her brother toured Scotland in 1803, they were offered herrings for breakfast at Cairndow, near Glen Kinglas. They enjoyed them, slightly to their own surprise:

Tuesday, August 30th: Breakfasted before our departure, and ate a herring fresh from the water, at our landlord's earnest recommendation – much superior to the herrings we get in the north of England.

Lucky Wordsworths! They were being treated to the best herrings Scotland can offer, caught in Loch Fyne, still famous today, and so plump and succulent that they are nicknamed 'Glasgow Magistrates'. Probably they were fried in oatmeal, for the Scots early discovered the affinity between these two foods which has created one of the world's great traditional simple dishes. Needless to say the fish should be fresh-caught, the oatmeal fresh also. Good quality dripping is traditional, but vegetable oil does perfectly well. Butter would be an affectation and a waste.

ANNETTE HOPE, *A Caledonian Feast* (1989)

Firm and erect the Caledonian stood;
Old was his mutton, and his claret good.
'Let him drink port!' the Saxon statesman cried.
He drank the poison, and his spirit died.

JOHN HOME (1722–1808)

High Tea

From the 1930s to the 1950s high tea was the evening meal of all but the professional and upper classes. For the servantless housewife with children it made sense to have a simple meal which could be enjoyed and shared by the whole family, and saved on the washing-up. If there were visitors it became the most hospitable of occasions.

In the industrial towns, Saturday teas were specially important family events, when married daughters and sons visited or were visited, and old ties with more distant relatives renewed. On Saturdays there was often more than one main course, and an impressive array of baking.

Main courses, frequently borrowed from the great Scottish breakfast, were usually simple – eggs, or finnan haddies, herrings in oatmeal, or kippers. Another favourite was cold meat: corned beef, tongue, or boiled ham. Fish and chips (home-made if the family was 'posh', otherwise bought from the 'Tallie') was a great standby. A very popular dish, especially in Glasgow, was the small mutton pies known as 'Twopenny Struggles'. Vegetables were never served, although 'posh' people sometimes ate tomato, cucumber, or cress sandwiches,

or used a lettuce leaf and half a tomato to garnish a main dish. Salads were rare indeed. Yet family high tea was, in its way, a splendid meal, making few demands on the palate and con-veying all the delightful security of the nursery and the tea-party . . .

For over 50 years, from the 1900s to the late 1950s, it was possible to go into any tea-room, anywhere in Scotland and, having asked for tea, to be met with the response 'Plain or High, Madam?' Whether the tea-room belonged to a chain or was a small family-run business, the quality of food and service were almost assured – tea was such a popular meal, and so many establishments were competing for custom. The toast was hot and golden, the butter came in small curls in a little pot, the jam and honey in glass or earthenware dishes, the milk, innocent of plastic and foil, in a proper jug. No microwave ovens waited malevolently to heat up cloned frozen scones. The haddock, plump and firm, was served with crisp chips in discreet portions so that one might do justice to the cake or biscuits. And the tea and hot water came in electroplated nickel-silver pots, enabling the customer to mix up the brew he preferred.

ANNETTE HOPE, *A Caledonian Feast* (1989)

Pre-war High Tea in Aberdeen

High tea in Aberdeen is like no other meal on earth. It is the meal of the day, the meal par excellence, and the tired come home to it ravenous, driven by the granite streets, hounded in for energy to stoke against that menace. Tea is drunk with the meal, and the order of it is this: First, one eats a plateful of sausages and eggs and mashed potatoes; then a second plateful to keep down the first. Eating, one assists the second plateful to its final home by mouthfuls of oatcake spread with butter. Then you eat oatcake with cheese. Then there are scones. Then cookies. Then it is really time to begin on tea – tea and bread and butter and crumpets and toasted rolls and cakes. Then some Dundee cake. Then – about half-past seven – someone shakes you out of the coma into which you have fallen and asks you persuasively if you wouldn't like another cup of tea and just *one* more egg and sausage . . .

LEWIS GRASSIC GIBBON, 'Aberdeen', *Scottish Scene* (1934)

Heather Ale

A Galloway Legend

From the bonny bells of heather
  They brewed a drink long-syne,
Was sweeter far than honey,
  Was stronger far than wine.
They brewed it and they drank it,
  And lay in a blessed swound
For days and days together
  In their dwellings underground.

259

There rose a king in Scotland,
   A fell man to his foes,
He smote the Picts in battle,
   He hunted them like roes.
Over miles of the red mountain
   He hunted as they fled,
And strewed the dwarfish bodies
   Of the dying and the dead.

Summer came in the country,
   Red was the heather bell;
But the manner of the brewing
   Was none alive to tell.
In graves that were like children's
   On many a mountain head,
The Brewsters of the Heather
   Lay numbered with the dead.

The king in the red moorland
   Rode on a summer's day;
And the bees hummed, and the curlews
   Cried beside the way.
The king rode, and was angry,
   Black was his brow and pale,
To rule in a land of heather
   And lack the Heather Ale.

It fortuned that his vassals,
   Riding free on the heath,
Came on a stone that was fallen
   And vermin hid beneath.
Rudely plucked from their hiding,
   Never a word they spoke:
A son and his aged father –
   Last of the dwarfish folk.

The king sat high on his charger,
   He looked on the little men;
And the dwarfish and swarthy couple
   Looked at the king again.

Down by the shore he had them;
   And there on the giddy brink –
'I will give you life, ye vermin,
   For the secret of the drink.'

There stood the son and father
   And they looked high and low;
The heather was red around them,
   The sea rumbled below.
And up and spoke the father,
   Shrill was his voice to hear:
'I have a word in private,
   A word for the royal ear.

'Life is dear to the aged,
   And honour a little thing;
I would gladly sell the secret,'
   Quoth the Pict to the King.
His voice was small as a sparrow's,
   And shrill and wonderful clear:
'I would gladly sell my secret,
   Only my son I fear.

'For life is a little matter,
   And death is nought to the young;
And I dare not sell my honour
   Under the eye of my son.
Take *him*, O king, and bind him,
   And cast him far in the deep;
And it's I will tell the secret
   That I have sworn to keep.'

They took the son and bound him,
   Neck and heels in a thong,
And a lad took him and swung him,
   And flung him far and strong,
And the sea swallowed his body,
   Like that of a child of ten;
And there on the cliff stood the father,
   Last of the dwarfish men.

'True was the word I told you:
  Only my son I feared;
For I doubt the sapling courage
  That goes without the beard.
But now in vain is the torture,
  Fire shall never avail:
Here dies in my bosom
  The secret of Heather Ale.'

R. L. STEVENSON (1850–94)

Pedantry about Booze

The Baron, drawing out a private key, unlocked the casket, raised the lid, and produced a golden goblet of a singular and antique appearance, moulded into the shape of a rampant bear, which the owner regarded with a look of mingled reverence, pride and delight, that irresistibly reminded Waverley of Ben Jonson's Tom Otter, with his Bull, Horse, and Dog, as that wag wittily denominated his chief carousing cups. But Mr Bradwardine, turning towards him with complacency, requested him to observe this curious relic of the olden time.

'It represents,' he said, 'the chosen crest of our family, a bear, as ye observe and *rampant*, because a good herald will depict every animal in its noblest posture: as a horse *salient*, a greyhound *currant*, and, as may be inferred, a ravenous animal *in actu ferociori*, or in a voracious, lacerating, and devouring posture. Now, sir, we hold this most honourable achievement by the wappen-brief, or concession of arms, of Frederick Redbeard, Emperor of Germany, to my predecessor, Godmund Bradwardine, it being the crest of a gigantic Dane, whom he slew in the lists in the Holy Land, on a quarrel touching the chastity of the Emperor's spouse or daughter, tradition saith not precisely which, and thus, as Virgilius hath it –

> Mutemus clypeos, Danaumque insignia nobis
> Aptemus.

Then for the cup, Captain Waverley, it was wrought by the command of St Duthac, Abbot of Aberbrothock, for behoof of another Baron of the house of Bradwardine, who had valiantly defended the patrimony of that monastery against certain encroaching nobles. It is properly termed the Blessed Bear of Bradwardine (though old Dr Doubleit used jocosely to call it Ursa Major), and was supposed in old and Catholic times to be invested with certain properties of a mystical and supernatural quality. And though I give not in to such *anilia*, it is certain it has always been esteemed a solemn standard-cup and heirloom of our house; nor is it ever used but upon seasons of high festival, and such I hold to be the arrival of the heir of Sir Everard under my roof; and I devote this draught to the health and prosperity of the ancient and highly-to-be-honoured house of Waverley.'

During this long harangue he carefully decanted a cobwebbed bottle of claret into the goblet, which held nearly an English pint, and at the conclusion, delivering the bottle to the butler, to be held carefully in the same angle with the horizon, he devoutly quaffed off the contents of the Blessed Bear of Bradwardine.

Edward, with horror and alarm, beheld the animal making his rounds, and thought with great anxiety upon the appropriate motto, 'Beware the Bear'; but at the same time plainly foresaw, that as none of the guests scrupled to do him this extraordinary honour, a refusal on his part to pledge their courtesy would be extremely ill received. Resolving, therefore, to submit to this last piece of tyranny, and then to quit the table, if possible, and confiding in the strength of his constitution, he did justice to the company in the contents of the Blessed Bear, and felt less inconvenience from the draught than he could possibly have expected. The others, whose time had been more actively employed, began to show symptoms of innovation, – 'the good wine did its good office'. The frost of etiquette, and pride of birth, began to give way before the genial blessings of this benign constellation, and the formal appellatives with which the three dignitaries had hitherto addressed each other, were now familiarly abbreviated into Tully, Bally, and Killie. When a few rounds had passed, the two latter, after whispering together, craved permission (a joyful hearing for Edward) to ask the grace-cup. This, after some delay, was at length produced, and Waverley concluded that the orgies of Bacchus were terminated for the evening. He was never more mistaken in his life.

SIR WALTER SCOTT, *Waverley* (1814)

Don't Hesitate

Three years ago, in an extremely swanky joint in London and after the most expensive meal I was ever paid to eat, I was bumbazed, when, in my innocent Scottish way, I asked what malts they had, to be given a look of withering incomprehension. While my eight fellow guests were happily sipping liqueurs I'd never heard of from eight separate countries, consultations and head-noddings resulted, ten minutes later, in a glass being set before me. No name was mentioned (nor had to be: it was Glen Grant). I believe they sent out for it.

The poor English. Yet they have improved, for I learn from Professor Daiches's book that there was a time when the whisky exported to England was actually rectified and turned into – gin. 'For goodness' sake' seems the wrong exclamation.

. . . When people compete in boasting about the oldest whisky they've drunk, I like to ask: what about the youngest? In my case it was half a minute old, a muscular infant that seemed old for its age.

Taking a salmon, shooting a stag, distilling a dram – these were an ordinary part of the life of the Gael, and to this day they see nothing wrong in it. The beady eye of the exciseman has made them realize, of course, it's illegal, which is a very different matter, and it took them some time to submit to that. An interesting statistic Professor Daiches gives us is that in 1823, when I suppose the total population of Scotland was round about two million, there were 14,000 official discoveries of illicit stills. Think of the others.

. . . I have noted with pleasure Professor Daiches's refusal to accept any mystique about the great malts (wine-bibbers, take note). Yet there comes a time when it has to be noticed that one whisky is almost certainly better than another. Next time you're in Tokyo and you're offered a choice between Talisker and King Victoria Finest Scotchman's Whisko, don't hesitate.

NORMAN MacCAIG, from his review of
David Daiches's *Scotch Whisky* in the *Listener* (1969)

A Toast

Scotland, my auld, respected Mither!
Tho' whyles ye moistify your leather,
Till when ye speak, ye aiblins blether;
    Yet deil-mak-matter!
Freedom and Whisky gang thegither,
    Tak aff your whitter.

from ROBERT BURNS, 'The Author's Earnest Cry and Prayer'

Freedom and Whisky

With a warm smile of pleasant embarrassment Donul investigated the liquor curiously and handed the tumbler to Old Hector.

'Now you can speak,' said Red Dougal, 'and I'll try not to interrupt you.'

Old Hector shook his head. 'What I have to say, you already know.'

'Are we deceiving the Revenue?' demanded Red Dougal.

'We are,' responded Old Hector.

'Are we breaking the law?'

'We are.'

'What would happen to us if the three gaugers were to descend upon us at this moment?' pursued Red Dougal.

'Because the largeness of the fine would be far beyond us, you and I would be put in prison for a very long time, but Donul would not be put in prison, for he had not anything to do with this, but only happened to light on us by chance. And you will both remember that story carefully,' said Old Hector.

Red Dougal laughed. 'Have I not cornered you now, hip and beard?'

'Not that I have noticed,' replied Old Hector mildly.

'Haven't I proved you the very fount and origin of law-breaking and all that's wrong?' demanded Red Dougal.

'Law-breaking, yes,' said Old Hector. 'But wrong is a difficult word. Many a day I have pondered over it, but I am not sure that I have found the answer. I only have a feeling about the answer and sometimes I go by that feeling. For, you see, laws are necessary, and to break them is wrong. Yet a law can be wrong.'

'And is a law wrong just because *you* find it wrong?' scoffed Red Dougal.

'Yes,' answered Old Hector.

'But the law that's wrong to you is sure to be right to the other fellow, or it wouldn't be in it. How then?' demanded Red Dougal.

'I still must judge for myself, just like the other fellow. That he may have the power to make me suffer does not, of itself, mean that he is right. It just means that he has the power to make me suffer. But it remains with me to judge for myself the outcome of all the elements and to come to a decision on the matter.'

'What are the elements here? Eh?'

'Many and varied they are,' replied Old Hector. 'This is our old native drink, made in this land from time immemorial. We were the first makers, as you have just said. For untold centuries we had it as our cordial in life, distilled from the barley grown round our doors. In these times, because it was free, it was never abused. That is known. Deceit and abuse and drunkenness came in with the tax, for the folk had to evade the tax because they were poor. The best smuggler in my young days was an Elder of the Church. Before he started making a drop, he used to pray to God, asking Him not to let the gaugers come upon him unawares.'

'I have heard of that,' said Red Dougal. 'Tell me,' he added with a curious look, 'did you put up a few words yourself before we started here?'

'I did,' replied Old Hector, looking back at Red Dougal with his gentle smile.

The laugh that had been ready to come out died inward in Red Dougal, and he looked downward.

'For we do not make this drink to profit by it at the expense of the tax,' proceeded Old Hector. 'We do not sell it. Just as Donul does not sell a saimon he takes out of the River. Nor would we even make it thus for our own use if we could afford to buy it. But we cannot buy it. We are too poor. The men who have made the law have taken our own drink from us, and have not left us wherewith to buy it. Yet they can buy it, because they are rich. I have the feeling that that is not just. I do not grudge them their riches and all it can buy for them.'

'And do you think,' said Dougal, lifting his head, 'that the Sheriff in his court will listen to your fine reasons?'

'I have no foolish notions about that,' replied Old Hector. 'But I am a man whose eightieth birthday is not so far distant, and I had to decide for myself whether my reasons might meet with understanding in a Court higher than the Sheriff's.' There was a pause, and Old Hector looked at the fire. 'There is only one thing,' he added quietly.

'What's that?' asked Red Dougal, eyeing the old man.

'I should not,' said Old Hector, 'like to die in prison.'

NEIL GUNN, *Young Art and Old Hector* (1942)

Toddy and Atholl Brose

Although whisky, in the Highlands at any rate, is still regarded as a spirit not to be adulterated or tampered with, I must admit that there were and are receipts for its use as a medicine and also for the final glory of a feast, receipts far more ancient than the blended whisky which we drink to-day. Of these the best known are toddy and Atholl brose. Toddy, excellent both as a cure for cold and as an elixir of life, requires careful preparation. The ingredients are sugar, boiling water and preferably a well-matured malt whisky. First, you heat the tumbler with warm water and, when the glass has reached a comfortable temperature, you pour out the water. Then into the empty glass you put two or three squares of loaf-sugar and add enough boiling water – a wine-glass should suffice – to dissolve the sugar. Then add a wine-glass of whisky and stir with a silver spoon; then another wine-glass of boiling water, and finally to crown this liquid edifice top it with another wine-glass of whisky. Stir again and drink the contents with slow and loving care. As a cure for cold, take your toddy to bed, put one bowler hat at the foot, and drink until you see two . . .

Atholl brose is a concoction which is drunk in company and on festive occasions like Hogmanay and St Andrew's Day. There are various receipts, but the simplest method is to mix an equal quantity of running heather honey and fine oatmeal in a little cold water. Then, according to the number of your guests, pour in very slowly a well-flavoured malt whisky. Stir the whole contents vigorously until a generous froth rises to the top. Then bottle and cork tightly, keep for two days and serve in the finest bowl that you possess. A pound of oatmeal and a pound of honey will need four pints of whisky, and the quantity required can be reduced or increased in these proportions.

Atholl brose is a giant's drink, and I have vivid memories of the St Andrew's Day I organized in Prague, when we left the making of the brose to the Military Attaché. It was the first St Andrew's Day dinner ever held in the Czechoslovak capital, and the M.A., a Sassenach, resolved that it should not be forgotten. For several days he worked in secret. When the brose was passed round in a magnificent loving cup with two handles, with a guest standing up on each side of the drinker, the fumes were almost overpowering. The M.A. had laced the brose with an over-generous measure of slivovice, the potent plum vodka of Slovakia. He suffered for his intervention in Scottish affairs. After the dinner there were several casualties and the only standing survivors were three Scots and Jan Masaryk.

SIR ROBERT BRUCE LOCKHART, *Scotch* (1951)

Athol Brose

Charm'd with a drink which Highlanders compose,
A German traveller exclaim'd with glee, –
'Potztausend! sare, if dis is Athol Brose,
How goot dere Athol Boetry must be!'

THOMAS HOOD (1799–1845)

Diaspora – Scots Abroad

Prussia

I

Besides the name Schott or Schotte, which came to signify throughout the German Empire a pedlar, and its derivations as 'Schottenkram', 'Schottenhandel', 'Schottenpfaffe', 'Schottenfrau', we have quite a number of traces of the old immigrants in local topography. There is a village called 'Schottland' in the district of Lauenburg, in Pomerania, with eighty-four inhabitants and ten houses; another Schottland in the Danzig lowlands in Western Prussia, numbering some 200 souls; a kirchdorf (village with a church), 'Schottland', in the district of Bromberg in Posen, also numbering about 200 inhabitants. A so-called Schottenkolonie exists near Neuhausen, in the district of Königsberg, Eastern Prussia. There are besides three so-called 'Schottenkrüge' = Scotch inns, one four miles distant from Marienburg, in the Danzig district, another in the district of Marienwerder, a third near the city of Culm, in Western Prussia. What the precise connection of these inns with the Scots was, whether they were at one time in the possession of Scotsmen, or because they were placed in a district where many Scots lived, or finally, because they were much frequented by the Scots – and who would deny the latter eventuality? – it would be difficult to say. They are there, at any rate, witnesses of a dim past, when the country was flooded by Scottish traders.

TH. A. FISCHER,
The Scots in Eastern and Western Prussia (1903)

269

II

A very characteristic element of the population of German towns in Eastern and Western Prussia is formed by the descendants of former Scotsmen. They being exposed to many dangers and persecutions as pedlars, gradually settled in the towns and married daughters of the citizens. The increase in strength and industrial capacity which this Scottish admixture instilled into the German was of the very highest importance, and it can scarcely be doubted that the peculiar compound of stubbornness and shrewdness which characterizes the inhabitants of the small towns of Eastern Prussia has its root in the natural disposition of the Scot.

F. SCHMIDT, *Geschichte des Deutsch Kroner Kreises*

III

The retail merchants of Thorn address a petition to the members of the governing Board of Prussia in 1556. They remind the crown of former prohibitions against Jews, Scots and pedlars who roam about the country to the ruin of the whole country, and they continue: 'These prohibitions are not obeyed. Much adulterated merchandise both in cloths and in silks and groceries is being carried into this land by the Jews and the Scots. They are also objectionable on account of their obstinacy, and their ways of selling. When they travel about the country and perchance arrive at a gentleman's estate, they sell to the steward or his wife not only pepper and saffron, and especially cloth, linen and macheier, but talk them into buying all sorts of groceries. Now when it so happens, and it does happen frequently, that the steward or the stewardess has no money, they· accept not only whey-cheese and butter and especially oats and barley, but all sorts of skins and furs which are secretly purloined from the owner of the estate and given to the Scots for their spurious goods, their false weight and measures. Everybody knows, moreover, how much of what has been spun by our honest womenfolk is pawned to the Scot.'

TH. A. FISCHER,
The Scots in Eastern and Western Prussia (1903)

The plantation of Ulster must be considered as the single successful experiment to the credit of purely Scottish colonization ...

What was the attitude of these Scottish settlers toward the 'natives'? There is no doubt about the answer. It embraces the perennial judgment of the Scot upon the Irishman. Their attitude was one of contempt for those who throughout the official correspondence of the time are referred to as 'the mere Irish'. And it seems that that attitude was encouraged from above. The colonists kept together and did not intermarry with the Irish. They were of a superior race and they meant to keep that race pure. How greatly they succeeded may be proved by a walk along a street in modern Belfast and a study of the names on shops or dwelling-houses. The Scottish visitor to Ulster is amazed to find himself, apparently, at home.

> The men who are driving the carts are like the men at home: the women at the cottage doors are in build and carriage like the mothers of our Southern Highlands: the signs of the little shops in the villages bear well-known names, Paterson, perhaps, or Johnstone, or Sloan. The boy sitting on the dyke with nothing to do, is whistling 'A Man's a Man for a' that'. He goes into a village inn and is served by a six-foot, loosely-hung Scottish borderer worthy to have served drams to the Shepherd and Christopher North: and when he leaves the little inn, he sees by the sign that his host bears the name of 'James Hay' and his wonder ceases ...

The Scottish plantation in Ulster was destined to have important consequences for the Empire. The strongly imperial sentiment in that part of Ireland put a heavy brake upon Ireland's career towards independence. The men of Ulster proved to be neither Scots nor Irishmen, but colonists *pur sang*, and as colonists of the approved pattern they would have none of separation from the Empire.

A. D. GIBB, *Scottish Empire* (1937)

I

In February, 1736, Governor Oglethorpe of Georgia paid a visit to the Highlanders at Darien and found them in their tartan plaids, armed after the fashion of their country with broad swords, small round shields and muskets. Forbidden to carry these weapons in the country from which they came, they were expected to do so on the Georgia frontier, whither they had been brought to provide a defense against the Spaniard and Indian. In compliment to them, Oglethorpe, during the whole time he was with them, dressed himself in Highland costume. Though the Scots had provided him with a fine soft bed, with holland sheets and curtains, the tactful governor chose to lie upon the ground in the open air, between two other gentlemen, wrapped in his cloak, so that all the rest were obliged to follow his example.

When Lachlan Campbell came to America in 1737, the Highland dress he wore 'was then a Novelty in the Country'. The Indians of the Saratoga region, where Campbell went to examine some lands, were so delighted by his unusual appearance that they pressed him and his friends to settle among them. It is said that a party of 350 Highlanders, who landed at Wilmington, North Carolina, threw such a fright into the town officials by their outlandish costume and language that the latter proposed imposing an oath upon the newcomers binding them to keep the peace . . .

The North Carolina settlers of the period 1740–1775 belonged to several clans, and they continued to wear their distinctive costume, including kilt, plaid, and sporran. When Allan Macdonald of Kingsburgh landed in the province in 1774, with his wife Flora, the famous preserver of Prince Charlie, he wore a tartan plaid over his shoulder, a large blue bonnet with a cockade of black ribbon, a tartan waistcoat with gold buttons, and tartan hose. When the *Hector* arrived at Pictou in Nova Scotia with its first cargo of Highland settlers, many of the younger men celebrated by donning their national dress, which some of them were able to round off with the dirk and claymore, while the only piper aboard prepared the way for disembarkation by clearing the neighbouring forests of wild life . . .

*

In 1717 Donald Macpherson, a prisoner of the 1715 rebellion, wrote from exile in Maryland to his father, who lived at Culloden in Inverness-shire. He entrusted the work of penning this remarkable letter to a Scots friend at Portobago, Maryland. The latter had come from Glasgow as a servant. He composed (or perhaps took down syllable for syllable what Macpherson said to him) the message to Scotland in the broad Scots tongue of the Lowlands, but phonetically spelled and with a Highland accent! This letter has been printed in the *Maryland Historical Magazine* without any attempt at translation into a more acceptable form of English. No wonder Macpherson's kindly master promised him a life of ease and supervision of the slaves if he would only learn to speak English like a Virginian, for Donald reported the promise in these words: 'My Mestir says til me, Fan I kan speek lyk de Fouk hier, dat I sanna pi pidden di nating pat gar his Plackimors wurk: for desyt Fouk hier dinna ise te wurk pat de first Yeer after dey kum in te de Quintry: Tey speak a lyke de Sogers in Inerness.' ['My master says to me, when I can speak like the folk here, that I shall not be bidden do nothing but make his blackamoors work; for decent folk here do not use to work but the first year after they come into the country; they speak like the soldiers in Inverness.']

As compared with the frequent references to Scottish loyalism in the period, one may find few examples of active sympathy for the American cause among the immigrants from Scotland. A number of individual careers are fairly well known. The reputations of John Paul Jones, John Witherspoon, James Wilson, Arthur St Clair, Hugh Mercer, and a few other American patriots among the Scots have given a misleading tone to much of what has been written of the so-called 'Scottish contribution' to American independence. These few swallows did not make a summer, and most of the Scots found the egalitarian climate of 1776 too chilly for comfort.

Even among the Virginia merchants, however, there was at least one notable supporter of the patriotic cause. James Hunter the elder of Fredericksburg put his large ironworks at the service of the Revolutionary armies. Although Hunter held aloof from Virginian society, another Scot, a young merchant named Jack Cunningham, 'noisy, droll, waggish, yet civil in his way and wholly inoffensive,' appeared in Virginia drawing rooms.

At one party he was observed to join a crowd who were toasting the Sons of America and singing 'Liberty Songs'. Cunningham was very much the exception to the rule. It has been said, indeed, that the failure of the Scots merchants to adapt themselves to the social life of Virginia and to become absorbed and accepted in Virginia society partly explains their inability to furnish a permanent mercantile class strong enough to survive the Revolution . . .

After the Revolution, Highland immigration to the United States grew in volume with each succeeding decade. Checked by the first French war (1793–1801) and by the War of 1812, the Highlanders recommenced the flow as soon as peace came.

Many of those who left during the nineteenth century, of course, went to more recently opened colonies of the British Empire. Canada was a favourite target of the Highlanders. The earliest settlements in Nova Scotia antedated the American Revolution, while those in Ontario and New Brunswick had been established in 1783, largely by Scottish loyalists from the south.

By 1890 so much of the Highlands had been depopulated that the sources of supply for immigrants were almost cut off. Many of the Western Isles of Scotland had lost three-quarters of their population. The monuments to this century of uprooting are the thousands of ruined cottages whose stunted walls now give shelter only to sheep.

Yet the greatest decade of Scottish emigration to the United States, so far as sheer numbers go, was the 1920s. In these ten years of postwar blight, the exodus consisted largely of unemployed Lowlanders. More than 300,000 of them went to America in that period, putting the whole movement of the eighteenth century in the shade.

In spite of the relatively small scale of the eighteenth-century migration, the influence of Scots as a national group, and even as individuals, was far greater than at any subsequent time. Filling political and administrative offices, the professions, and the ranks of commerce with energetic leaders, the Scots of the Age of Reason aroused the envy and malice of many Englishmen and Americans. In the nineteenth century, the Scots immigrants, in spite of their greater numbers, were lost in the general ferment of mass movement to the New

World and the rapid growth of the United States. The names of a few important individuals alone have stood the test of time in the history books – Frances Wright, Andrew Carnegie, Alexander Graham Bell, Philip Murray.

IAN C. C. GRAHAM, *Colonists from Scotland* (1956)

II

The boy born at Arbigland in Scotland on 6 July 1747 and christened John, who later added Jones to his surname Paul, and who was generally known as Paul Jones during the height of his naval career, had a complex character and far from a simple career. Born in obscurity and poverty, he rose through his own efforts to be a distinguished naval officer and a prominent figure at the Court of Versailles. He professed to have fallen in love with America at first sight, and declared undying allegiance to the new nation; but the last five years of his life were spent in Europe. On many occasions he wrote that he had drawn his sword from pure love of liberty as a 'citizen of the world'; but he drew it for the last time in the service of the greatest despot of Europe, Imperial Catherine. He affected contempt for family and rank; but he longed to be accepted by the county families of Scotland, and his happiest years were spent in Paris under the shadow of royalty as *le Chevalier Paul Jones*. He professed to be indifferent to wealth; but no naval officer strove longer and more strenuously than he to exact the last penny due to him and his men for prize money. He could be tougher and rougher than the most apelike sailor on his ships; yet, when entertaining ladies on board or ashore, his manners were those of a very fastidious gentleman. He pretended total indifference to fame, but he took every possible means to place a far from modest estimate of himself before the public of two continents.

And well did he succeed in this effort. Today, for every one who has heard of his fellow captains of the young Continental Navy, such as Manley, Wickes, Barry and Biddle, thousands have heard of John Paul Jones. Benjamin Disraeli, an early biographer, remembered that 'the nurses of Scotland hushed their crying charges by the whisper of his name', and called attention to the penny chapbooks in which Paul Jones was depicted 'in all the plenitude of terrific glory, the rival of

Blackbeard and the worthy successor of the Buccaneers'. A ballad exalting him was struck off the press while the smoke of battle was still hovering off the English coast, and a Dutch song, 'Here comes Paul Jones, that fine fellow', is still sung by schoolchildren in the Netherlands. With women he was a seagoing Casanova; and the untangling of his many love affairs is an exacting, if amusing, task for a biographer. His remains, buried in a forgotten cemetery outside Paris, were disinterred over a century after his death, transferred with due ceremony to the United States, and placed in a marble sarcophagus under the Naval Academy chapel in a setting comparable to Napoleon's at the Invalides.

Yet, first and always, Paul Jones was a fighting sailor. In the history of the United States Navy, whose rise to be the greatest navy in the world he desired and foretold, Paul Jones now occupies a place comparable only with that of Nelson in the Royal Navy of Great Britain. And, although he never had Nelson's opportunities for fame, I have no doubt that, given them, he would have proved himself to be a great naval tactician and strategist. In the board-to-board, hand-to-hand sea fights in which he did engage, he was without peer.

SAMUEL ELIOT MORISON, John Paul Jones (1959)

III

Against the crimes of the French Revolution and of Bonaparte may be set two compensating benefactions: the Revolution broke the chains of the *ancien régime* and of the Church, and made of a nation of abject slaves a nation of freemen; and Bonaparte instituted the setting of merit above birth, and also so completely stripped the divinity from royalty, that whereas crowned heads in Europe were gods before, they are only men, since, and can never be gods again, but only figure-heads, and answerable for their acts like common clay. Such benefactions as these compensate the temporary harm which Bonaparte and the Revolution did, and leave the world in debt to them for these great and permanent services to liberty, humanity, and progress.

Then comes Sir Walter Scott with his enchantments, and by his single might checks this wave of progress, and even turns it back; sets the world in love with dreams and phantoms; with decayed and swinish forms of religion; with decayed and degraded systems of government; with the sillinesses and emptinesses, sham grandeurs, sham gauds, and sham chivalries of a brainless and worthless long-vanished society. He did measureless harm; more real and lasting harm, perhaps, than any other individual that ever wrote. Most of the world has now outlived good part of these harms, though by no means all of them; but in our South they flourish pretty forcefully still. Not so forcefully as half a generation ago, perhaps, but still forcefully. There, the genuine and wholesome civilization of the nineteenth century is curiously confused and commingled with the Walter Scott Middle-Age sham civilization; and so you have practical, common-sense, progressive ideas, and progressive works, mixed up with the duel, the inflated speech, and the jejune romanticism of an absurd past that is dead, and out of charity ought to be buried. But for the Sir Walter disease, the character of the Southerner – or Southron, according to Sir Walter's starchier way of phrasing it – would be wholly modern, in place of modern and mediæval mixed, and the South would be fully a generation further advanced than it is. It was Sir Walter that made every gentleman in the South a Major or a Colonel, or a General or a Judge, before the war; and it was he, also, that made these gentlemen value these bogus decorations. For it was he that created rank and caste down there, and also reverence for rank and caste, and pride and pleasure in them. Enough is laid on slavery, without fathering upon it these creations and contributions of Sir Walter.

Sir Walter had so large a hand in making Southern character, as it existed before the war, that he is in great measure responsible for the war. It seems a little harsh toward a dead man to say that we never should have had any war but for Sir Walter; and yet something of a plausible argument might, perhaps, be made in support of that wild proposition. The Southerner of the American Revolution owned slaves; so did the Southerner of the Civil War: but the former resembles the latter as an Englishman resembles a Frenchman. The change of character can be traced rather more easily to Sir Walter's influence than to that of any other thing or person . . .

A curious exemplification of the power of a single book for good or harm is shown in the effects wrought by 'Don Quixote' and those wrought by 'Ivanhoe'. The first swept the world's admiration for the mediæval chivalry-silliness out of existence; and the other restored it. As far as our South is concerned, the good work done by Cervantes is pretty nearly a dead letter, so effectually has Scott's pernicious work undermined it.

MARK TWAIN, Life on the Mississippi (1883)

IV

As he was ultimately one of the wealthiest men the world has known, and as his biography is one of the outstanding success stories of all time, he can hardly be described as typical, yet there are many features in his career which were typical of nineteenth-century Scottish emigration. Born in Dunfermline in 1835, the son of a damask weaver, he came of a family which knew the vicissitudes consequent on industrial changes: his grandfather, a leather merchant, was ruined, like many others, when peace and demobilization came in 1815; his father had prospered to the extent that he had four or five looms in the lower storey of the house, with the living quarters upstairs, until 'The change from hand-loom to steam-loom weaving was disastrous to our family'. His father found himself without employment, his mother had to open a small shop, but two sisters of hers were already in Pittsburgh, and the Carnegies made the decision to sell off their looms and other movables and emigrate too. Even after they had realized all they could, they still had to borrow £20 to make up the sum they required. When they left in 1848, they travelled from Glasgow on a sailing ship, rather than a steamship, in order to economize, and had a seven weeks' voyage. These were the beginnings of the man who during his later life gave away over 350,000,000 dollars.

Carnegie's family had a strong tradition of radicalism and unorthodoxy. Some of his kinsmen had been involved in agitation against the Corn Laws, and Dunfermline was something of a radical centre, where it was not uncommon to express a preference for republican America. Even when Carnegie prospered and himself lived in a castle, he never surrendered his dislike of monarchy, as was discovered by those who once asked him to subscribe to a memorial to Scotland's patriot king, Robert Bruce. He replied as follows:

Dungeness, Ga., Mch. 12.87

My Dear Sir,

I cannot feel much interest in Kings or in any who occupied or do occupy positions, not by merit, but by Birth. Let the successors of such build monuments to their predecessors, or those who can live contentedly under institutions which deny them equality.

I am too staunch a Republican, Hate with a bitter hatred and resent as an insult to my manhood, the Monarchical idea.

A king is an insult to every other man in the land.

You see, my dear sir, why, entertaining such sentiments, I cannot give you 30£ to commemorate even one who was better than his class. Perish Kings and Queens and privilege in all its forms.

If you have a Man of the People who is thought worthy of a monument – or of assistance and you obtain subscriptions for this man, I'll send my 30£ to that fund, but not a penny for all the Kings and Queens in Christendom.

Sincerely yours,

Andrew Carnegie

. . . In his boyhood in Dunfermline, Carnegie had often admired the beautiful grounds of Pittencrieff Glen, which were in private hands, and he fulfilled a long-standing ambition when his wealth ultimately allowed him to purchase these grounds and present them to his native town. In his early days in America, when he was educating himself, he owed much to the generosity of a gentleman who opened his library to working boys, and this determined the line in philanthropy with which Carnegie's name is perhaps most often linked – the provision of Free Libraries. It was noble, too, in a man who himself had no professional training, that he established the Carnegie Trust for the Universities of Scotland, which for many years assisted the majority of Scottish students to pay their fees, in the days before grants from other sources were available, and which more recently has concentrated on aiding research. Carnegie's other benefactions were many and various, but his native town was always closest to his heart: it was in

Dunfermline that he established his first free public library, as early as 1881, and the Carnegie Dunfermline Trust continues to benefit the town in a variety of ways. He remarked that 'what Benares is to the Hindoo, Mecca to the Mohammedan, Jerusalem to the Christian, all that Dunfermline is to me'.

GORDON DONALDSON, *The Scots Overseas* (1966)

Canada – Southern Ontario

Not even in the Western Isles are the Scotch to be found in more concentrated solution. Beginning at the Currie Road were first the McPhails and Grahams, then more Grahams, McFarlanes, the McKeller property, Camerons, Morrisons, Gows, Galbraiths, McCallums, more McPhails, more Morrisons, Pattersons, and, among others, the McLeods. Along the way were the Gilroys, who may not have been Scotch, and a man by the name of Malone. He had moved out from town in very recent times, it was said for his health. But Hogg Street was not exceptional in its commitment to the Highlands, and many parts of the township were much more specialized as to clan. To the north, around a hamlet called Cowal, nearly everyone was named McCallum. The Campbells were similarly grouped around another minute village bearing the not inappropriate name of Campbellton. One or two roads were occupied more or less exclusively by Grahams. In the larger towns, those of four or five hundred people and upward, one encountered a measure of racial diversity. Along the Lake, a few families of Irish extraction fished and supported a small Catholic church. And a few prosperous farmers on the immediate shore traced their ancestry to the disgruntled Tories who came to Canada after the American Revolution. In Canada the Tory émigrés are called United Empire Loyalists, and it is known that they migrated out of affection for the King and a deep commitment to personal liberty. Elsewhere there was a scattering of English and Irish names. But nearly everyone was Scotch. Certainly it never occurred to us that a well-regulated community could be populated by any other kind of people. We referred to ourselves as Scotch and not Scots. When, years later, I learned that the usage in Scotland was different it seemed to me rather an affectation ...

An enduring problem among the Scotch was that of personal nomenclature. As I have noted, a certain number of the clans transported themselves to Canada in bulk or, in any case, reformed their ranks quickly on arrival. McCallums, Campbells, Grahams, and McKillops were exceptionally numerous. That so many had the same surname would not have been serious had they not so often had the same Christian names as well. To call a son something other than John was to combine mild eccentricity with unusual imagination. And even an unusual imagination did not normally extend beyond Dan, Jim, Angus, Duncan, or Malcolm. A fair proportion of the people we knew were called John McCallum. The John Grahams and the John Campbells were almost equally numerous.

The Scotch eliminated the danger of confusion by giving everyone a nickname. The parents having failed, the neighbours stepped in. The nickname might turn on some feature of a man's farm or location; most often it was inspired by some prominent personal trait. Since an unpleasant trait invariably makes a stronger impression than an agreeable one, the nicknames were usually unflattering and often offensive.

There were Big Johns and Little Johns and once there had been Wee Johns, but this form had gone out of use. There was also Black John and Johnny Ruah, the latter being Gaelic for red and referring not to politics but to beard and complexion. More regrettably there was (or within recent memory had been) a Lame John, a Dirty John, a Lazy John, numerous Old Johns, a Bald John, a Nosey John, and a Piggy John who was named for the number of, and his own resemblance to, his livestock. Most of the McCallums were Presbyterians; one who was not bore the proud name of John the Baptist ...

One of the great McKillop clan was always known as Codfish John. (Dried codfish was the cheapest form of protein available in the winter months. It was universally detested and a man who fed it to his family, hired hand or the neighbour who, in accordance with the custom of the community, might drop in unannounced for a meal, was suspected of stinginess.) Many stories were told of Codfish John's economies. When he was finally being lowered into his grave at Black's cemetery west of Wallacetown, it was said that he lifted the cover of the coffin and handed out his coat, waistcoat, pants, and under-shirt. That was not widely believed. But he did warn his wife to take up the parlour carpet before the funeral.

Interestingly, it was always said of Codfish John, as of any-one else who was excessively frugal, that he was 'very Scotch'.

J. K. GALBRAITH, The Non-potable Scotch (1967)

Australia

I

The Scots, along with the Jews, have probably been the great ethnic success story in Australian history. Some Irish Australian friends of mine once demanded to know what the Scots, as compared with the Irish, had achieved in Australia. 'Well,' I replied, 'we own it.' The enormous number of Scots and Scottish descendants, in proportion to our share of the population, who have been leaders in commerce, in politics, in education, in military matters and in the pastoral industry is pretty well known, even in the absence of any really compre-hensive and respectable study of the Scottish part in Australian history. Which is an amazing lack, when you think about it. Even though Australian politics has sometimes seemed a per-petual struggle between one Irish and two Scots parties, it has been the Irish who have attracted the historians and the explainers of our nation's culture. The Irish have been more visible, and more tragic, though there is a sadness at the heart of Scottish success which might yield much to a scholar prepared to probe deeply. And this sadness may also have a bit to do with my first surprising claim, namely, that another field in which we have been active and successful in a measure way out of proportion to our numbers is poetry. Just under one-tenth of Australia's population has so far produced between a fifth and a quarter of the country's poets. Ethnic satisfaction quite aside, this is a mystery and a breach of stereotype, which I am con-cerned to understand. And it leads into other mysteries which are anything but comfortable.

LES A. MURRAY, 'The Bonnie Disproportion'
in Persistence in Folly: Selected Prose Writings (1984)

More successful, more ruthless, and with a better head for business, Angus Macmillan of Bushy Park had been born in Glenbrittle in Skye in 1810, the fourth of 15 sons. A man of substance, he had paid £55 for a cabin in which he emigrated to Sydney in 1838 with a letter of introduction to another Skyeman, Captain Lachlan Macalister, and quickly gained employment as a station overseer at Camden in New South Wales. Very soon he looked south to new lands for settlement on his own account. Financed in part by Macalister, and animated by a self-confessed godly mission, Macmillan undertook much arduous and exacting exploration in the southern limit of the colony. With the aid of aboriginal guides (he possessed 'a peculiar capacity for winning the fidelity of the natives') this hardened frontiersman opened up large tracts of country and earned the title of 'the Gippsland pioneer'. Eventually he carved out a territory for himself at Bairnsdale. It was land for cattle and sheep, hard won from the aborigines. When, during 1843, he came across the mutilated body of Ronald Macalister (the fifth white in the locality so treated) the Skyeman assembled a posse of 20 settlers (mainly Scots – called 'Macmillan's Highland Brigade') and surprised a body of blacks at Warrigal Creek. It was thought that 150 aborigines died in the slaughter. Macmillan himself thought that the country thereabouts was a suitable refuge for his fellow Highlanders: it was 'Country capable of supporting all my starving countrymen'. Indeed the district attracted a cluster of *emigré* Highlanders, usually men of means, but their record, here at least, was not one of financial success. Hal Porter's opinion was that

> seemingly intoxicated by space and affronted by freedom, their wits dislocated, they plunged too many irons in the fire, found themselves momentary lords of tracts of land too far-spreading properly to look after, and victims of their own tangled visions.

Perhaps the leap from land-hunger in Scotland to Victoria was too much for the mind.

ERIC RICHARDS,
'Australia and the Scottish Connection 1788–1914'
in ed. R. A. Cage, *The Scots Abroad: Labour,
Capital, Enterprise, 1750–1914* (1985)

I

It was in 1842 that the concept of planting a 'New Edinburgh' in New Zealand originated in the mind of George Rennie, a sculptor. According to his ideas, the colony, as befitted a Scottish one, was to be Presbyterian, but there was no notion at this stage of making it narrowly sectarian. In 1843, however, came the Disruption and the formation of the Free Church of Scotland, and the plan for a 'New Edinburgh' fell into the hands of men who set aside Rennie's broader views in favour of a strictly Free Church settlement. Otago was selected as the objective in 1844, and the Lay Association of the Free Church of Scotland arranged to buy from the New Zealand Company 2,400 lots, each of 60 acres, or 144,000 acres in all. These lots were to be sold to emigrants at £2 an acre.

Active leadership passed to the Reverend Thomas Burns (1796–1871) and Captain William Cargill (1784–1860). Burns, a nephew of the poet Robert Burns, had withdrawn from the Church of Scotland in 1843 to join the Free Church; Cargill was a veteran of the Peninsular War who characteristically claimed descent from the covenanting 'martyr' Donald Cargill, although the martyr had no recorded legitimate descendants. Burns sailed, with 247 persons, in the *Philip Laing* from the Clyde on 27th November 1847 and had a voyage of 117 days, arriving on 15th April 1848. Life during the voyage was carefully regulated, to provide for public worship, the education of the children, sound feeding and medical attention, but inevitably there was a good deal of misery when stormy conditions prevailed. Captain Cargill sailed, with ninety-seven persons, on the *John Wickliffe* from the Thames on 24th November 1847, and had a slightly shorter voyage, arriving on 22nd March 1848. On the *John Wickliffe*, as on the *Philip Laing*, careful provision was made for the health of the emigrants – the surgeons were each to receive a gratuity of £25, less £1 in respect of each death which took place on the voyage – and the *John Wickcliffe* had, among the stores for the colony, a considerable quantity of religious and informative books; but the *John Wickliffe*'s passengers were so mixed that the religious and moral standards of the *Philip Laing* could not be maintained on board her . . .

Although growth in Otago was at first slow, and in 1854 the total population was only 2,400, of whom 700 were in Dunedin, the area continued, thanks to the propagandists, to attract a certain flow of emigrants direct from Scotland, before as well as after a fresh attraction arose with the discovery of gold in Otago in 1861. Individual examples of colonists are – James Barr, from Glasgow, 1849; James Macandrew, from Aberdeen, 1850; John Barr, from Paisley, 1852; Alexander Begg, from Edinburgh, 1859; William Barron, from Edinburgh, 1861; Alexander and John Bathgate, from Edinburgh, 1863. But, in addition to Scots direct from home, such a peculiarly Scottish settlement as Otago drew a certain number of Scots from other parts of New Zealand: James Allan, for instance, who had settled with his parents at Nelson in 1842, when he was eighteen, subsequently became a successful farmer and stockbreeder in Otago; and Archibald Anderson, one of the 1839 immigrants to Port Nicholson, moved to Otago in 1845 and took land at Inch Clutha and Stirling. Some came even from outside New Zealand: Arthur Beverley had emigrated from Aberdeen to Melbourne in 1852 and came on to Dunedin in 1856; Edward McGlashan was in Adelaide, Melbourne and Sydney before he reached Dunedin in 1850; Donald Ferguson, from Argyll, joined his uncle on a sheep farm in Australia in 1851 and in 1862 went on to Otago, where he was a successful cattle-breeder. Fewer colonists seem to have left Otago, but George Thomson Chapman, after being a missionary teacher in Otago, went off to the Victoria goldfield and finished up in Auckland.

The peculiar appeal of the Dunedin area did not, however, mean that no Scots went to other parts of New Zealand in the middle of the nineteenth century. In the extreme south end of South Island, in what came to be the separate province of Southland, there was a Scottish settlement at Invercargill, formed in 1857. And in the far north of North Island, the Nova Scotian Highlanders, under the leadership of Norman MacLeod, settled at Waipu, north of Auckland, where by 1860 there was a community about a thousand strong. Apart from such settlements, individual Scots made their way to a variety of places . . .

A remarkable illustration of the attraction of New Zealand is provided by the career of James Meiklejohn. He was an

Edinburgh sea-captain who for years had been engaged in building ships in Prince Edward Island and sailing them to Great Britain, where he sold them. In 1856 he embarked his family on a ship he had built and put to sea, determined to cruise until he found a place which specially appealed to him. After a year or more he came to New Zealand, where he decided to settle, and acquired land at Big Omaha in North Island, where he resumed ship-building.

GORDON DONALDSON, *The Scots Overseas* (1966)

II

When to New Zealand first I cam,
Poor and duddy, poor and duddy,
When to New Zealand first I cam,
It was a happy day, sirs,
For I was fed on parritch thin,
My taes they stickit thro' my shoon,
I riggit at the pouken pin,
But I couldna mak it pay, sirs.

Nae mair the laird comes for his rent,
For his rent, for his rent,
Nae mair the laird comes for his rent,
When I hae nocht tae pay, sirs.

Nae mair he'll tak me aff the loom,
Wi' hanging lip and pouches toom,
To touch my hat and boo to him,
The like was never kent, sirs.

At my door cheeks there's bread and cheese,
I work or no, just as I please,
I'm fairly settled at my ease,
And that's the way o't noo, sirs.

JOHN BARR,
Poems and Songs, Descriptive and Satirical (1861)

India is the corn chest for Scotland where we poor gentry must
send our younger sons as we send our black cattle to the south.

SIR WALTER SCOTT, in a letter (1821)

'Henry IX, King of Scotland' was the nickname given to Henry
Dundas, later Lord Melville, the most powerful man in Scottish
politics from 1766 onwards, when he was appointed Solicitor-
General for Scotland. A Tory and a despot, given a free hand by
George III's government in London, there were many who had
little cause to love him in Scotland. Yet he had immense
powers of patronage in his hands, and it was thanks to him that
the Scots began to play a major part in the administration of
British India.

The series of wars which broke out in the last quarter of the
18th century were dominated by some of the great names from
Scottish military history. First, there was Sir Hector Munro, the
commander-in-chief, who had already gained great fame at
the battle of Buxar in 1764, which may rank as one of the most
decisive battles for the British in India by asserting definitive
control over Bengal. His career in the south was less auspicious,
however, and in 1780 the British suffered one of their worst
defeats at the hands of Hyder Ali, the Raja of Mysore, which
resulted in the imprisonment of the British officers under
extremely harsh conditions. An interesting sidelight on the
Scottishness of the senior command of the army in India is
Munro's remark that he had not preserved copies of his notes to
Colonel Baillie, 'except one or two Erse ones. . . . The having no
cypher made me write those in Erse, as they were of some consequence.' Sir Hector came from Novar, in Ross-shire, where he
was buried in 1805, and a neighbouring hill is still crowned by
the 'Indian Temple', erected on his instructions as a means of
alleviating local unemployment. Sir Hector had a tragic personal loss when his only son, who was picnicking with a group
of friends on Sagar Island, near Calcutta, was suddenly carried
off by a tiger. A member of the party related how 'in a moment
his head was in the beast's mouth and it rushed into the

287

jungle with him, with as much ease as I could lift a kitten'.

David Baird of Newbyth had just arrived in India when Colonel Baillie's force was overwhelmed by Hyder Ali's army in 1780, and it was only after three and a half years' imprisonment that he and about thirty other survivors were allowed free from Seringapatam. The British prisoners taken by Hyder Ali were chained together in pairs. 'I pity the man wha's chained to oor Davie', commented his mother laconically. In the meantime, Hyder Ali had been succeeded by his son, Tipu Sultan, a man of an equally sadistic nature. His favourite toy was a full scale mechanical tiger engaged in the act of devouring a European. By means of the moveable parts, the tiger could be seen to enjoy its feast and the European his appropriate anguish, and devices like those of an organ made suitable roaring and shrieking noises. Curiously enough, the British delighted in a Sheffield-ware figure – though not full-scale – of Sir Hector Munro's son being mauled by a tiger . . .

Bishop Heber, who wrote the hymn 'From Greenland's icy mountains, From India's coral strand', records a meeting with Sir David in 1823. 'We passed Sir David Ochterlony and his suite on his road to Bhurtpoor. There certainly was a very considerable number of led horses, elephants, palanqueens, and covered carriages, belonging chiefly, I apprehend (besides his own family), to the families of his native servants. There was an escort of two companies of infantry, a troop of regular cavalry, and I should guess forty or fifty irregulars, on horse and foot, armed with spears and matchlocks of all possible forms; the string of camels was a very long one, and the whole procession was what might pass in Europe for that of an eastern prince travelling.' The Bishop probably knew, but forebore to tell his readers, that Sir David's family consisted of several wives (thirteen, it was said) whom he used to parade round Delhi, each on the back of an elephant . . .

John Malcolm was the son of a Borders farmer. When he was interviewed by the Directors of the Company in 1781, at the age of twelve, he was asked, 'My little man, what would you do if you were to meet Haidar Ali the Sultan of Mysore?' Malcolm replied promptly, 'Do? Why, I'd oot wi' my sword and cut aff his heid!' He was immediately accepted for service into the Company's army. For the rest of his life, he was known as 'Boy' Malcolm, even when he rose to become Governor of Bombay . . .

Mountstuart Elphinstone arrived in India in 1795 at the age of sixteen, with all the confidence of the son of one of Scotland's greatest noble families, the Lords Elphinstone of Elphinstone in Stirlingshire, and a nephew of one of the Company's Board of Directors. He started what was to be one of the most important careers in the governance of India at the Residency of Poona. His career coincided with one of Britain's expansionist periods. The Governor-General was supreme from Calcutta to Delhi, and the south was secure. In the middle was the huge Maratha confederacy which was about to disintegrate, with Britain moving into the power vacuum, and Elphinstone was centrally situated as Resident at Nagpur. His purely Indian activities were interrupted by his mission to the King of Kabul in 1808, another small part in the global conflict between Britain and France. Nothing of diplomatic value resulted, but he left to posterity a very important book, *Account of the Kingdom of Cabool*, a work in which he was encouraged by Sir James Mackintosh 'the learned Recorder of Bombay'. Along with Malcolm, he presided over the final stage of the break-up of the Maratha confederacy, and from his Residency at Poona dealt with the court of the Peshwa, the ruler of the state which immediately surrounded Bombay. The campaign was not a particularly brilliant one, but it ended with the utter defeat of the Peshwa, and the end of any possible revival of the Marathas. Another splash of red was added to the map of India . . .

Whether Alexander Gardner was a lovable rogue or merely a rogue is a question that cannot be easily answered. Accounts of his life, including his own, suggest that he was of Scottish, Irish and Aztec ancestry (the first two being probable; the latter most unlikely), and had a beautiful Afghani wife who disappeared in a massacre. He was basically an adventurer, who took advantage of the complete breakdown of Moghul power in northwestern India, the various forays by the Afghanis in their eastwards expansion, and the attempt by Ranjit Singh to develop a western-style army of Sikhs which would occupy the vacuum. Gardner appears to have arrived at Lahore in 1831, and was subsequently involved in many of the murders and atrocities which were connected with the period of anarchy that followed the death of Ranjit Singh, and, indeed, personally performed the mutilation of one of his enemies, Jodha Ram. As Sikh power was gradually reduced, he entered into the profitable trade of purchasing old cannonballs, retired northwards to the service of the Kashmiri army, and died at Sialkot in 1877. Confusing things to the last, he gave his age as 98, although he was at least twenty years younger. The celebrated photograph of him taken in old age portrays him in a garment entirely of his own invention, 'clothed from head to foot in the 79th tartan, but fashioned by a native tailor. Even his pagri was of tartan, and it was adorned with the egret's plume, only allowed to persons of high rank.'

James Skinner was, to say the least, an unexpected figure. His father, Hercules Skinner, was a Scotsman in the service of the East India Company, the son of a Provost of Montrose. Another branch of the family was the commercial firm of Skinner and Co., one of the most eminent in Bombay. Hercules Skinner distinguished himself not only in the field, rising to be a Lieutenant-Colonel, but also by marrying a Rajput princess, known to the family as 'Jeany'. The early days of the Company had seen many mixed marriages, and, indeed, they had been encouraged in the absence of British women ('better a Hindu or a Muslim than a Portuguese Roman Catholic', would have been the sentiment at the Company's headquarters), but with the increase in the numbers of British women coming out to India, such marriages and liaisons were actively discouraged. From 1792 onwards, 'no person, the son of a native Indian, shall henceforth be appointed by this Court to appointments in the Civil, Military, or Marine services of the country'. Young James Skinner's military career was, therefore, dependent on his joining the army of a native prince, so in 1796 he joined in with the Scindia of Gwalior, leader of the Marathas, who, at that time, was in fact master of Delhi, and a threat to British security.

However, the Scindia found himself unable to rely on loyalties which might be in conflict, so all British or Anglo-Indian officers in his service were dismissed. Skinner, in the company of two other Scotsmen, Captain Kenneth Stuart and Captain George Carnegie, had to seek the protection of the British Army. Welcomed by the Commander-in-Chief, General

Lake, Skinner was asked if he would care to raise a regiment of irregular horse in the British service. It would be an entirely new type of unit, distinct from the regular cavalry but trained for skirmishing. Though at first doubtful, Skinner agreed, and 1803 saw the foundation of Skinner's Horse, to this day the crack regiment of the Indian cavalry. Sikander Sahib's Yellow Boys, as they became known, were a striking regiment, in their yellow tunics with a red turban and cummerbund edged with silver for the men. For the officers, he chose a dark blue jacket with silver facings, a red and gold striped cummerbund, white buckskin breeches, black Wellingtons, and a dragoon helmet with a white cockade. Their flag bore the griffin's head and bloody hand of the Skinner family, which was also tattooed on the stomach – a means of identification in case the head should be severed from the body.

The abolition of discrimination against Anglo-Indians in 1833 permitted full integration into British Indian society. Visitors came to see Lieutenant-Colonel Skinner, 'Nasir-ud-Dowlah Colonel James Skinner Bahadur Ghalib Jang', according to the title given him by the Emperor of Delhi: 'Most exalted victorious in war'. The Eden sisters, Emily and Fanny, found that he was the person they liked best in Delhi, though Emily described him in *Up the Country* as 'very black', and said that he spoke broken English. In fact he spoke Persian fluently, and wrote his memoirs in that language. He has a permanent memorial in the Church of St James in Delhi, opposite his house at the Kashmir gate. Opposite his church, he had also built a mosque, 'because he said that one way or the other he should be sure to go to heaven', said Emily Eden. Emily Metcalfe, daughter of the Delhi Resident of the time, wrote in a letter: 'It was difficult to tell what the religion of the family was . . . One son called Joe Skinner was a marvellous creation, as you may imagine when I tell you that his visiting dress consisted of a green cloth cutaway coat, with gilt buttons (or possibly gold as they were very pretty), very light claret-coloured trousers, patent leather boots, white waistcoat, and gilt buttons, and a white necktie. He always carried a gold-mounted Malacca cane.' Skinner was thought to have at least fourteen wives, though by what kind of ceremony he married them was not always clear.

ALEX M. CAIN, *The Cornchest for Scotland: Scots in India* (1986)

I

We believe it is Sir Archibald Alison who mentions how, when Marshal Keith was combating the Turkish forces under the Grand Vizier, the two generals came to a conference with each other; the Grand Vizier came mounted on a camel, in all the pomp of Eastern magnificence; the Scotch Marshal Keith, who originally came from the neighbourhood of Turiff, in Aberdeenshire, approached on horseback. After the conference the Turkish Grand Vizier said to Keith that he would like to speak a few words in private to him, in his tent, and begged that no one should accompany him; Marshal Keith accordingly went in, and the moment they conferred, the Grand Vizier threw off his turban, tore off his beard, and running to Marshal Keith, said, 'Oh, Johnnie, foo's a' wi' ye, man?' and he then discovered that the Grand Vizier of Turkey was a schoolfellow of his own who had disappeared about thirty years before from a parish school near Methlic. And we remember to have met with an anecdote of a Scotchman from Perth, who had penetrated into some far interior of Asia – we forget where; he had to see the Pasha, or Bashaw. He was introduced to the comely man in his tent. They gathered up their knees, and sat down upon their carpets. They drank their strong coffee, and smoked their hookahs together in solemn silence; few words, at any rate, passed between them, but, we may trust, sufficient for the occasion; but when the man of Perth was about to leave, the Pasha also arose, and, following him outside the tent, said, in good strong Doric Scotch, 'I kenned ye vera weel in Perth; ye are just sae and sae.' The Perth man was astonished, as well he might be, until the Pasha explained, as he said, 'I'm just a Perth man mysel'!' He had travelled, and he had become of importance to the Government there. His story was not very creditable. In the expectation of the post he filled, he had become a Mohammedan. But he was an illustration of the ubiquity of his race.

PAXTON HOOD, *Scottish Characteristics* (1883)

As a postscript to the story of both missions we may quote from an incident recounted by the historian and journalist D. Mackenzie Wallace, who was travelling through the Caucasus in the 1870s. He had noticed the name 'Shotlandskaia koloniia' on a map of the district he was in. His curiosity aroused, he visited the place itself but could obtain no information on any Scots living there until advised to consult an old man who lived at the end of the village. He then recalls:

> . . . I found a venerable old man, with fine venerable features of the Circassian type, coal-black sparkling eyes, and a long grey beard that would have done honour to a patriarch. To him I explained briefly, in Russian, the object of my visit, and asked whether he knew any Scotsmen in the district.
>
> 'And why do you wish to know?' he replied, in the same language, fixing me with his keen, sparkling eyes.
>
> 'Because I am myself a Scotsman and hoped to find fellow-countrymen here.'
>
> Let the reader imagine my astonishment when, in reply to this, he answered in genuine broad Scotch, 'Oh, man, I'm a Scotsman tae! My name is John Abercrombie. Did you never hear tell o' John Abercrombie, the famous Edinburgh doctor?'
>
> I was fairly puzzled by this extraordinary declaration. Dr Abercrombie's name was familiar to me as that of a medical practitioner and writer on psychology, but I knew that he was long since dead. When I had recovered a little from my surprise, I ventured to remark to the enigmatical personage before me that, though his tongue was certainly Scotch, his face was as certainly Circassian.
>
> 'Weel, weel,' he replied, evidently enjoying my look of mystification, 'you're no far wrang. I'm a Circassian Scotsman!'

It turned out that Abercrombie had been one of the children purchased by the Karass missionaries to be brought up as a Christian. As the money for his purchase had been subscribed by Dr John Abercrombie he had, on being baptized, taken the latter's name. Having learnt the trade of printing at Karass, he had worked for the missionaries at Selenginsk in that capacity for several years until the mission closed. Afterwards he had returned to the Caucasus and remained there as one of the last living relics of two heroically unsuccessful enterprises.

J. R BOWLES,
'From the Banks of the Neva to the Shores of Lake Baikal'
in *The Caledonian Phalanx: Scots in Russia* (1987)

Transported Jacobites

The Colonies of North America and the islands of the Caribbean swallowed up the prisoners. They sweated in labour or died in fever. They worked under indentures for the rest of their lives or were given a conditional liberty after seven years. In the West Indies their Highland blood was often mixed with African, and two centuries later their descendants brought back to Britain the lost names of Lochaber, Badenoch and the Isles.

JOHN PREBBLE, *Culloden* (1961)

San Andrés

I remember once, coming long years ago to an outlying settlement in the province of Buenos Aires, where all the people came, I think, from Inverness-shire; but, anyhow, once on a time they had been Scotch. Their names were Highland, but were pronounced by those who bore them after the Spanish way, as Camerón, and McIntyré, McLeán, Fergusón, and others, which they had altered in the current of their speech, so as to be unrecognizable except to those who spoke the language and knew the names under their proper forms.

None of these Scoto-Argentines spoke English, although some knew a few words of Gaelic, which I imagine they pronounced as badly as their names.

Four generations – for most of them had left their glens after Culloden – had wrought strange changes in the type. They all were dark, tall sinewy men, riders before the Lord, and celebrated in the district where they lived as being *muy guacho* – that is, adroit with bolas and lasso, just as the Arabs say a man is a right Arab, when they commend his skill in horsemanship.

Having left Scotland after the Forty-Five, most of their forebears had been Catholics, and their descendants naturally belonged to the same faith, though as there was no church in all their settlement I fancy most of them believed rather in meat cooked in the hide and a good glass either of Caña or Carlón, than dogmas of their creed.

R. B. CUNNINGHAME GRAHAM, *Charity* (1912)

Singular that I should fulfil the Scots destiny throughout, and live a voluntary exile, and have my head filled with the blessed, beastly place all the time!

R. L. STEVENSON to Sidney Colvin (1893)

Requiem

Under the wide and starry sky,
Dig the grave and let me lie.
Glad did I live and gladly die,
   And I laid me down with a will.

This be the verse you grave for me:
Here he lies where he longed to be;
Home is the sailor, home from the sea,
   And the hunter home from the hill.

R. L. STEVENSON

ACKNOWLEDGMENTS

The wood engravings in this anthology have been contributed by:

Lesley Bathgate, pages ix and 78; Andrew Christmas, pages 126 and 178; Claire Dalby, page 128; Andrew Davidson, pages 219 and 232; Jonathan Gibbs, page 110; Paul Kershaw, pages x and 256; Gwyneth Leech, pages 95 and 117; Winifred Mackenzie, page 74; Alyson MacNeill, pages 204, 262 and 299; Oliver and Boyd Publishers for the work of Joan Hassell, pages 48 and 172; Hilary Paynter, pages 59 and 60; and Jozef Sekalski, page 65.

We are grateful to the following authors, owners of copyright, publishers and literary agents who have kindly given permission for poems and passages of prose to appear:

Aberdeen University Press for 'Farmer's Wife' from *Poems*, John C. Milne (1976);

Angus & Robertson Ltd for extract from 'The Bonnie Disproportion' in *Persistence in Folly: Selected Prose Writings of Les A. Murray* (1984);

B. T. Batsford Ltd for extract from *The Heart of Scotland* by George Blake (1934);

Basil Blackwell Ltd for extract from *Enemies of God: The Witch Hunt in Scotland* by Christina Larner (1981);

Blackie & Son Ltd for extract from *The Scots Kitchen* by F. Marian McNeill (1929);

Bloomsbury Publishing Ltd for extract from *A Case of Knives* by Candia McWilliam (1988);

The Bodley Head for extract from *Scotch* by Sir Robert Bruce Lockhart (1951);

Bill Bryden for extract from his piece '"Member" at ?' in *Jock Tamson's Bairns* ed. Trevor Royle (Hamish Hamilton, 1977);

Campaign for a Scottish Assembly for extract from *A Claim of Right for Scotland* by Owen Dudley Edwards (1988);

Carcanet Press Ltd for 'Canedolia' by Edwin Morgan in *Poems of Thirty Years* (1982), 'Hallaig' by Sorley MacLean in *From Wood to*

Ridge (1989), 'Old Woman' by Iain Crichton Smith in *Selected Poems* (1985), and 'A Glasgow Cemetery' by Luis Cernuda, trans. Edwin Morgan in *Rites of Passage* (1976);

Canongate Press for extracts from *Whereabouts* (1987) and 'Scotland' in *Weathering* (1978) by Alastair Reid, *Fergus Lamont* by Robin Jenkins (1979), *Lanark* by Alasdair Gray (1981), and for the poems 'Strathnaver' by Ruaraidh MacThomais from *Modern Scottish Gaelic Poems*, ed. Donald MacAuley (1976) and 'In Galloway' from *Surviving Passages* by Andrew Greig (1982);

Chatto & Windus Ltd for extracts from 'John Logie Baird' in *A Scottish Assembly* by Robert Crawford (1990), and for the poems 'Old Edinburgh', 'Heron', 'Crossing the Border' and 'Crofter's Kitchen, Evening' from *Collected Poems* by Norman MacCaig (1985);

Croom Helm Ltd for extract from 'Australia and the Scottish Connection' in *The Scots Abroad*, ed. R. A. Cage (1985);

Cornell University Press for extract from *Colonists from Scotland* by Ian C. C. Graham (1956);

W. & R. Chambers Ltd for the poem 'A per se' by David Rorie in *The Lum Hat Wantin' the Croon* (1935);

Faber & Faber for extracts from *Highland Pack* (1949), *Highland River* (1937) and *Young Art and Old Hector* (1942) by Neil Gunn, 'What Images Return' by Muriel Spark in *Memoirs of a Modern Scotland* ed. Karl Miller (1970), *Selected Letters of Somerville and Ross* ed. Gifford Lewis (1989), *Lowland Lairds* by James Fergusson (1949), and for the poem 'Rannoch, by Glencoe' by T. S. Eliot in *Collected Poems*, 'The Silver City', *Sun and Candlelight* (1927) and 'Alas, Poor Queen' in *Selected Poems* by Marion Angus (1950);

Galloping Dog Press for the poems 'Unrelated Incidents' and 'The Voyeur' by Tom Leonard in *Intimate Voices* (1984);

Grafton Books for the poem 'The Prows O'Reekie' by Lewis Spence in *Plumes of Time* (1926);

Michael Grieve for extracts from *Lucky Poet* by Hugh McDiarmid (1943);

Robert Hale Ltd for extracts from *North East Lowlands of Scotland* by J. R. Allan (1974) and *The Scots Overseas* by Gordon Donaldson (1966);

Hamish Hamilton Ltd for extract from *The Thistle Rises*, ed. Alan Bold (1984);

HarperCollins Publishers for extracts from *Summer in Scotland* by Ivor Brown (1952), and *Memories* by Thomas Johnson (1952);

Harrap for the poem 'Childhood' from 'The Story and the Fable' in *Autobiography* by Edwin Muir;

A. M. Heath for extracts from *Collected Essays of George Orwell*, vol. 4 (1970);

Routledge for extracts from *Scott & Scotland* by Edwin Muir (1936) and *The Lion and the Unicorn* by Eric Linklater (1935);

Society of Authors for extracts from a radio talk by Sir Compton Mackenzie (1928), and 'Safety Last' by Sir Compton Mackenzie in *Scotland in Quest of Her Youth*, ed. David Cleghorn Thomas (1932);

Virago Press for extract from *Nothing Sacred* by Angela Carter (1982);

Gordon Williams for extract from his book *From Scenes Like These* (1968);

Yale University Press for extract from *Caught in the Web of Words* by Elizabeth Murray (1979);

Alison Young for extract from *A Prospect of Flowers* by Andrew Young (1945) and for the poem 'In December' from *The Poetical Works* of Andrew Young (1985).

Every effort has been made to contact the copyright owners of material included in this anthology. In the instances where this has not proved possible, we offer our apologies to those concerned.

INDEX

Home, John, 257
Hood, Paxton, 292
Hood, Thomas, 268
Hope, Annette, 256-9
Hopkins, Gerard Manley, 53
Hume, David, 18, 20, 22, 232,
Hutton, Professor James, 19-20,
    22

India, 287-91
Inverness, 125-6
Iona, 136
Irving, Washington, 70
'Ivanhoe', 278

Jacob, Violet, 207-8
James IV, 42, 69, 167
James Maxton, 163
Jenkins, Robin, 42-7
Jews in Scotland, 202-4
Joffre, General, 41
Johnson, Dr Samuel, 7, 26, 65,
    66, 67, 70, 79, 136, 224, 231-2
Johnson, Thomas, 161-3
Jones, John Paul, 273, 275-6
Joyce, James, 239-40

Kant, Immanuel, 18
Keats, John, 227-8
Keith, Sir Arthur, 22, 87
Kelvin, Lord William Thomson,
    18
Kennaway, James, 11
Kennedy-Fraser, Marjorie, 245
Kilt, the, 41-8, 126
Kipling, Rudyard, 205
Kirkwood, David, 162
Knollys, Sir Francis, 180
Knox, John, 66, 174-8
Kyles of Bute, 53-6

Larner, Christina, 190
Law, Robert, 7
Lawrence, D. H., 143, 241
Leith, W. F., 184

Leonard, Tom, 237, 238
Lewis, Gifford, 116
Leyden, Dr John, 234
Lindsay, Davie, 157
Linklater, Eric, ix, 24-5, 166-8,
    179-81
Livingstone, David, 13
Lloyd George, David, 165
Loch Ness monster, 87-8, 96
Lockhart, John Gibson, 224
Lockhart, Sir Robert Bruce,
    267-8
Lockhart, William, 7
Lorimer, Robert, 4
Lorimer, W. L., 176
Lowe, David, 161
Lyon, Reverend Robert, 194-6

Macadam, John Loudon, 21
Macaulay, Thomas, Lord, 41
MacAuley, Donald, 139
Macbreck, Father James, 183-4
MacCaig, Norman, 9, 61-2, 88-
    9, 114, 142-3, 264
McCallum, Neil, 17-23
Mac Colla, Fionn, 123-4
MacDiarmid, Hugh, 40, 56-7,
    72, 83, 84, 116-17, 127, 239-
    41, 242, 245
Macdonald, Alexander, 161
Macdonald, Allan, 272
Macdonald, Flora, 272
MacDonald, Ramsay, 162-3
McGilchrist, John, 191
MacIntyre, Lorn, 9
MacIver, Hector, 129-35
Mackenzie, A. M., 6
Mackenzie, Sir Compton, 11, 79,
    127, 128-9
Mackenzie, Henry, 232
Mackintosh, Charles Rennie, 4,
    21, 97-8
McLaren, Moray, 25-8, 200, 237
MacLean, Sorley (Somhairle
    MacGill-Eain), 245-6, 248-51

MacLean, Willie, 9
MacLeod, Kenneth, 245
MacNeice, Louis, 2
McNeill, F. Marian, 254–5
MacPherson, James, 224, 245
MacThomais, Ruaraidh *see*
    Derick Thomson
McWilliam, Candia, 49–51
Malcolm, Col-Gen Sir J., 234
Malcolm of Lochore, Sir
    Michael, 172
Mary Queen of Scots, 5, 69, 174,
    177, 178–81, 223
Massie, Allan, 204–5
Maxton, James, 163
Maxwell, James Clerk, 18–19
Meiklejohn, Francis, 166–8
Melville, Herman, 11–12
Menteith, 51–2
Mercer, Hugh, 273
Meredith, George, 241
Miller, Hugh, 22
Miller, Karl, 120
Milne, J. C., 75
Miłosz, Csesław, 2
Moncrieff, George Scott, 124,
    135
Montgomerie, Alexander, 182
Morgan, Edwin, 97, 246–7
Morison, Samuel Eliot, 275–6
Muggeridge, Malcolm, 163
Muir, Edwin, 60–1, 68, 93–4,
    148–9, 174, 176, 223–4, 228–9,
    242–5
Munro, Sir Hector, 287, 288
Murdock, William, 18
Murray, Gilbert, 164
Murray, Sir James, 234–5
Murray, K. M. Elisabeth, 234–5
Murray, Les A., 11, 282

Nairn, Ian, 97–8
Nairn, Tom, 1, 2
Nairne, Colonel, 66–7
Napier, James, 215

Napier, John, 23
Nasmyth, James, 19, 21
Nationalism, 166–9, 200, 228
New Zealand, 284–6
Nicoll, W. Robertson, 1, 174

Ord, John, 77
Orwell, George, 168–9

Payn, James, 112
Perth, 121–2, 292
Pope, Alexander, 197
Prebble, John, 294
Presbyterianism, 22, 37, 134,
    167, 193–4, 195, 281, 284
Proust, Marcel, 241
Prussia, 269–70
Pryde, G. S., 155

Ramsay, Allan, 243
Ramsay, E. B., 246
Ramsay, Sir William, 18
Reid, Alastair, 3, 13–14, 25, 28,
    31–2
Reith, John, 234
Renwick, James, 30
Richards, Eric, 282–3
Robertson, William, 227
Rorie, David, 125
Rosebery, Lord, 26, 194
Royle, Trevor, 48, 205
Russia, 293–4
Rutherford, Samuel, 189–90

St Andrew, 173–4
St Andrews, 65–7
St Clair, Arthur, 273
Salmon, Annette Hope, 256
Schmidt, F., 270
Scott, Sir Walter, 2–3, 9, 12–13,
    21, 25, 31, 57, 70, 156–7, 158–
    61, 186–8, 223–4, 228, 242–3,
    253, 255–6, 262–3, 276–8, 287
Selver, Paul, 114
Sharp, Alan, 33–4, 101, 201–2

303

Shaw, Christian, 7, 190–2
Shiant Islands, 79, 127, 128–9
Simpson, Professor, 19
Sinclair, Alex, 9
Sinclair, Sir John, 207
Skye, 120, 141–2
Smith, Adam, 18, 20, 22
Smith, Alexander, 120
Smith, G. Gregory, 239
Smith, Iain Crichton, 135–6, 138
Soutar, William, 121–2
Spark, Muriel, 8, 117–20
Spence, Lewis, 115, 208–11
Stevenson, Robert Louis, 3, 9,
   17, 21, 49, 108–9, 146–8, 177–
   8, 233–4, 244, 259–60, 294,
   295
Stewart, Douglas, 145–6
Stewart, Dugal, 111
Stirling, 120
Stuart, Charles Edward *see*
   Charlie, Bonnie Prince
Sutherland, Halliday, 38–9
Swan, Sir Joseph Wilson, 18
Swift, Jonathan, 156
Symington, William, 21
Symon, Mary, 236

Tancock, L., 194
Taylor, Rachel Annand, 16–17
Taylor, Wilfred, 32–3
Telford, Thomas, 7, 20–1
Tennyson, Alfred, Lord, 70
Thompson, H. W., 232
Thomson, David Cleghorn, 11
Thomson, Derick (Ruaraidh
   MacThomais), 138–9

Toman, Karel, 148
Trevelyan, G. M., 224–5
Turkey, 292
Twain, Mark, 276–8

Ulster, 271
Uniformity, 166
Union of England and Scotland,
   7–8, 41, 153–4, 155–7,
   158–61
Urquhart, Sir Thomas, 36–7, 37–
   8, 180–1
USA, 166, 272–80, 294

Voltaire, 193–4

Wallace, Sir William, 15, 157,
   223
Walsh, Dr Walter, 240
Watt, James, 20
Wedderburn, John, 181–2
West Indies, 294
Wilkes, John, 159
Wilkie, J., 206–7
Williams, Gordon, 81–2
Wilson, James, 273
Witchcraft and folklore, 7, 190–
   2, 206–22
Witherspoon, Sir John, 7, 273
Woolf, Virginia, 141–2
Wordsworth, Dorothy, 256–7
Wordsworth, William, 256–7

Young, Andrew, 69–71, 74–5
Young, Douglas, 47, 200–1
Young, Thomas, 18